Palgrave Studies in the History of Subcultures and Popular Music

Series Editors

Keith Gildart
University of Wolverhampton, UK

Anna Gough-Yates
University of Roehampton, UK

Sian Lincoln
Liverpool John Moores University, UK

Bill Osgerby
London Metropolitan University, UK

Lucy Robinson
University of Sussex, UK

John Street
University of East Anglia, UK

Pete Webb
University of the West of England, UK

Matthew Worley
University of Reading, UK

From 1940s zoot-suiters and hepcats through 1950s rock 'n' rollers, beat-niks and Teddy boys; 1960s surfers, rude boys, mods, hippies and bikers; 1970s skinheads, soul boys, rastas, glam rockers, funksters and punks; on to the heavy metal, hip-hop, casual, goth, rave and clubber styles of the 1980s, 90s, noughties and beyond, distinctive blends of fashion and music have become a defining feature of the cultural landscape. The Subcultures Network series is international in scope and designed to explore the social and political implications of subcultural forms. Youth and subcultures will be located in their historical, socio-economic and cultural context; the motivations and meanings applied to the aesthetics, actions and manifesta-tions of youth and subculture will be assessed. The objective is to facilitate a genuinely cross-disciplinary and transnational outlet for a burgeoning area of academic study.

More information about this series at
http://www.springer.com/series/14579

David Wilkinson

Post-Punk, Politics and Pleasure in Britain

palgrave
macmillan

David Wilkinson
Department of English
Manchester Metropolitan University
United Kingdom

Palgrave Studies in the History of Subcultures and Popular Music
ISBN 978-1-137-49779-6 (hardcover)   ISBN 978-1-137-49780-2 (eBook)
ISBN 978-1-349-69807-3 (softcover)
DOI 10.1057/978-1-137-49780-2

Library of Congress Control Number: 2016937717

Cover illustration: © Jon Savage. Adapted from the cover of City Fun fanzine Vol 2 issue 14,
1981

Printed on acid-free paper

This Palgrave Macmillan imprint is published by Springer Nature
The registered company is Macmillan Publishers Ltd. London

PREFACE

One issue that I do not explicitly deal with elsewhere in this book is the experience at the root of the questions I ask of post-punk. It is a difficult one to fully account for. Nevertheless, I think it is worth summarising. This is because the influence of the work of Raymond Williams on what follows extends beyond its intellectual and political dimensions to encompass its abiding concern with experience. The following preface, then, is not biography, but aims to enrich understanding of the book's arguments by clarifying a broader generational 'structure of feeling' behind them.

Throughout my childhood, under the successive Tory governments of the 1980s and 1990s, my parents and grandparents brought me up with a set of values and a kind of love that were an often unacknowledged expression of their socialist convictions. I am certain I am not alone in this; as I argue in Chap. 3, the British public was not wholeheartedly 'Thatcherised' over the course of the 1980s. Growing up with oppositional, prefigurative values is, I think, one source of this book's concern with comparable projections entangled within the left of British post-punk.

On 15 February 2003, my sixth-form friends and myself boarded a coach put on from Stockport to London by largely female baby boomers. I remember them swirling in the sartorial remnants of a countercultural past. We joined the biggest protest in British history—around two million—against the imminent war on Iraq. There is a pessimistic tendency on today's left concerning the anti-war movement of the early 2000s. Given that it did not stop the war either in Iraq or in Afghanistan, and considering the continuing vertiginous spiral of ideological opposition between radical Islamism and neoliberal capitalism, this pessimism might seem justified.

The commonly remembered slogans of the time are usually phrased in the negative, capturing the defensive position of the left after decades of defeat: 'No blood for oil' and 'not in my name'. However, I remember another one that was floating around at the time, which summed up the fact that many did not stop at saying 'no': 'Another world is possible.' The blatant imperialism of the war helped unlock a broader and deeper critique of the kind of politics that led to it, encouraging young people to mix with older generations who had spent years honing this critique. In one critical moment, the long efforts of the radicals of the past produced the radicals of the future. Here, I think of this book's claim that, as a development of the counterculture and the libertarian left of the 1960s and 1970s, post-punk retained a utopianism that contrasted valuably with its crisis-ridden and ultimately pessimistic moment.

The anti-war movement also taught many young people that politics does not have to be boring or dutiful. I experienced the dual frissons of rebellion and collective ethical certitude during a road-blocking sit-in. It was a creative time involving midnight graffiti, eccentric songs and chants. There was also the moment on the 15th February demo when, seeing all the effort people had put in and wishing I had done something in advance, I grabbed an abandoned placard and scrawled lyrics onto it from Marvin Gaye's 'What's Goin' On'. Having been caught up in this deeply felt, liberating and culturally informed variety of political action helps account for the way I put post-punk in dialogue with (1) theoretical arguments on the relationship between culture, politics and sensibility and (2) a historical argument for the enduring significance of struggles over the meaning of freedom and pleasure in postwar and contemporary Britain.

As I have hinted, the cultural aspect of the anti-war protests owed a debt to the legacy of successive postwar countercultures. At the same time as all this was going on, I was discovering post-punk in conjunction with a media-driven revival of interest in it. Possibly part of the last generation whose teenage tastes were shaped significantly by print music journalism, I could not get enough of reading about post-punk's world of alternative institutions; its aesthetic and political radicalism. At some level, I associated this new cultural consciousness with my developing political consciousness. Others must have done similar; post-punk influences can often be detected amongst today's global network of small-scale 'DIY' bands and their audiences, many of whom seem to share a broadly progressive political outlook.

The post-punk revival of the early 2000s, however, did not really link up more generally with the anti-war movement. One memory always acts for me as a reminder of Sarah Thornton's theory of 'subcultural capital': an acquaintance at my college came in the day after attending a gig by a post-punk revival band. Nu-metal, they declared, a musical genre that had previously drawn many of us together, was 'over' (now *Noisey*, the musical arm of taste-making online magazine *Vice*, declares that nu-metal is back: http://noisey.vice.com/en_au/blog/the-nu-metal-revival-is-real). The memory feeds into the way that the book draws on Pierre Bourdieu's work on distinction to explore the political complexities of post-punk. The revival also corresponded with the 'regeneration' strategies of post-industrial cities, which (especially in Manchester, my home city) drew on post-punk history and aesthetics to market urban space. Another guiding theme of this book thus began to dawn on me around this time—the recognition that culture is always politically contested.

I left college and started university later in 2003, benefiting from the cumulative postwar expansion of higher education. Like many students, the experience profoundly influenced me, and it has informed two central threads of the book.

The first is my attention to the importance of previously oversimplified issues of class and education in relation to post-punk, given my first-hand understanding of the way in which the extension of education in an unequal society produces a complex mesh of class fractions, often mutually suspicious of each other even as they overlap. The second is the book's cultural materialist theoretical framework. I was fascinated by the pick 'n' mix of cultural theory introduced to me on my degree, especially the way it interwove with my political outlook. As I continued my studies, however, I started to feel that, with a few welcome exceptions, this pick 'n' mix was a 'selective tradition'. Its cultural politics often tended—and still tend—to flip between an ultimately pessimistic 'resistance' and the compensatory, excessively optimistic stance of celebrating the majority of popular culture as inherently democratic and subversive.

Apportioning blame for this situation would be unhelpful. The problems of contemporary cultural theory have, after all, been determined in part by the historical defeat of the left over the past three decades. But my experience of childhood and of the anti-war movement, among other things, gave me an intuitive sense that this frustrating, see-sawing structure of feeling was specific, not total. Eventually, this led me to cultural materialism. Williams' work acknowledges how deeply rooted and difficult to change dominant power relations can be. Yet its stress on agency and creativity, and its understanding of society and culture as human-made processes rather than all-pervasive structures, allows for reasonable hope. Such a view informs my historical analysis of post-punk's politics. Overall, my judgements are cautiously, guardedly optimistic. I hope to offer a reasoned but hopeful socialist cultural perspective on the conjuncture of post-2008 austerity Britain.

ACKNOWLEDGEMENTS

This book has been made possible by funding from the Arts and Humanities Research Council and the Leverhulme Trust.

Thanks Matthew Worley and John Street, my brilliant, supportive colleagues on the Leverhulme project 'Punk, Politics and British Youth Culture 1976–1984', without whom the book would not exist. Combining team meetings with Pop Group gigs has been pretty much my dream job. Thanks also to David Alderson who has been in it for the long haul, having offered invaluable advice from the earliest stages of what would become *Post-Punk, Politics and Pleasure in Britain* up to its completion.

The ideas of the book have been informed and tested by a number of conferences and events, including various workshops organised by the Subcultures Network, the 2014 'PopLife' conference at the University of Northampton organised by Nathan Wiseman-Trowse, the commemorative CCCS50 conference at the University of Birmingham, the 2014 workshop '1979 Revisited—The Cultural Production of Structures of Feeling Under Thatcherism' held at Birkbeck organised by Herbert Pimlott, and the 2015 'Keep It Simple, Make It Fast' conference at the University of Porto organised by Paula Guerra. I still find it faintly surreal to recall talking to Dick Hebdige about swimming pools in the Casa de Música.

Beyond their unwavering love and support, I am grateful to my mum and dad for passing on the values that inform this book; there are not many better gifts that parents could give their kids.

The following people have all contributed in various important and often crucial ways too. Patrick Gannon, Jon Gardner, Sara Shepherd, Caroline Blase, Jen Morgan, Lucy Jackson, Abigail Ward, Kieran Curran,

Marcus Barnett, Andrew Moor, Lucy Burke, Jason Toynbee, Eithne Quinn, David Hesmondhalgh and my fellow Manchester Left Writers Natalie Bradbury, Steve Hanson and Bob Dickinson.

Thanks Helen Brown for donating her prized post-punk record collection to me, Liz Naylor for post-punk-related insight and Stockport-related gossip, and Una Baines and Martin Bramah for being fantastic, generous interviewees.

Special gratitude is due to Jon Savage for granting me permission to use the image on the cover—it is adapted from a collage he created for *City Fun* vol 2 no 14, 1981.

Sections from this book have appeared in earlier forms in:

'Prole Art Threat: The Fall, the Blue Orchids and the Politics of the Post-Punk Working Class Autodidact', *Punk & Post-Punk* 3:1 (2014): 67–82

'Is Natural In It? Gang of Four, Scritti Politti and Gramsci' in Rachel Carroll and Adam Hansen (eds), *Litpop: Writing and Popular Music* (Farnham: Ashgate, 2014) 141–156

'We all have good intentions/but all with strings attached: Post-punk and Marxism on the cusp of neoliberalism', *The Journal of Research on Marxist Aesthetics* (2012:2) 52–64 (translated into Mandarin)

I am grateful for permission to re-publish this material.

I also want to celebrate the gem that is the Working Class Movement Library—maybe the only archive where staff members invite you for comradely tea breaks.

Thanks to Palgrave Macmillan for their support and patience, especially Angharad Bishop and Emily Russell.

CONTENTS

1 Introduction: Shake Your Cosy Attitudes   1

2 Post-Punk and the Politics of Postwar Popular Music   11

3 Post-Punk, Thatcherism and the Libertarian Left   37

4 Is Natural in It? Radical Theory and Educational Capital   77

5 The Politics of the Post-Punk Working Class Autodidact   115

6 Desires Bound with Briars: Freedom, Pleasure
   and Feminism   155

7 Agents of Change: Post-Punk and the Present   189

Bibliography   205

Index   221

CHAPTER 1

Introduction: Shake Your Cosy Attitudes

In November 1978, midway between the break-up of the Sex Pistols and the election of Conservative prime minister Margaret Thatcher, 19-year-old *NME* journalist Ian Penman reviewed a clutch of singles with cautious optimism. Punk, it seemed, far from being dead, was mutating to better bridge the gap between 'functions and heart, political abstracts and personal alienation…"messages" and "art"'. There were no 'Bo Diddley riffs' here.[1] That was not all: these records were independently released, suggesting punk's original injunction to 'do it yourself'[2] had not degenerated into the apparent irony of 'EMI financed revolutionary statements'. Where punk's filth and fury had burned brightly and briefly, it was hoped that this new underground might result in 'the right manner of public aggravation':[3] a sustained and constructive challenge at the levels of music, politics and production.

Penman was not alone. Pre-emptive manifestos on the 'new musick' in rival weekly *Sounds* had begun to appear even before the Pistols' implosion.[4] There was a sense of renewed excitement about what would be dubbed 'post-punk'[5] at a broader subcultural level too. Manchester's *City Fun*, with a circulation estimated to be in the thousands by 1980, was one of a raft of fanzines that sprang up in the wake of *Sniffin' Glue*'s demand for a grassroots punk media: one that could rival an established press viewed as 'so far away from the kids that they can't possibly say anything of importance'.[6] Around the time of Penman's singles round-up, a *City Fun* gig review of PragVEC and The Normal at Tony Wilson's Factory club found the crowd receptive and the bands both 'intellectual' and 'danceable'. It noted a pattern emerging: 'This is one place the energy of '76 is going ... coming soon, the energy of '79, fucking brilliant i'nt it.' In typical fanzine style, the review then veered off—not entirely tangentially, as we will see—on an anti-consumerist rant.[7] 1979 would indeed produce lauded debut albums by Gang of Four, The Slits, The Raincoats, The Fall and many others, now critically regarded as classics.

By January 1981, the tone was somewhat different. In a wayward style peppered with allusions to post-structuralist philosophy, Penman dismissed the 'rhythmic antiquity' of post-punk band the Blue Orchids.[8] There was no reference to oppositional politics or challenges at the point of production. Instead, he puckishly celebrated US chart-pop imports like Fantasy—the exact kind of 'disco, boogie and pop' that Buzzcocks had wished would 'stop' back in 1978. A month later, Paul Morley made a similarly provocative gambit, hyping the MOR balladry of husband and wife duo Dollar and luxuriating in the fact that 'they don't pretend to be profound saviours'.[9] Within a year, he would propose them as a model for post-punk progression.[10]

These were not just the daydreams of feverish young countercultural scribblers: many post-punk bands, including squat collective Scritti Politti, had responded to and even anticipated journalists' articulation of a 'new pop' in reaction against post-punk's sometimes testing trajectories. Even *City Fun*, which delighted in chippy Mancunian satire of the trend-driven London-based music press, now sounded disenchanted. It lambasted with equal scorn the 'cosy attitudes' of punk's diaspora. Die-hard 'real punks', experimental 'post punks' and pop-embracing 'new romantics' alike—all, it claimed, were mistaken if they thought they had avoided being 'ripped off', or were 'contributing something to social awareness that will actually change events'. Importantly, all this was apparently no fun anymore: 'The kid in the club with the wide sleeved frilly lace shirt looked just plain miserable.'[11]

With the arrival of 1984, punk and post-punk practices stubbornly persisted, nurtured by a network of grassroots local scenes and collectives. Morley, though, had long since moved on, managing Frankie Goes To Hollywood to a number one hit. Penman, meanwhile, was recoiling from the charts, wondering how the new pop he and Morley helped create had got so 'dumb'.[12] *City Fun* folded that year, and although post-punk bequeathed its independent infrastructure and sometime oppositional politics to the emergent indie scene, many of those bands' musical reference points looked back nostalgically to the 1960s.[13] Since the rise of electronic pop, hip-hop and the multiple subgenres of dance, it is debatable whether British rock has ever successfully re-united formal, political and economic radicalism with such collective verve and relative impact. What happened to post-punk, and why does it matter?

This book aims to answer those questions. An inquiry into leftist post-punk in Britain, it focuses on the bands Gang of Four, Scritti Politti, The Fall, the Blue Orchids, The Slits and The Raincoats as case studies, with a particular emphasis on the independent record label Rough Trade. I investigate how far post-punk was bound up with political moves towards libertarian left and feminist alternatives in the face of the collapse of welfare-capitalism.[14] I also consider how far it had affinities with broader public moods captured by Thatcherism, with those fractions of the left that capitulated to Thatcherism's neoliberal logic, and with 'post-feminist' developments. Throughout, I focus on the themes of freedom and pleasure, which I argue were central to the political struggles of the era. Perhaps most importantly, I aim to emphasise the continuity of such struggles with the present and conclude by reflecting on the lessons of leftist post-punk for oppositional cultural production and politics today.

Inevitably, this raises the question of how we value popular music. Recently, David Hesmondhalgh has sympathetically critiqued the assumption of many scholars that popular music matters most when it aids progressive political causes.[15] Because of this, such studies have disproportionately focused on the moments when popular music has directly linked up with campaigns for political change. But the question of how we might value popular music in ways that go beyond profitability and status-seeking is more complex. It demands the kind of thorough socio-historical, cultural and psychological analysis that Hesmondhalgh engages in. He makes a nuanced case for music's value in contributing to intimate and collective 'human flourishing'.[16]

I empathise with this argument: ultimately, the value of popular music relates to one of the central functions of culture, which is the communication of social experience.[17] Whilst that is a left-leaning view in the way it stresses our necessary dependence on one another, it accepts that popular music's value extends beyond the directly political. I might put Leonard Cohen on when I feel petty and cynical, to remind myself that others have found more profound takes on the world. I might put Cyndi Lauper on if I want to re-connect with memories of childhood, when my cousin and I used to dance on the settee to her greatest hits.

However, the following chapter shows that historically, the politics of pop have gone beyond obvious instances of 'protest songs' and commitment to movements. And they have often done so in ways that meet up with Hesmondhalgh's focus on flourishing. We should also recall that the scholars Hesmondhalgh alludes to have been rightly working, as he does, against the persistent common-sense assumption that pop and politics do not mix—or that things will not end well if they do. These are assumptions that often work to preclude attempts to align progressive causes and popular music. They also tend to conceal pop's frequent (political) implication in the maintenance of the status quo. Indeed, journalist Simon Reynolds, the leading popular historian of post-punk, does not think its engagement with the left ended well. This is in spite of his belief that the most valuable aspect of post-punk was its 'commitment to change'[18]—musical and political—and his excellent and compelling overview of its complexities. For Reynolds at his most pessimistic, post-punk 'tried to make politics and pop work together but failed'.[19] Without overstating post-punk's impact or its left credentials, I think it is worth telling a different story.

Hesmondhalgh's reassessment of music's value accompanies his doubt about the way the rebellion of rock in particular has been mythologised and exaggerated. Does rock's oppositional stance mean nothing nowadays, when ruling figures express their love for it?[20] Again, I empathise: David Cameron still publicly adores the anti-Thatcherite Smiths, despite guitarist Johnny Marr's attempt to 'forbid' him from doing so on Twitter.[21] Nonetheless, the mythology is there and Hesmondhalgh acknowledges that rock has been socially important in the lives of millions. Rock continues to be a key battleground in a wider process of socio-cultural reproduction and change, driven in part by struggle between dominant and subordinate groups. In Britain, we can deduce this from the very fact that Cameron thinks it worth repeatedly telling the media that he likes The Smiths—not to mention staking claims on subcultural expressions of creativity, as in the instance of him making a 'mixtape' for world leaders at a G8 global summit.[22] The point is that rock's history is contested; it demands politicised engagement. That is one objective reason for writing this book—I have gestured to my subjective reasons in the preface.

This is not an alternative popular history; it has been written from within academia. But my approach to popular music and subcultural studies is comparable to that of Keith Negus, who argues that research in this field should not be confined to insular academic preoccupations, given the democratic promise suggested by the very term 'popular music'.[23]

The book draws on the theoretical resources of cultural studies, the close analysis of literary studies and the archival grounding of history, but I have aimed to write in such a way that its conclusions might resonate further.

I have also done so out of sympathy with the approach proposed by Alan Sinfield as one way for those on the left studying cultural production to 'make themselves useful' in conditions where neoliberalism has overturned many of the political gains of the postwar settlement. This is the suggestion that our efforts should 'work with and through ... a subcultural constituency'.[24] In Sinfield's case, this is lesbians and gay men; in my own, it is those involved in the production and consumption of popular music who have in some way inherited the hopes of the postwar counterculture that popular music can be a force for progressive cultural, social and political change. In the long run, such an approach cannot be a substitute for a broader cultural strategy rooted in a renewed class politics. Nonetheless, engagement with those who are marginalised by the dominant culture would seem to be an important and complementary task.

This is not always easy; it is wise to recall Dick Hebdige's hesitant conclusion to the classic *Subculture: The Meaning of Style*, in which he frets that the language of institutionalised intellectuals 'threaten[s] to kill with kindness the forms which we seek to elucidate'.[25] There are grounds for optimism, though. The expansion of higher education means that the kind of work this book does is not quite so marginal as it might once have been. Those who write on popular music and subcultures, too, usually have some form of lived connection to their subject. Sinfield calls the literary culture he scrutinises 'a resource that I share with friends and people I love; a repertoire of stories for thinking through'.[26] Much the same could be said of my relationship to popular music and subcultures.

The work of Raymond Williams, one of Sinfield's main influences, is a key 'resource of hope'; especially the later cultural materialist theory, but also Williams' more political writings like *Towards 2000*, written and published during the period covered by this book. As my concern is with the politics of post-punk, Chap. 2 situates post-punk within a more general argument regarding the political pertinence of popular music in postwar Britain. It provides a longer historical view on the politics of post-punk, the collapse of welfare-capitalism and the rise of neoliberalism, offering a theoretical framework through which to understand this history. In so doing, I draw on and develop key cultural materialist tools to stress the salience of popular music's production, its historical concern with disaffected aspirations to freedom and pleasure, the connotations of the particular forms that successive musicians have created and reworked, and the importance of authorship and reception. Throughout subsequent chapters, the balance shifts the other way: the framework is foregrounded less but nevertheless underlies my points.

In Chap. 3, I elaborate two parallel and connected histories of postwar Britain. The first is an account of what I refer to throughout the book as 'the libertarian left'. The chapter defines the term in detail, but in brief it refers to a historical strand that can be traced to the New Left of the 1950s and onwards, also encompassing 1960s student protest, the new social movements of the 1970s, developments on the intellectual left, and elements of Eurocommunism and libertarian socialism. These disparate elements shared an emphasis on grassroots democracy, the building of alternative institutions and ways of life qualitatively distinct from those valued under capitalism. The second history is an account of the development and political concerns of post-punk. It focuses the previous chapter's reflection on the politics of postwar popular music. We will see that leftist post-punk was concerned with the political in certain key ways, including engagement with overtly political themes and movements, the radical transformation of sensibility, gender, personal relations, and the popular music industry. These were filtered through tensions of class and education, resulting in a formation that was fairly distinct from other breakaway factions from punk, such as Oi!'s pursuit of a populist working class authenticity and the new pop's aspirational, postmodern turn.

The chapter contributes to a central claim of the book: that leftist post-punk was often informed by and contributed to the libertarian left, and that this particular synergy is one from which we can learn in present circumstances—along with the harder lessons of various other directions taken by the bands I analyse. My historical turn is also a practical way of framing the more in-depth studies of particular bands in successive chapters. It gestures, too, towards the substantial archival research that underpins many of the book's claims.

I then move on to three chapters of close analysis. Each case study compares two bands with similar backgrounds and concerns in order to bridge the divisions between individual and historical study of cultural production and examine the internal variation and tensions within leftist post-punk.

In the first of these, on Gang of Four and Scritti Politti, I challenge the existing critical consensus that incorporation of radical theory into their practice threatened pleasurable engagement with their music. Most analyses are also relatively uncritical of the decision of both bands to abandon post-punk economic independence in favour of major labels, a decision I examine in more depth. The chapter concentrates on the connection of the bands' class backgrounds and education to their cultural practice. Each band experienced education as class mobility, with contradictory political implications. Parallels are drawn between the development of these bands and that of the British left into the 1980s and beyond, leading to the emergence of New Labour. I point out that Gang of Four and Scritti Politti were informed by comparable intellectual currents to those that provided the rationale for one section of the left's accommodation with neoliberalism. With hindsight, some of their actions can be seen as an early example of this trend.

Class and education take centre stage once more in Chap. 5, which focuses on The Fall and the Blue Orchids. I argue that the bands' working class autodidact background is crucial to an understanding of their visions of fulfilment and their negotiation of the era's politics. My comparison of the two bands also shows how their approaches were rooted in contrasting working class ways of life: after an early period of sympathy with the left, Mark E. Smith of The Fall leant towards a contradictory hybrid of working class conservatism and countercultural individualism. The Blue Orchids, meanwhile, married working class traditions of mutual aid and collective self-education with an interest in the esoteric. Each band's relationship to post-punk and to emergent Thatcherism thus played out very differently, despite their common origin as teenage school friends in North Manchester. The chapter is partly informed by original interviews conducted with original Fall members and co-founders of the Blue Orchids, Una Baines and Martin Bramah.

An attention to gender and feminism features throughout, but comes to the fore in the penultimate chapter on the all-female bands The Slits and The Raincoats. I discuss them in relation to the women's movement of the era, arguing that this is a necessary move in order to better understand the politics of each band. The Slits' individualism and sometime wariness of feminism as a movement could be read as prototypical of today's neoliberal incorporation of feminism as individual success. However, their ecological mysticism echoed trends within the women's movement that challenged the desirability and sustainability of capitalist growth. The Raincoats, meanwhile, have been viewed as puritanical in terms very similar to those often invoked to dismiss the 'anti-sex' turn of feminism at this time. Yet the band developed a sophisticated stance on erotic liberation that challenged both sexist objectification and the puritanical response to it.

The conclusion engages with recent media and academic speculation on the legacy of British post-punk, the contemporary music industry and the current political conjuncture. I point out that post-punk labels like Rough Trade have much to teach those who want to see the emergence of more democratic and egalitarian outcomes from the shift to online, digital music. What is more, the ethos and working methods of Rough Trade gave a practical grounding to the utopian urges of leftist post-punk bands. The content of these urges, informed by residual countercultural influences and libertarian left politics, could, I claim, prove informative and productive for the British left. For years, it has been unable or unwilling to articulate a practical, convincing and desirable political strategy with which to oppose the dominance of neoliberal policy. However, we are now living through a moment in which neoliberalism is being challenged increasingly in the wake of global economic crisis. More soberly, I summarise the manner in which the historic shift to neoliberalism limited leftist post-punk's utopian urges, and pressured it into accommodation. The way this was often mediated by broadly postmodernist perspectives that fulfilled similar functions in the spheres of politics and academia prompts me to gesture to the enduring critical relevance of cultural materialism.

NOTES

1. Ian Penman, 'Singles', *NME*, 18 November 1978, p. 31.
2. Caroline Coon, 'Parade of the Punks', *Melody Maker*, 2 October 1976, pp. 26–27.
3. Penman, 'Singles'.
4. Jon Savage and Jane Suck, 'New Musick', *Sounds*, 26 November 1977, p. 23; Vivien Goldman, 'New Musick: Dub', *Sounds*, 3 December 1977, pp. 22, 24; Davitt Sigerson, 'New Musick: Disco', *Sounds*, 3 December 1977, p. 28.
5. Possibly the first use of the term 'post-punk' is Jon Savage and Jane Suck, 'New Musick'. It was used fairly often in all three music weeklies during the period covered by this book, especially *NME*, as well as in subcultural discourse, such as fanzines. There has been some contention over whether the kind of cultural production I discuss was conventionally understood as 'post-punk' at the time, questioning the apparent revisionism and 're-branding' of Simon Reynolds' influential bestseller *Rip It Up and Start Again: Postpunk 1978–1984* (London: Faber, 2005). See Alex Ogg, 'Beyond Rip It Up: Towards a New Definition of Post-Punk?', *The Quietus*, 1 October

2009, available online at http://thequietus.com/articles/02854-looking-beyond-simon-reynolds-rip-it-up-towards-a-new-definition-of-post-punk, accessed 5 October 2014. For those interested in terminology and definitional boundaries, I clarify the features of the particular tendency with which I am concerned in Chap. 3, and have stuck to 'post-punk' on the basis that, for good or ill, it is now common parlance.

6. Mark Perry, 'Editorial', *Sniffin' Glue* 1 (1976), 2. For an overview of punk fanzines, see Matthew Worley, 'Punk, Politics and British (Fan)zines, 1976–84: "While the World was Dying, Did You Wonder Why?"', *History Workshop Journal* 79 (2015), 76–106.

7. Anonymous, 'PragVec and the Normal at the Factory', *City Fun* 1, no. 3 (1978).

8. Ian Penman, 'Singles', *NME*, 17 January 1981, pp. 19–20.

9. Paul Morley, 'Singles', *NME*, 7 February 1981, p. 27.

10. Paul Morley, 'Dollar in Wonderland', *NME*, 2 January 1982, pp. 17, 30.

11. Anonymous, 'Shake Your Cosy Attitudes', *City Fun* 2, no. 14 (1981).

12. Ian Penman, 'Into Battle—Declaring War on the Pop State', *NME*, 8 September 1984, pp. 30–31.

13. Reynolds, *Rip It Up and Start Again*, p. 519.

14. 'Welfare-capitalism' is the phrase used by Alan Sinfield to describe the postwar consensus—see Alan Sinfield, *Literature, Politics and Culture in Postwar Britain*, 3rd ed. (London: Continuum, 2004), p. xxxi. Sinfield argues that because of the left's tendency to see the state as ameliorating the worst effects of capital, the postwar consensus was often viewed as tending towards socialism. This is not the case; the consensus is better characterised as a kind of corporatism which temporarily stabilised capitalism (p. 316) The term also sidesteps the problems of 'social democracy' or 'social democratic' as descriptions; it is arguable that postwar Labour governments' degree of concession to capitalist interests meant that social democracy was never fully achieved in Britain, and more or less certain that Conservative consensus governments never saw their aims in terms of social democracy.

15. David Hesmondhalgh, *Why Music Matters* (Oxford: Wiley Blackwell, 2013), p. 142.

16. Hesmondhalgh, *Why Music Matters*, pp. 170–171.

17. Raymond Williams, *The Long Revolution* (Harmondsworth: Penguin, 1965) [1961], p. 40.

18. Reynolds, *Rip It Up and Start Again: Postpunk 1978–1984*, p. 527.

19. Simon Reynolds, *Totally Wired: Post-Punk Interviews and Overviews* (London: Faber, 2009), p. 431.

20. Hesmondhalgh, *Why Music Matters*, p. 143.

21. Jo Adetunji, 'Johnny Marr Tells David Cameron to Stop Saying He Likes the Smiths', 3 December 2010, http://www.theguardian.com/politics/2010/dec/03/johnny-marr-david-cameron-twitter, accessed 5 October 2015.

22. Tom McTague, 'Cameron Insists His Love for the Smiths "Will Never Go Out" Despite the Band "Banning" Him from Listening to Their Music', *Daily Mail*, 9 January 2015, http://www.dailymail.co.uk/news/article-2903557/Cameron-insists-love-Smiths-never-despite-band-banning-listening-music.html, accessed 5 October 2015.
23. Keith Negus, *Popular Music in Theory* (Cambridge: Polity, 1996), p. 224.
24. Sinfield, *Literature, Politics and Culture in Postwar Britain*, pp. xxxv–xxxvi.
25. Dick Hebdige, *Subculture: The Meaning of Style* (London: Methuen, 1979), p. 139.
26. Sinfield, *Literature, Politics and Culture in Postwar Britain*, p. xix.

CHAPTER 2

Post-Punk and the Politics of Postwar Popular Music

Cultural Materialism, Popular Music and Post-Punk

Why cultural materialism? The theory originated in Raymond Williams' rapprochement with Marxism in the 1970s. Williams' recognition that culture is material, and is shaped by the way it is produced in particular circumstances, is a crucial one in any context. But it is especially relevant in an era that has been marked by the intensified commodification of cultural production. Cultural materialism, then, theorised not only its subject matter but also the historical conditions of its own emergence.[1] These are the same historical conditions that produced post-punk, which, as we will see, was often comparably self-aware of the political significance of how music gets made.

The cultural materialist attention to specific contexts of production is one of its key strengths over the theoretical tendencies that have dominated cultural studies since the 1980s. Another is Williams' adaptation of Antonio Gramsci's theory of hegemony. Hegemony is the 'saturation' of 'relations of domination' into 'the whole process of living' so that 'the pressures and limits of a specific economic, cultural and political system' like capitalism often seem like 'common sense'.[2] Although hegemony goes deep, significant and potentially transformative dissidence is still possible. This is because hegemony is by nature partial and selective. It does not and cannot account for all 'human practice [and] ... intention'.[3] Thus,

© The Editor(s) (if applicable) and The Author(s) 2016
D. Wilkinson, *Post-Punk, Politics and Pleasure in Britain*,
DOI 10.1057/978-1-137-49780-2_2

hegemony 'has continually to be renewed', being 'continually … challenged by pressures not all its own'. One hegemonic response to such cultural and political challenges is the attempt to *incorporate* them.[4] In Britain, in the 1970s and 1980s, this was the response of the New Right to the qualitative disaffection expressed by the postwar counterculture, its punk and post-punk descendants, and various strands of leftist opposition (a case I make in the following chapter).

Williams' interpretation of hegemony contrasts sharply with a more influential version of the concept rooted in the work of the structuralist Marxist philosopher Louis Althusser.[5] It derives from the gradual anti-humanist turn of the intellectual left throughout the 1970s, as thinkers began to advocate 'theory with a capital T'.[6] This version of hegemony continues to crop up in contemporary intellectual production, most of which now owes little else to Marxist sources.[7] Rather than hegemony being rooted in material production and reproduction—in what we simultaneously do, make, think, communicate and feel—it is more commonly understood as a pervasive ideological structure, upon which even our notion of ourselves as individuals is dependent. 'Ideology' understood as 'false consciousness' and the beliefs of a dominant social group becomes elided with 'ideology' understood as 'the general production of meanings and ideas'.[8] Such work usually combines an emphasis on close reading, neglecting analysis of the significance of cultural production, with a reduced sense of the scope for dissidence.[9] This reduction of scope is a consequence of the downplaying of human agency in post-Althusserian theory,[10] a trait that was the result of philosophically abstracting a particular historical era of defeat for the left.

Although this theoretical–political difference might seem like a slightly esoteric detour from the question of post-punk and politics, it is fairly central in two respects. Firstly, following Williams on hegemony allows us to see that left-post-punk's 'increasingly out of synch relationship'[11] with the shift to neoliberalism in Britain did not mean that its transformative efforts simply 'failed'.[12] Instead of just being crushed, absorbed and rendered irrelevant by broader structural transformation, post-punk dissidence may still offer a residual resource of hope. The word 'residual' is key here, pointing towards Williams' historically layered sense of hegemony. For Williams, the dominant culture coexists with 'residual' and 'emergent' elements, each of which may feature alternative or actively oppositional counter-hegemonic traits.[13] 'Hope', too, is important—Alan Sinfield notes that Williams' model of hegemony offers an alternative to understandings of dominance as 'unbreakable continuum' derived from Althusser and post-structuralists such as Michel Foucault.[14] Secondly, cultural materialism provides a critical vantage point on the fact that structuralist Marxist and post-structuralist theories often provided direct justification for post-punk's instances of political compromise, as they diffused from higher education, radical bookshops and political activism into post-punk subculture.

Such intellectual production did not just mediate the political compromises of post-punk. Especially in Chap. 4, I explore the way that these compromises foreshadowed the direction of influential left intellectual work in the 1980s—work that was to have a bearing, for example, on the future direction of the British Labour Party. By contrast, the connection between cultural theory and political alignment for Williams was far less historically contingent. His theoretical bearings complemented fairly neatly his support for 'the radical libertarian and socialist currents within the labour movement' and the new social movements of the 1970s and early 1980s.[15] These are the same forces that shaped the political context of leftist post-punk. I expand further on the links between Williams' theory, his politics, and the moment of Thatcherism and post-punk in the next chapter.

Although Williams' work was hugely influential in the opening up of the humanities to the study of popular culture, he rarely engaged with popular music and alternative youth culture. The study of subcultures is dominantly traced back to the Birmingham Centre for Contemporary Cultural Studies, and the way that work was breaking theoretically from Williams' influence at the time, even as it still drew occasionally on his thought,[16] has meant that he has not been the most obvious 'go-to' thinker for the field. Williams, did, however, make a hopeful passing comment during the post-punk era. He noted that some forms of popular music did not originate with the market, even if market imperatives eventually claimed them, and contrasted popular music's 'vitality' and social engagement with more nostalgic and navel-gazing examples of contemporary cultural production.[17] And there has been a current within cultural studies and sociological analyses of popular music and subcultures that bears the influence of cultural materialism.[18] Below, I engage with this current to explain how the way popular music was made within the historical context of postwar Britain gave it three broad and overlapping orientations in relation to politics. These I refer to as *culturalism, populism* and *anti-culturalism*.

I then account for popular music's recurrent concerns with freedom and pleasure in similar terms, considering the political implications of these concerns. I engage with Williams on structures of feeling, humanism and utopianism, discussing too the work of Frankfurt School philosopher and unlikely figurehead of the New Left, Herbert Marcuse. I also draw on and expand Alan Sinfield's argument that rock subculture was from the beginning invested with utopian qualities by young people. With the coming of the 1960s counterculture from which post-punk in part derived, this investment began to interlace more strongly with libertarian left ideals of qualitative social change.

Finally, there is the question of the close reading that features in Chaps. 4–6. A key goal of cultural materialism is 'a fully elaborated account of cultural process'.[19] The aim is to bridge political economy, sociology and history, which often leave out cultural analysis, and literary and cultural studies, which tend to focus exclusively on it. Musical forms are actively made and re-made within particular circumstances. We should therefore analyse the politics of popular music such as post-punk by attending to the meanings that are likely to have been made of its forms in such circumstances, and in the circumstances that have followed since its production. I also draw on Pierre Bourdieu's concept of 'habitus' to emphasise the way in which the social background of post-punks shaped what they produced. I conclude by discussing the issue of audience, arguing that communication is completed only by reception, and summarising the forces that have shaped reception of post-punk.

THE INSTITUTIONAL BASIS OF POSTWAR POPULAR MUSIC

Societies need to produce ... to continue—they need food, shelter, warmth ... a transport and information structure ... and so on. Also, they have to produce culturally. They need knowledges to keep ... production going ... and they need understanding, intuitive and explicit, of a system of social relationships within which the whole process can take place. Cultural production produces ... apparently 'natural' understandings to explain who we are ... [and] how the world works. Social conflict manifests itself as competition between stories.[20]

To understand popular music as part of this conflict, we need to consider the particular institutions through which it has been produced.[21] In the following chapter, I focus on the post-punk music industry alongside the significance of institutions such as the British music press and higher education to the politics of post-punk. But it is necessary to step back a little from the instance of post-punk here in order to gain perspective, especially in the case of the music industry. A longer view of the productive processes at play in postwar popular music gives us an essential sense of the ground on which the political conflicts of post-punk took place.

Within the music industry, popular musicians operate within the dominance of a 'corporate professional' system, with residual elements of 'post-artisanal' and 'market professional' production.[22] *Post-artisanal* describes a situation where cultural producers enjoy a degree of autonomy at the same time as being partly reliant on others to help them make their work. They then sell their work to further intermediaries, who sell it on for profit. We can identify this in the popular music industry in the instances of distribution companies, studio production and manufacture of music in various listening formats. *Market professionalism* involves the move to copyright and royalties, with the producer developing an investment in the market as a whole in the form of sales figures, rather than simply receiving a lump sum for their work. The *corporate professional* system involves direct and sustained employment by large companies and commissioning from above 'of planned saleable products' for 'a highly capitalised market'.[23] Whilst this is more formally organised in industries like publishing, it is a central feature of the music industry, embodied, for example, in contracts and marketing.

Jason Toynbee calls the relative freedom of the post-artisanal elements of popular musical production 'institutional autonomy'. He argues that historically, companies have often ceded control of cultural production to musicians. This production has often been 'spatially dispersed in small units', and there is 'a strong continuity between consumption and production (often within an over-arching subculture)'.[24] Because of this distance from straightforward capitalist functionality, Toynbee notes that although 'musicians aspire to enter market relations ... at the same time the market is held to corrupt the non-commercial values to which successive corps of music makers ... have subscribed'.[25] Geoff Travis, founder of post-punk independent label Rough Trade, recalls the 'disappointing' moment when The Clash and the Sex Pistols signed to major labels.[26]

Culturalism

We could also frame this by arguing that much popular music has tended to inherit the *culturalist* distinction of the arts from commerce and civilisation. This distinction is critically analysed in its English, largely literary, form in Williams' classic first book *Culture and Society 1780–1950*. It is part of a broader European tradition of aesthetics,[27] which, as Francis Mulhern summarises, 'took shape in the later eighteenth century as a critical, usually negative, discourse on the emerging symbolic universe of capitalism, democracy and enlightenment … a process of social life for which a … French coinage furnished the essential term: *civilisation*'.[28] Culturalism has taken many forms and adopted various political hues. In Britain, it has been present in romanticism, modernism, and the postwar nexus of the counterculture and the New Left, amongst other formations. It is usually rooted in 'middle class dissidence'; disdain for the 'philistine' branches of the middle class—'businessmen, industrialists and empire-builders'—to which it opposes a celebration of 'good' culture.[29] This is not to say that culturalism cannot be adapted and taken up by other classes, as we will see especially in the case of working class bands The Fall and the Blue Orchids.

The reasons for culturalism's emergence and the shapes it has taken are complex. It was in large part, though, a reaction to the growing subordination of cultural production to the vagaries of the market rather than the previous positions of cultural producers within state and religious hierarchies or as the beneficiaries of patronage.[30] Stripped of higher purpose in a marketplace that reduced the qualitative specifics of use value to the quantitative commensurability of exchange value, cultural producers required a new justification for their work. Amid the anxieties produced by the expanding and rapidly changing world of industrial capitalism, culture began to be explained both as a product of 'the "inner life"… in effect a metaphysics of … the imaginative process' and organic 'ways of life', distinct from the march of abstract, rational 'civilisation'.[31]

It might seem like a stretch to detect the workings of culturalism at play within postwar popular music. Culturalism's tendency to elitism and authority claims about cultural value meant that even influential left-leaning versions of the discourse in postwar Britain advocated a state-funded extension of supposedly 'good culture' (literature, drama, fine art, classical music, etc.) to all, through institutions such as school, the Arts Council and public service broadcasting. Those who held this attitude usually stood in direct opposition to 'commercial' forms such as popular music.[32] Yet by the 1960s, these assumptions were challenged by the class mobility, the new forms of popular culture, and the expanded consumerism and educational opportunities of the postwar political settlement. Sinfield notes that 'young people had acquired the confidence not to compromise ... the kind of attention usually given to "good" culture was lavished on popular and commercial forms'.[33]

Simon Frith and Howard Horne relate this in institutional terms to the art schools that produced many of the key figures of British popular music in the 1960s, including The Who and Pink Floyd. They argue that 'the idea that artists are natural rebels gained wide cultural exposure during the student occupation of Hornsey College of Art in 1968', which incidentally included the key New Left thinker Tom Nairn. With their bohemian beliefs of living 'spontaneously' and 'creative autonomy', the students resented new pressures to direct their skills towards feeding the culture industry, in a classic example of the culturalist distinction of culture from commerce. The Hornsey occupation, Frith and Horne claim, 'reflected specific institutional contradictions, but fed into a much wider counter-culture ... By 1968 ... the loose "hippie" movement had created its own version of aesthetic revolt.'[34] Paul Willis' ethnographic research on the 1970s hippie subculture in the West Midlands observes an antipathy towards a 'ratio-technical order', held responsible 'for the complete impoverishment of human sensibilities'.[35] The following chapters explore in more detail how post-punk came to inherit these culturalist attitudes.

Culturalism's distinction of culture from commerce is an untenable one if we are discussing cultural production embedded in capitalist market relations. Theodor Adorno's critique of popular music acutely observes that the very elements of culture which are said to be opposed to commerce are sold back to us,[36] or, as Gang of Four succinctly put it, 'ideal love a new purchase/a market of the senses'. Also, culturalism's distinction of culture from civilisation can tend to discourage straightforward analysis of the politics of culture. Often, culture actually comes to stand in for politics in culturalist discourse.[37] Furthermore, notions of artistic genius, individualism, and outsider status associated with culturalist movements like romanticism may chafe against leftist hopes for democracy, egalitarianism, solidarity and co-operation. Despite all this, there is something highly valuable from a left perspective in the prevailing belief that popular music should be about more than capitalist imperatives[38]—specifically, about aspects of human life neglected or suppressed by such imperatives. It is surely what Ari Up of The Slits was getting at when she claimed: 'When you're into a thing for money then your heart drops out and the heart is made out of rhythm and if you ain't got the heart, then the rhythm ain't there.'[39] Culturalist attitudes are also at the heart of popular music's concern with freedom and pleasure, as we will see below.

Populism

Culturalism, already a fraught political battlefield, does not exhaust the institutional determination of the politics of popular music. Arguing that popular music rests on the ideal that 'popular musicians come from the common people', Toynbee claims that the political agency of popular musicians requires an engagement with *populism*.[40] As early as 1960, Ray Gosling, writing in *New Left Review*, characterised young British rock 'n' roll figures like Marty Wilde, Cliff Richard and Billy Fury as representatives of the preoccupations of a new era: 'He is your son, the nation's hope, the child of the emancipated common man, the idol of a moneyed age, the hope in a world full of fear. His face comes out in the third dimension from the screen to appeal to the mother, the daughter, the youngest son; to epitomise this new glossy world of boom.'[41]

There are various sources of this ideal of the popular musician as everywoman and man. First and foremost, there has been no official and potentially elitist route through qualifications to become a popular musician.[42] Secondly, there has been a historical trend of collective self-management that includes 'the notion of a direct relationship between audience and musicians'. Toynbee dates this as far back as swing bands and contrasts it with the individualist role of 'pop star'.[43] Thirdly, we should add, popular music is a mass-market cultural form that potentially reaches many people. The royalties system means that there is a financial incentive to reach more people too.

These factors have given popular musicians the opportunity of a public platform for political debate, the ability to act as a representative force for progressive political movements and marginalised groups, and the potential to act as a reminder that 'ordinary people are creative too', often in a 'structurally democratic' manner at odds with the hierarchies and individualist ideologies of capitalist production.[44] Toynbee notes, though, that popular music often underlines inequality by failing to represent marginalised groups. Furthermore, because of the commodification of the creative self involved in the pop process, vainglory and elitist individualism threaten democratic ideals. We should observe, too, that popular musicians have used their public platform to intervene in politically reactionary ways—as in the case of Eric Clapton's racist comments that helped provoke the Rock Against Racism movement, which would go on to shape the political context of post-punk.

Post-punk's sometime support for causes such as feminism and anti-consumerism meant that at times it represented the concerns of the libertarian left. It gave broad exposure to such ideas not only in songs but also in the published discourse of the music weeklies upon which it was reliant. Post-punk's continuation of punk's hostility to stars, and of punk's egalitarian injunction to 'do it yourself', was a particularly pronounced form of populism. There was sometimes a desire for populist reach at the level of consumption as well as production, expressed in Mark E. Smith's claim that 'The Fall had to appeal to someone who was into cheap soul as much as someone who liked [the] avant-garde. I even wanted the Gary Glitter fans.'[45] As will become clear, though, post-punk was challenged on this score by its 'new pop' outgrowth, which ironically revived stardom at the same time as it staked a claim to populism. This was a tension in which the broader political stakes were high.

Anti-Culturalism

Culturalism and populism help frame much of the politics of post-punk. However, there is a third institutional factor to the political possibilities of popular music. Its history has been further characterised by what I call *anti-culturalist* tendencies—an umbrella term for any position that consciously recognises the weakness of the culturalist distinction of culture from commerce and civilisation. The most obvious determining element of anti-culturalism is the dominance of corporate professionalism within the music industry; popular musicians are usually the contracted employee of a business, with all the insecurity and exploitation this has historically involved. They experience first-hand the power of the music industry to define what counts publicly as musical creativity in its construction of specific markets, its policing of genres, and its influence over what does and does not get released.[46] We should note, in other words, that the 'creative freedom' of institutional autonomy is only a relative condition. In the face of this, it is not difficult to see how doubt might creep in about one's role as an artist whose concerns transcend the grubbiness of the commercial world.

There have also, however, been institutional influences on anti-culturalism from outside the music industry itself. Pop Art in Britain combined the formal techniques of modernism with the 'danger of US popular culture' and an acknowledgement of commerce and consumerism. In so doing, it focused the challenge of the 1960s generation to the 'nannying' institutions of 'good culture', influencing bands like The Who and the

Beatles.[47] Pop Art presumptions would consolidate themselves in the educational institutions and milieus that went on to influence later waves of British popular music. Here, the work of Simon Frith is again instructive; with Howard Horne, he has highlighted the centrality of the British art school to the formation of punk and post-punk.[48]

Frith and Horne, though, tend to overemphasise the potentially conservative consequence of anti-culturalism: once culturalism is sacrificed, popular music can tend to get equated with capitalist imperatives. This is an issue, and it is a theme that often haunted post-punk's new pop turn. But anti-culturalism has also been marked by more incisively critical strands: Pop Art 'facilitated a ... breakthrough into political work' through 'its disrespect for the dignity of art'.[49] And more straightforwardly politicised approaches to culture, including Marxism and feminism, also circulated within the same milieus, as the counterculture divided between devoted radicals and more non-committal hedonists.[50] At times, this strand of anti-culturalism has produced acute awareness and criticism of the unjust economic processes of popular musical production (thus dissolving the distinction of culture from commerce) and of the social and political significance of creative practice and form (thus dissolving the distinction of culture from civilisation). In an early interview, Gang of Four guitarist Andy Gill argued, 'I believe that all art is political. Whether it's a painting, a movie, or a song, you're making some kind of statement.'[51] This was only one example of the prevalence of 'demystification' in post-punk discourse.[52] I explore the specific determining factors of post-punk anti-culturalism in the following chapters.

FORMATIONS AND STRUCTURES OF FEELING

Though attention to the institutions that shaped postwar popular music in Britain gives a broad idea of its political scope, an understanding of cultural processes 'is also a question of *formations*; those effective movements and tendencies, in intellectual and artistic life, which have significant ... influence on the active development of a culture, and which have a variable ... relation to formal institutions'.[53] By considering how formations like post-punk relate to their historical circumstances and how they contain internal differences and tensions, this kind of analysis acts as a bridge between generalised accounts of cultural production and studies of individual contributions.[54]

In the next chapter, I look at post-punk as a specific formation, and as a broader subculture. This is crucial to an understanding of its politics. Existing histories of post-punk have sometimes oversimplified its internal variations of class background, educational experience, cultural influences and political stance. In contrast, I attempt a more accurate account, before identifying a specifically leftist current that forms the basis of subsequent analysis.

A stress on formations, bound by shared aims and practices, also helps to get over a sense of more immediate and personal investment in popular musical production than institutional analysis; a feel for the values and the moods that brought post-punks together as a retrospectively recognisable tendency. Here, Williams' concept of 'structure of feeling' is also useful. The term avoids the notion of a 'formalised belief system' implied by 'ideology'. It captures the more complex and often contradictory nature of social experience whilst acknowledging that our feelings as well as our thoughts are socially determined.[55] The term 'structure of feeling' later developed another usage in Williams' work: a way of describing inchoate historical developments that could not be ideologically pigeonholed.[56] This usage informs the way I go on to show that certain elements of what post-punks did remain difficult to place ideologically, or hinted at cultural and political developments yet to come.

The concept of structure of feeling also frames my emphasis on freedom and pleasure as key issues that mediated the political concerns of post-punk and its broader historical conjuncture. Freedom and pleasure are surely amongst the most deeply, personally 'felt' experiences within an encompassing hegemonic process. They are irreducible to purely abstract and conceptual understandings if their varied expressions—dominant, alternative or oppositional—are to have any genuine hold.

FREEDOM, PLEASURE AND POPULAR MUSIC

We have already touched on why freedom has been a common theme in popular music in the discussion of the creative freedom allowed by institutional autonomy. The concern with pleasure in popular music comes largely from the same source. Culturalism tends to view the arts as the terrain of individual experience, the imagination and the bodily senses.[57] Such a focus is highly conducive to questions of pleasure and personal fulfilment. Historically, rock, in particular, captured the frustration and longing of young people to whom postwar welfare-capitalism had extended schooling, even as it maintained class stratification.[58] Education was only part of the story—welfare-capitalism generated aspirations on a far greater scale than its capability to fulfil them, producing widespread disaffection.[59] Ray Gosling quoted a young soldier who claimed that 'life is a permanent wank inside you'.[60] Thus, popular music became a way to imagine alternative fulfilment, however hazily defined.[61] Martin Bramah of The Fall and the Blue Orchids recalls that 'we were really just factory fodder. It was our way out from what the world was offering us.'[62]

Freedom and pleasure's shared origin in the institutional autonomy of popular musical production, and their twin historical articulation in the disaffection of postwar youth, mean that they are often inextricable themes within popular music, as in the case of post-punk. The emphasis on musical experiment that marked post-punk was often inseparable from a sense that this creative freedom was not simply formal self-indulgence. Rather, it was tied to an interrogation of the freedoms and pleasures associated with certain creative practices and an attempt to suggest new ones, sometimes with utopian intent.

The pleasure of popular music, though, cannot be abstracted from hegemony.[63] It is wise, if depressing, not to be too optimistic about pleasure's radical potential. Just as culturalist creative freedom may work against leftist collectivism, despite disdaining 'commercialism', so the pleasures and fulfilments promoted by popular music are often marked by dominant articulations of these themes, even as they express disaffection. 'Rock music', Sinfield argues, is in many instances 'consumer capitalism writ too large ... developing its recommended values (conspicuous consumption, material aspirations, masculine aggression) with an unacceptable excess'. This excess is one that does not seriously disturb the dominant culture.[64] Indeed, it may even rejuvenate it; Jim McGuigan has argued convincingly that we live now in an era of 'cool capitalism', which has incorporated disaffected countercultural appeals to pleasure and autonomy as an appealing 'front' region concealing a more unpleasant, exploitative 'back region'.[65]

However, given the long history of popular music's embroilment with progressive politics, it would be hasty and overly pessimistic to write off popular music's potential as a forum for the exploration of alternative and oppositional freedoms and pleasures. In Jon Savage's account of the deep roots of British punk, he notes that the upheavals of 1968 'turned aesthetic style into political gesture. The violent intensity of the pop that had flooded the world from 1964 was translated into a public demonstration of the utopian promise: that the world could be transformed.'[66]

In the following chapter, I historicise the fraught positioning of post-punk between residual libertarian, New Left, and countercultural ideals of freedom and pleasure and the process of their capture by emerging Thatcherite neoliberalism. Here, I emphasise the significance of a key figurehead of the New Left, who often focused its ideals. The work of Herbert Marcuse is dominantly looked upon as being tied to an era now past. The activist, intellectual and ex-student of Marcuse Angela Davis attributes this situation to the way Marcuse's later writings were so closely bound up with the New Left's ascendancy. She notes the nostalgia evoked in 1960s and 1970s radicals by mention of his name, arguing that such a reaction threatens to relegate Marcuse's insights to a status that is 'meaningful only in the context of our reminiscences'.[67] However, Marcuse's concern with a qualitative critique of capitalism remains bitingly relevant and thus deserves serious contemporary engagement.[68] Marcuse's work is, with some revision, compatible with a cultural materialist approach to understanding qualitative critiques of capitalism like those of post-punk in terms of freedom and pleasure. Its utopian[69] projections also have a direct historical connection with the moment of post-punk.

How are cultural materialism and Marcuse's work related, and how do they throw light on post-punk's qualitative critique? Both Williams and Marcuse can broadly be described as Marxist humanists; they desired political change based on the recognition that capitalism was not only economically unjust but also ultimately inadequate for a specifically human kind of self-fulfilment. In this, they shared the concerns of the broader libertarian left that shaped post-punk. Williams' recognition that capitalist hegemony reaches the 'fibres of the self'[70] and his acceptance that the biological was a determining factor of social life[71] echo Marcuse's understanding that dominant social systems must work at a biological level to be effective. We are 'libidinally and aggressively' bound to 'the commodity form'.[72]

The flipside of these fairly grim-sounding arguments is that both thinkers built on Marx's theory of human 'species being' and alienation[73] to argue that we are simultaneously creative and social creatures.[74] When capitalist social relations predominate, private owners are the main beneficiaries of our collective work. Furthermore, production is largely organised on the basis of the reproduction of capitalism, rather than on a democratically decided fulfilment of social needs and the chance for everyone to put their various capabilities into play. Thus, we often experience conscious productive activity—one of the main things that makes us human—as something to be got through. Even if we are lucky enough to experience 'job satis-faction', work is still usually an external obligation, a means to the wage that sustains us. As a commodity, it is excessively quantified and calculated, alienating us from full investment in it.[75] Rarely is it a liberating, enjoyable and fully sociable activity. For both Williams and Marcuse, though, as for the New Left more broadly, cultural production occasionally offered a glimpse of how things could be otherwise.[76]

Here, we can see that Williams and Marcuse also owed their arguments to a culturalist inheritance, with its stress on bodily senses and its celebra-tion of culture as transcending capitalist instrumentalism. In Williams' case, this came from the influence of the avowedly culturalist literary critic F.R. Leavis; in Marcuse's, it came from a long line of German aesthetic philosophy.[77] As philosophical materialists and Marxists, though, neither went along with the culturalist mystification of human creativity. Williams negotiated this better than Marcuse, however, with the latter maintaining a lingering mistrust of explicitly politicised cultural production.[78]

If Williams is more advanced than Marcuse on culture as key to politi-cal struggles over freedom and pleasure, why draw on Marcuse to look at post-punk? My rationale here has to do with the actual content of Williams' suggestions for a qualitative alternative to capitalism. *Towards 2000*, for example, is fascinatingly suggestive in its acknowledgement of the ecological critique of limitless capitalist growth.[79] It also contains practical suggestions for how new technologies might be used in socialist cultural policy to democratise access to cultural consumption and pro-duction.[80] We could see these as contributions to what Williams termed 'systematic' utopianism: starting to sketch the future practicalities of a dif-ferent society.[81]

But Williams has less concrete suggestions when it comes to what he refers to as 'heuristic utopias', those whose 'purpose is to form desire', and which are 'imaginative encouragement[s] to feel and relate differently';[82] in other words, those projections which devote greater consideration to issues of freedom and pleasure. In fairness, this reticence comes from Williams' valuable and all too rare concern with 'the problem of how to establish democratic socialism as the political pre-condition for a common culture, rather than with the attempt to identify the specific content of any such culture'.[83] It is a concern that I have attempted to do justice to through my identification of the record label Rough Trade as central to leftist post-punk in its prefiguration of socialist cultural production. Nevertheless, we cannot do without the heuristic utopia; its 'strongest centre', Williams argues, 'is ... the conviction that people can live very differently, as distinct from having different things and from becoming resigned to endless crises and wars'.[84]

It is on this score that Marcuse comes into his own. He argued that 'the emergence of ... new needs and satisfactions [cannot] be envisaged as a mere by-product ... of changed social institutions'. The solution he proposed, to a countercultural audience during the Dialectics of Liberation conference at the Roundhouse in London in 1967, was the necessity of innovating ways of life that prefigured new definitions of freedom and pleasure.[85] Marcuse's rootedness in the movements of the New Left and the counterculture meant he avoided the elitist cultural prescriptivism of some sections of the left that had earlier worried Williams.[86] Although certain elements of the 'new sensibility' Marcuse proposed pre-dated the upsurge in radicalism of the late 1960s, it was this lived moment that provided him with a means of concretising its content.

The point is that heuristic utopias must be popularly rooted in order to carry weight. It may seem unusual, then, that in successive chapters, Marcuse's work is drawn upon to frame oppositional freedoms and pleasures in the cultural production of post-punk, given the historical gap between the late 1960s and the late 1970s and early 1980s. However, post-punk was in many ways an emergent development of the same countercultural movements from which Marcuse drew inspiration and upon which he was hugely influential. Published by large companies in affordable paperback form, his work also circulated significantly: the first edition of *One-Dimensional Man* alone sold 300,000 copies.[87] Even if those I go on to write about had not read such work, they were most certainly moving in circles with some connection to its ideas. It should be stressed, though, that I do not want to imply that post-punks were simply ventriloquising Marcuse. Marcuse's ideas are helpful because they condense many more general preoccupations of the libertarian left: issues such as sexuality, the human relationship to the natural world, and the nature of work.

The historical shift in mood on the left between the late 1960s and the late 1970s and early 1980s may also seem to count against such reasoning; even before the rise of neoliberalism, hopes for radical change had begun to subside in the face of economic crises, preliminary conservative backlashes represented by the governments of Edward Heath in the UK and Richard Nixon in the USA, and the beginning of the long rolling back of the historical gains of the labour movement. Post-punk was bound up with 'the sense of dread and tension' in Britain at the close of the 1970s with the resurgence of the far right, the election of Margaret Thatcher and the re-escalation of the Cold War.[88] Herbert Pimlott has called this structure of feeling 'crisis music'.[89] The following chapters, though, show that post-punk was also nourished by the residual survival of libertarian left and countercultural structures of feeling.

How were these structures of feeling expressed? A theory of close cultural analysis will allow us to get a handle on the cultural forms in which these notions were embedded as social processes of production and interpretation.

FORM, AUTHORSHIP AND RECEPTION

Form

For cultural materialists, forms of cultural production such as popular songs are historical, social and material in and of themselves.[90] Jason Toynbee has developed an understanding of forms as social processes and products specifically in relation to popular music.[91] He builds on the Marxist linguist Mikhail Bakhtin's theory of heteroglossia. Heteroglossia is the 'multiplicity of languages and verbal-ideological belief systems' found in the novel, which correspond to their broader social usage.[92] Toynbee's use of Bakhtin can be supplemented by Williams' profoundly important point that such formal elements of cultural production are not reflective or derivative of a separate social world, but are active and shaping elements of it.[93]

Toynbee draws an analogy between elements of musical form and the kinds of language combined in heteroglossia.[94] Music, he points out, can be socially and historically rooted too, due to the fact that it originates as 'a site of production, in other words a specific throat, instrument, recording studio', and via textual location in terms of class, place, gender, sexuality, race and so on. Toynbee gives as examples 'Motown girl groups', the 'Smoke On The Water' riff, and the four-on-the-floor beat of house music.[95] To draw on such elements, then, often invokes or unsettles particular connotations, as we will see in the following chapters in relation to post-punk's expansive musical experiment.

Music, in contrast to the linear flow of the novel, entails experiencing various signifying elements simultaneously as well as sequentially. There are also extra parameters to consider such as timbre, tempo and time signature.[96] We should note, too, that popular music with lyrics actually combines both processes. When analysing songs, it is necessary to investigate not only the significance of placing certain musical elements in synchronicity with one another but also their interaction with the accompanying lyrics. Thus, heteroglossia as it relates to language underpins my analysis, whilst bearing in mind the different formal conventions associated with song lyrics in contrast to the novel.

So far I have focused on the production of popular musical meaning without expressly considering its political significance. Here, the concept of 'multiaccentuality' is useful. It was developed by Bakhtin's associate V.N. Voloshinov to convey the multiple meanings generated within individual linguistic signs.[97] Such meanings, though, are not relative and potentially limitless. Rather, multiaccentuality is part and parcel of hegemonic struggle. In the process of communication, signs have contested, varied and evolving meanings.[98] Much the same can be said of music, given that it is largely comprehended through language; elements of musical form are always invested both consciously and unconsciously with a variety of contested meanings that at some point are bound to have political connotations. One example from British post-punk was the attempt by certain bands to integrate rhythms adapted from disco, funk, and reggae into their music as a means of challenging the perceived macho connotations of more typical rock rhythms. To summarise, popular music contains a heteroglossic assortment of musical and linguistic elements in interaction with one another, and each of these elements is multiaccentual.

When thinking about cultural production, we also need to look at authorship and reception. Otherwise, there is a risk of forming opinions according only to one's own belief in, and often desire for, a particular interpretation. This is a familiar phenomenon in cultural studies: Todd Gitlin has argued that the discipline has often exaggerated the radical potential of popular culture as a compensatory move in response to the declining fortunes of the left.[99]

Authorship

Whilst authorial intent does not guarantee meaning, it is an important link in the process of negotiating it. Some attention to authorial intent is therefore necessary in the understanding of cultural production that is 'implicated in relations of power'.[100] Placing the author to one side also unduly absolves them of any responsibility for what is made of the meaning encoded into cultural production.

Historically, authorship has been a valued component of popular music. This has had both positive and negative political consequences that deserve investigation.[101] The value of authorship was commonly retained in British post-punk, despite a culture of intense scepticism and scrutiny of common-sense notions of popular music. Even Green Gartside of Scritti Politti, perhaps the most likely post-punk candidate to dismiss the concept of authorship due to the anti-humanism of his structuralist Marxist and post-structuralist influences, was elevated to the status of 'theory guru'; Buzzcocks' manager Richard Boon recalls Scritti Politti's songs and Gartside's interviews being scrutinised by admiring members of the Manchester Musicians' Collective.[102] Meanwhile, as I go on to argue, a deeply romantic conception of Mark E. Smith of The Fall as unfathomable genius has developed in commentary on the band, stifling political analysis of the band's cultural production.

It is not only that authorship remains politically significant in the interpretation of songs; this is also the case in terms of the process of their production. The interaction between the social world that has shaped individual authors and the cultural forms with which they work is key to understanding the politics of what they do.[103] This includes popular music.[104] Here the work of Pierre Bourdieu is helpful.

Toynbee uses Bourdieu's concept of habitus as a way of thinking about how individual musicians approach cultural production. Habitus is the particular, and adaptable, disposition produced in a person by their social experiences of class, race, sexuality, gender, education, employment and so on.[105] As well as shaping their approach to politics, it disposes musicians 'to play, write, record or perform in a certain way'.[106] In the cases of Gang of Four and Scritti Politti, The Fall and the Blue Orchids, and The Slits and The Raincoats, I consider how factors such as class, education and gender shaped their dispositions within the context of post-punk and the broader historical conjuncture. 'Habitus' is valuable shorthand for Williams' concern with 'the real sense of living individuals in every kind of relationship'[107]—for understanding authorship as a social phenomenon. The term can be divested of its tendency towards abstraction in Bourdieu's work and enriched by Williams' more humanistic attention to experience and structures of feeling by being placed within a cultural materialist framework.

Bourdieu is often concerned with the fact that not all cultural practices consist in a struggle between dominant and subordinate elements; some take place within the dominant culture over the best way to respond to a changing world, leading him to state ominously: 'permanence can be assured by change'.[108] Here, his position is commensurate with Williams' argument that hegemony is neither static nor uniform and must constantly adapt.[109] Andrew Milner, though, notes that over the whole span of Bourdieu's work, the emphasis on the dominant is overplayed.[110] In *Distinction*, Bourdieu even characterises those working within the counterculture, a central residual component of post-punk, simply as hoping to raise their own cultural, social and economic position.[111]

There is an element of truth here, and Bourdieu's concern with education and social advancement has informed the argument of Chap. 4 that the trajectories of the leftist bands Gang of Four and Scritti Politti were marked by their experience of class mobility. However, Bourdieu's view of the counterculture is an overly pessimistic summary of a movement whose alternative and sometimes oppositional features were self-evidently embodied in its name. The following chapter explores a faultline in the counterculture over the meaning of freedom and pleasure, one that would have consequences for its post-punk successors.

Reception

Sinfield has noted that whilst a cultural materialist approach devotes appropriate attention to authorship and the institutions of cultural production, its concern is with 'the effects of the text in the world';[112] hence the questions I put to post-punk in this book. Although the meaning of a text does not end with authorship and production, we should not consider audience interpretation as a free-for-all. The ways in which we interpret cultural production are subject to just as many determining factors as the process of production itself, and this is as true of popular music as of other kinds of cultural production.

This leads us to the predominant ways in which post-punk has been interpreted historically. Have audiences of post-punk really listened so closely as to have consciously and unconsciously extracted the variety of political meanings that successive chapters attribute to various bands' work? Despite having been unable to pursue the kind of empirical research that might more concretely ascertain this, I would argue that it is often likely to be the case.

Why is this so? Dave Laing has drawn on Bourdieu's theory of the 'cultural intermediary' to consider the way music journalism has shaped audience interpretation. He notes that music journalists have mediated interpretation in a variety of ways. They have often colluded 'with the culture industries' definition of listeners as consumers'. But journalists sourced from the underground press of the 1960s and 1970s framed popular music in countercultural terms, invested it with culturalist values of 'personal involvement' and 'immersion', and critiqued the record industry.[113] Simon Reynolds has pointed to the centrality of the weekly music press in audience understandings of post-punk. Reynolds accurately characterises key journalistic mediators of post-punk as 'activist critics' and immediate successors to their countercultural and punk forebears.[114] It is also worth noting that many writers had comparable backgrounds either in terms of higher education or in having written for punk and post-punk fanzines that formed the emergent continuation of the countercultural underground press. Political dissent, too, was channelled through the music press. Style journalist Peter York observes: 'It reached the kids ... who never saw ... [libertarian left magazine] *The Leveller* ... quite ordinary working or lower middle class kids who nonetheless wanted to be in touch with *something else*.'[115]

What this meant for the interpretation of post-punk during the era of its production was that it was predominantly understood to *matter* profoundly on a personal and political level, demanding the kind of engagement which might yield the understandings that I go on to suggest. The power of the music press to mediate audiences' engagement with post-punk accounts for the amount of attention I devote to archival sources from publications such as *NME*, *Melody Maker* and *Sounds* throughout subsequent chapters. I also engage with fanzines in recognition of broader subcultural participation in post-punk.

What about contemporary interpretation of the politics of post-punk? With the waning of the counterculture and the advent of multiple new media formats, traditional popular music journalism now has far less influence over interpretation than it once had. It faces 'an uncertain future in the twenty-first century'.[116] This view would seem to be confirmed by the amount of British music magazines which have folded, begun to devote coverage to topics other than music or publish with reduced frequency over the past 20 years.

Nevertheless, individual music journalists who have managed to establish a dominant media position still have considerable sway over audience understandings. A key example is Reynolds himself; his book-length history of post-punk *Rip It Up and Start Again* became a bestseller.[117] There has been an incorporative element to the post-punk 'revival' that has been in force from the early 2000s onwards, something I look at in more detail in Chap. 7. However, Reynolds' commitment to documenting both the politics of post-punk and those of its era, as well as his belief that it was being a teenager during post-punk which has made him take popular music so seriously,[118] has maintained a continued popular understanding of post-punk as explicitly countercultural. Even advertising reflects this: a vinyl reissue of Cabaret Voltaire's *Red Mecca* on sale in 2015 featured a promotional sticker written by record shop staff, claiming that the LP's 'soundscapes evoke an economy spiralling out of control … It is an album that deals with … all that is and was evil about the society in which these musicians lived.' The influence of Reynolds on interpretations of post-punk accounts for my sustained engagement with his work, along with popular biographies of specific bands and existing academic work on them in acknowledgement of their part in shaping current understandings.

Notes

1. Andrew Milner, *Re-Imagining Cultural Studies: The Promise of Cultural Materialism* (London: SAGE, 2002), pp. 104–105.
2. Raymond Williams, *Marxism and Literature* (Oxford: OUP, 1977), p. 110.
3. Raymond Williams, 'Base and Superstructure in Marxist Cultural Theory' [1973], in *Culture and Materialism* (London: Verso, 2005), p. 43.
4. Williams, *Marxism and Literature*, pp. 112–114.
5. Louis Althusser, *On Ideology* (London: Verso, 2008). Particularly influential conduits included the work of the Centre for Contemporary Cultural Studies—see, for example, CCCS, *On Ideology* (London: Hutchinson, 1978), the Centre's influence on historians via writers such as Richard Johnson—especially the article 'Edward Thompson, Eugene Genovese, and Socialist-Humanist History', *History Workshop* 6 (Autumn 1978), 79–100, the 1970s output of Terry Eagleton in literary studies—see *Criticism and Ideology* (London: New Left Books, 1976), the work of the journal *Screen* in film and visual studies and the social and political theory emanating from the University of Essex. See Barry Hindess and Paul Hirst, *Mode of Production and Social Formation* (London: Palgrave Macmillan, 1977) and especially Ernesto Laclau and Chantal Mouffe, *Hegemony and Socialist Strategy* (London: Verso, 1985).
6. Dennis Dworkin, *Cultural Marxism in Postwar Britain* (Durham: Duke University Press, 1997), p. 219.
7. David Alderson offers a nuanced and convincing critique of the ways in which Althusser's work was taken up and subsequently drawn upon to move 'beyond' Marxist cultural theory into a broadly post-structuralist ambit, even as some of Althusser's most unsubtle and politically disabling notions were simultaneously preserved by those who did so. Importantly, Alderson's account is sensitive to the historical and institutional determinations of this process, reflecting too on its political consequences. David Alderson, 'Back

to the Future', *English Studies in Canada* 30, no. 4 (December 2004), 167–187.

8. Williams, *Marxism and Literature*, p. 55.
9. Milner, *Re-Imagining Cultural Studies*, p. 115.
10. Milner, *Re-Imagining Cultural Studies*, p. 84.
11. Simon Reynolds, *Rip It Up and Start Again: Postpunk 1978–1984* (London: Faber, 2005), p. xxv.
12. Simon Reynolds, *Totally Wired: Post-Punk Interviews and Overviews* (London: Faber, 2009), p. 431.
13. Williams, 'Base and Superstructure in Marxist Cultural Theory'.
14. Alan Sinfield, *Faultlines: Cultural Materialism and the Politics of Dissident Reading* (Berkeley: University of California Press, 1992), p. 9.
15. Milner, *Re-Imagining Cultural Studies*, p. 173.
16. Dworkin, *Cultural Marxism*, p. 163.
17. Raymond Williams, *Towards 2000* (London: Chatto and Windus, 1983), pp. 145–146. ITV's serialisation of *Brideshead Revisited* and the 'nominal' radicalism of postmodernist art came in for particular stick.
18. See, for example, Jason Toynbee, *Making Popular Music: Musicians, Creativity and Institutions* (London: Arnold, 2000), pp. x–xii; Keith Negus, *Popular Music in Theory* (Cambridge: Polity, 1996), p. 220; and *Music Genres and Corporate Cultures* (London: Routledge, 1999), p. 151; David Hesmondhalgh, 'Post-Punk's Attempt to Democratise the Music Industry: The Success and Failure of Rough Trade', *Popular Music* 16, no. 3 (October 1997), 255–274.
19. Milner, *Re-Imagining Cultural Studies*, p. 130.
20. Alan Sinfield, *Literature, Politics and Culture in Postwar Britain*, 3rd ed. (London: Continuum, 2004), p. 29.
21. For institutions, see Williams, *Marxism and Literature*, pp. 115–118 and Williams, *Culture* (Glasgow: Fontana, 1981), pp. 33–56.
22. These terms are taken from Williams' discussion of cultural production and the market, *Culture*, pp. 44–52.
23. Williams, *Culture*, p. 52.
24. Toynbee, *Making Popular Music*, p. 1.
25. Toynbee, *Making Popular Music*, p. 2.
26. Reynolds, *Rip It Up and Start Again*, p. 93.
27. Terry Eagleton, *The Ideology of the Aesthetic* (Oxford: Blackwell, 1990), p. 11.
28. Francis Mulhern, *Culture/Metaculture* (London: Routledge, 2000), p. xv.
29. Sinfield, *Literature, Politics and Culture in Postwar Britain*, p. 46.
30. Williams, *Culture*, p. 72.
31. Williams, *Marxism and Literature*, pp. 15–17; Milner, *Re-Imagining Cultural Studies*, p. 14.

32. See Sinfield, *Literature, Politics and Culture in Postwar Britain*, especially chapter 11, 'The Rise of Left Culturism'.
33. Sinfield, *Literature, Politics and Culture in Postwar Britain*, p. 323.
34. Simon Frith and Howard Horne, *Art into Pop* (London: Methuen, 1987), pp. 51–52.
35. Paul Willis, *Profane Culture* (London: Routledge, 1978), p. 93.
36. Theodor Adorno, 'On the Fetish Character in Music and the Regression of Listening', in *The Culture Industry: Selected Essays on Mass Culture*, ed. J.M. Bernstein (London: Routledge, 1991), pp. 33–35.
37. Mulhern, *Culture/Metaculture*, p. xix.
38. Toynbee, *Making Popular Music*, p. 2.
39. Adrian Thrills, 'Up Slit Creek', *NME*, 8 September 1979.
40. Toynbee, *Making Popular Music*, pp. ix–x.
41. Ray Gosling, 'Dream Boy', *New Left Review* 1, no. 3 (May–June 1960), 30–34.
42. Toynbee, *Making Popular Music*, p. 26.
43. Toynbee, *Making Popular Music*, p. 25.
44. Toynbee, *Making Popular Music*, pp. xi–xii.
45. Lisa Verrico, 'Are You Talking to Me?', *Dazed and Confused*, December 1998, pp. 56–60.
46. Negus, *Music Genres and Corporate Cultures*, p. 178.
47. Sinfield, *Literature, Politics and Culture in Postwar Britain*, pp. 324–325.
48. Frith and Horne, *Art into Pop*, p. 180.
49. Sinfield, *Literature, Politics and Culture in Postwar Britain*, p. 325.
50. Jon Savage, *England's Dreaming: Sex Pistols and Punk Rock*, 2nd ed. (London: Faber, 2005), p. 43.
51. Tony Parsons and John Hamblett, 'Leeds: Mill City', *NME*, 5 August 1978, pp. 7–8.
52. See, for example, Steve Taylor, 'The Popular Press or How to Roll Your Own Records', *Time Out*, 2 February 1979; Paul Morley and Adrian Thrills, 'Independent Discs', *NME*, 1 September 1979, p. 23; Chris Burkham, 'Cabaret Voltaire: Prepare to Meet Your Mecca', *Sounds*, 25 July 1981; Anonymous, 'Scam', *City Fun* 1, no. 7 (1979).
53. Williams, *Marxism and Literature*, p. 117.
54. Williams, *Culture*, p. 86.
55. Milner, *Re-Imagining Cultural Studies*, p. 73.
56. Milner, *Re-Imagining Cultural Studies*, p. 94.
57. Eagleton, *The Ideology of the Aesthetic*, p. 13.
58. Sinfield, *Literature, Politics and Culture in Postwar Britain*, p. 179.
59. Sinfield, *Literature, Politics and Culture in Postwar Britain*, p. 319.
60. Gosling, 'Dream Boy'.
61. Sinfield, *Literature, Politics and Culture in Postwar Britain*, p. 193.

62. Simon Ford, *Hip Priest: The Story of Mark E. Smith and The Fall* (London: Quartet, 2003), pp. 14–15.
63. Richard Middleton, *Studying Popular Music* (Milton Keynes: Open University Press, 1990), p. 247.
64. Sinfield, *Literature, Politics and Culture in Postwar Britain*, p. 202.
65. Jim McGuigan, *Cool Capitalism* (London: Pluto, 2009), p. 1.
66. Savage, *England's Dreaming*, p. 27.
67. Angela Y. Davis, 'Preface: Marcuse's Legacies', in *Herbert Marcuse: The New Left and the 1960s*, ed. Douglas Kellner (London: Routledge, 2005), p. vii.
68. Davis, 'Preface: Marcuse's Legacies', p. xiii.
69. The term is used in the sense of a 'vision of the future on which a civilisation bases its projects, establishes its ideal goals and builds its hopes', following Marcuse's friend and fellow New Left thinker André Gorz—see André Gorz, *Critique of Economic Reason* (London: Verso, 1989), p. 8.
70. Williams, *Marxism and Literature*, p. 212.
71. Williams, *Politics and Letters: Interviews with New Left Review* (London: Verso, 1981), pp. 340–341.
72. Herbert Marcuse, *An Essay on Liberation* (Harmondsworth: Pelican, 1972), p. 20.
73. Karl Marx, *Early Writings* (Harmondsworth: Penguin, 1975), pp. 327–330.
74. Williams, *Marxism and Literature*, p. 212; Marcuse, *Counterrevolution and Revolt* (Boston: Beacon Press, 1972), p. 64.
75. Andre Gorz, *Critique of Economic Reason*, p. 22.
76. Williams, 'On Reading Marcuse', *Cambridge Review*, 30 May 1969, pp. 366–388; Paul Jones, *Raymond Williams' Sociology of Culture* (Basingstoke: Palgrave Macmillan, 2004), p. 64.
77. Milner, *Re-Imagining Cultural Studies*, p. 8.
78. Marcuse, *Counterrevolution and Revolt*, p. 106.
79. Williams, *Towards 2000*, p. 18.
80. Williams, *Towards 2000*, pp. 146–147.
81. Williams, *Towards 2000*, p. 13.
82. Williams, *Towards 2000*, p. 14.
83. Milner, *Re-imagining Cultural Studies*, p. 64.
84. Williams, *Towards 2000*, p. 14.
85. Herbert Marcuse, 'Liberation from the Affluent Society', transcript of Marcuse's contribution to the Dialectics of Liberation conference in *Herbert Marcuse: The New Left and the 1960s*, pp. 76–86 (p. 78).
86. Raymond Williams, 'Culture is Ordinary', in *Resources of Hope: Culture, Democracy, Socialism*, ed. Robin Gable (London: Verso, 1989), p. 96.
87. Ronald Aronson, 'Marcuse Today', *Boston Review*, 17 November 2014, available online at http://bostonreview.net/books-ideas/ronald-aronson-herbert-marcuse-one-dimensional-man-today, accessed 25 June 2015.
88. Reynolds, *Rip It Up and Start Again*, p. xxv.

89. Herbert Pimlott, '"Militant Entertainment"? "Crisis Music" and Political Ephemera in the Emergent "Structure of Feeling", 1976–1983', in *Fight Back: Punk, Politics and Resistance*, ed. The Subcultures Network (Manchester: MUP, 2015), pp. 268–286.

90. Williams, *Marxism and Literature*, pp. 187–188.

91. Williams, *Culture*, p. 120.

92. Mikhael Bakhtin, *The Dialogic Imagination*, ed. Michael Holquist (Austin: University of Texas Press, 1981), p. 311.

93. Williams, *Culture*, p. 142.

94. Toynbee, *Making Popular Music*, p. 43.

95. Toynbee, *Making Popular Music*, p. 44.

96. Toynbee, *Making Popular Music*, pp. 43–44.

97. V.N. Voloshinov, *Marxism and the Philosophy of Language* (Napier: Seminar Press, 1973).

98. Williams, *Marxism and Literature*, p. 39.

99. Todd Gitlin, 'The Anti-political Populism of Cultural Studies', in *Cultural Studies in Question*, ed. M. Ferguson and P. Golding (London: Sage, 1997), p. 27.

100. Toynbee, *Making Popular Music*, pp. xiv–xv.

101. Toynbee, *Making Popular Music*, pp. 31–32.

102. Reynolds, *Rip It Up and Start Again*, p. 204.

103. Williams, *Marxism and Literature*, p. 187.

104. Toynbee, *Making Popular Music*, p. xiv.

105. Toynbee, *Making Popular Music*, p. 171.

106. Toynbee, *Making Popular Music*, p. 36.

107. Williams, *Marxism and Literature*, p. 197.

108. Pierre Bourdieu, *Distinction: A Social Critique of the Judgement of Taste*, trans. Richard Nice (London: Routledge and Kegan Paul, 1984), p. 164.

109. Williams, *Marxism and Literature*, p. 112.

110. Milner, *Re-imagining Cultural Studies*, pp. 168–169.

111. Milner, *Re-imagining Cultural Studies*, p. 6.

112. Sinfield, *Literature, Politics and Culture in Postwar Britain*, p. 41.

113. Dave Laing, 'Anglo-American Music Journalism: Texts and Contexts', in *The Popular Music Studies Reader*, ed. Andy Bennett, Barry Shank and Jason Toynbee (London: Routledge, 2006), pp. 333–339 (pp. 335–337).

114. Reynolds, *Rip It Up and Start Again*, p. xxvii.

115. Peter York, *Style Wars* (London: Sidgwick and Jackson: 1980), p. 27.

116. Laing, 'Anglo-American Music Journalism: Texts and Contexts', p. 339.

117. Faber website listing for *Totally Wired* by Simon Reynolds, available online at http://www.faber.co.uk/catalog/totally-wired/9780571235490, accessed 5 October 2015.

118. Reynolds, *Rip It Up and Start Again*, p. xvi.

CHAPTER 3

Post-Punk, Thatcherism and the Libertarian Left

Thatcherism, Welfare-Capitalism and the Libertarian Left

Anyone who opposes the neoliberal project that dominates British parliamentary politics might have understandable objections to Margaret Thatcher's 'humbug' misquotation of St Francis of Assisi as she entered 10 Downing Street on 4 May 1979: 'Where there is discord, may we bring harmony'.[1] After all, the 18 years of Conservative rule that her victory had set in motion were consistently and brutally divisive.[2] But there is a sense in which the quotation has become painfully accurate. Recent popular historical accounts of the 1970s tend heavily towards fatalism when reflecting upon the reasons for Conservative victory at the close of the decade. This is due largely to the hegemonic status achieved by neoliberalism in Britain since the election of New Labour in 1997.

From the right, Dominic Sandbrook portrays leftist regret at the breakdown of working class solidarity as puritanical nostalgia which 'refused to see' that this was 'the choice of working class people themselves... [they] unashamedly relished the new consumerism ... [and] deserted the Labour Party for Mrs Thatcher's Conservatives'.[3] As in prior instalments of Sandbrook's account of postwar Britain, the libertarian left is largely given short shrift in *Seasons in the Sun*. Afforded just a few pages, it is mocked as humourlessly earnest and hypocritically authoritarian. Though Sandbrook acknowledges that the libertarian left briefly institutionalised

© The Editor(s) (if applicable) and The Author(s) 2016
D. Wilkinson, *Post-Punk, Politics and Pleasure in Britain*,
DOI 10.1057/978-1-137-49780-2_3

itself in local government, he reduces its contemporary influence and relevance to academia.[4] Instead, the book largely concentrates on the crisis of welfare-capitalism, depicting Thatcherism as its inexorable consequence.

Even Alwyn W. Turner, writing from a broadly centre-left position, concludes that 'the truth was that it was Thatcher's moment', opposing her focus on the future to the 'tired, ineffectual' succession of Edward Heath, Harold Wilson and Jim Callaghan. Turner is a little more willing to recognise the influence of the libertarian left on parliamentary politics, noting the Tories' incorporation of its rhetoric of freedom and its suspicion of statist paternalism.[5] Nevertheless, his discussion of the libertarian left's development in the 1970s is mainly relegated to a chapter entitled 'Fringes', which tellingly places it alongside tales of the most credulous esoteric excesses of the counterculture and a cult of intergalactic Trotskyism.[6]

The fatalism of popular historians like Sandbrook and Turner might seem justified when we consider that Stuart Hall's influential analysis of Thatcherism identified that it brought together powerful collective resentments dating back to the late 1960s.[7] Sandbrook and Turner's focus, too, on the collapse of welfare-capitalism is arguably vindicated by Hall's methodical identification of Thatcherism's successes with the failings and contradictions of postwar Labourism.[8] On this point though, we should also recall Raymond Williams' argument that the drift to the right in Britain was not some 'essence of the people' distilled by Thatcherism, but a response to the 'dislocation' produced by the gradual decline of welfare-capitalism. This was a dislocation that could potentially be politically redirected.[9] Indeed, Hall recognised in *The Great Moving Right Show* that Thatcherism's ideological gains over Labourism had had to be consciously and pro-actively achieved.[10] Nor did they achieve instant hegemony.[11]

My point here is that the political moment of the 1970s and early 1980s was, like all historical periods, one of active struggles rather than inevitable development. It was open to contest, and this contest was one that occurred not only between welfare-capitalism and Thatcherism but also between Thatcherism and the libertarian left. The complacent ridicule directed at these political movements by Sandbrook and Turner is indicative not of their self-evident implausibility and marginality, but rather the success of a persistent ideological battle waged against the libertarian left.

The media was a key battleground, an arena that the left had neglected at its peril.[12] Ben Jackson notes that the neoliberal think-tanks which influenced the New Right fostered intimate connections with the British media through exclusive dinners, seminars and so on, playing on the resentments of media executives and journalists who had a 'professional identity... similar to that of self-employed skilled workers' against the influence of the print unions.[13] The term 'loony left' is often associated with the mid-1980s and the right-wing media's demonisation of those local Labour councils where the libertarian left had taken refuge. Yet the process of portraying the left as deranged had begun much earlier (even Labour newspaper the *Daily Mirror* was using the term 'loony left' as early as 1976),[14] and was part of a well-honed media art of dismissing oppositional forces, one which had deep historical roots.[15]

Popular culture was another significant arena, especially television and film. In the context of the media's attacks, the sitcom *Till Death Us Do Part*, though assembled by a left-leaning team, inadvertently offered a sympathetic portrayal of its reactionary 'everyman' main character Alf Garnett. One episode, broadcast following the years of gay liberation activism earlier in the 1970s, shows Garnett uncomfortably humiliated by a camp pub entertainer after a series of homophobic outbursts to the effect that gay people are 'taking over'.[16] *Carry On Girls*, meanwhile, climaxed with the disruption of a seaside beauty contest by a group of feminists named 'Operation Spoilsport'. Later in the decade, *Citizen Smith* satirised would-be young radicals, squatters and rock musicians the Tooting Popular Front. Even the surreal early 1980s student sitcom *The Young Ones*, emerging from the left-wing 'alternative comedy' scene covered by the music weeklies alongside post-punk,[17] auto-critiqued itself with the character of Rik: an infantile middle-class brat whose anarchist pretensions and luxuriant enunciations of the word 'revolution' are somewhat undermined by his petty selfishness. Yet the fact that the libertarian left received such attention was proof that its influence went far deeper than we have recently been expected to believe.

Direct attacks, combined with gentle mockery from within and without, were undoubtedly powerful and lasting in their effects. This is something we will see in later analyses of those post-punks who broadly shared libertarian left ideals. Especially common amongst their critics were accusations of hypocritical authoritarianism and joylessness, suggesting the era's hegemonic struggle over freedom and pleasure. Ann Leslie, for instance, recounted her student Marxist days wryly in a sensationalist *Daily Mail* article that speculated on why so many 'nicely brought up middle class girls' gravitated to the radical left. Leslie evoked a world of 'dreary bedsits', claiming that 'I'd like to say it was good sense that brought me round, but more likely it was sheer boredom and irritation at the joyless squalor'. Notably, she also suggested that her former male comrades' political activities were hypocritically motivated by a desire for 'girlish admiration' and a 'snobbish … prestige at having won some Annabel or Sarah Jane over to their side'.[18]

The libertarian left was undoubtedly a weaker opponent than Labourism in terms of direct political power; it was fragmented due to its favouring of autonomy and the difficulties of making deep and sustained alliances with either the wider labour movement or the sectarian huddles of the revolutionary left.[19] Ultimately, too, many who practised this kind of politics were 'closet Keynesians': revolutionary in intent but somewhat optimistically framing their demands in terms of a delivery on Labour's parliamentary socialist 'promises of 1945'.[20] This was captured in the influence of Marxist thinkers such as Ken Coates on the Bennite wing of the Labour Party.[21] Nevertheless, the libertarian left was far more advanced than Labourism in terms of its oppositional notions of freedom and pleasure. Thus not only did it need to be ridiculed and dismissed by the right in order to gain the political advantage, but also significantly incorporated.

This issue requires a little back story. Williams identified as far back as the start of the 1960s that both the Labour Party and labour movement were succumbing to defining their activities in terms of the market and consumerism. To do so was a fatal weakness, because it abandoned the oppositional, co-operative practices within the labour movement that might form the basis for a transformed society. Instead, 'patterns of crude economic cynicism' arose on the left.[22] Collectivism never took hold deeply enough; even state welfare was usually valued in terms of individual need rather than shared provision.[23] Hall later argued that Thatcherism had successfully identified popular aspirations with individual wealth and status, ideologically opposing these aspirations to the very 'interventionist state' that in reality had helped spread prosperity and opportunity around.[24] In other words, Thatcherism operated on the same terrain as postwar Labourism regarding freedom and pleasure. It cynically positioned itself as the natural inheritor and means of fulfilment for the consumerist desires fostered by welfare-capitalism, yet which, beset by economic crisis, the latter could no longer grant. 'We will make it possible for people to earn more so they can buy more', declared a 1979 Conservative election broadcast.[25] 'There are great industries in other people's pleasures', Thatcher later claimed, ominously.[26]

Williams, though, framed the problem in less pessimistically structuralist terms than Hall with the concept of 'mobile privatisation'. The phrase aimed to capture a pervasive structure of feeling with its roots in the consumerism of welfare-capitalism. 'Mobile privatisation' is the investment of freedom and pleasure, including 'many of the most productive, imaginative impulses of people', into private consumption, especially within the spheres of home, family, and friends. It is 'a shell which you can take with you', insulating against 'those big things, in whatever colour of politics they appear to come, [which] are interpreted as mere ... abstractions ... boring interferences with this real life'.[27]

Williams noted that 'mobile privatisation' was an ambivalent phenomenon, expressing in part the huge advance in mobility and material comforts for the many created by welfare-capitalism. But it depended on unsustainable economic conditions and policies, and was now being co-opted by Thatcherism, despite the fact that 'it is only in certain marginal and superficial ways that the Right has ever really offered this opportunity to people'. It meant that the labour movement was often pressured to adopt a discourse of 'collective provision'. This was difficult to oppose on moral grounds, but alone it was an insufficient response. The left was ceding the ground of 'freedom and achievement' to the right, falling back on an unattractively impersonal and puritanical position of duty to the public good which wrongly and arrogantly generalised a diagnosis of 'deluded, selfish, greedy, aggressive mass behaviour' on the part of the electorate.[28] This left freedom and pleasure open for colonisation by the traditional consumerist appeal to the private individual. As André Gorz has noted, this appeal usually defines satisfaction against precisely any feeling of obligation or solidarity as part of its compensatory function, making up for the way we are forced to sacrifice our autonomy to capitalist interests.[29]

By contrast, it was precisely the ground of freedom and pleasure that the libertarian left had built many of its oppositional notions upon, making it a direct threat to emerging Thatcherism. A brief history of the libertarian left and its oppositional definitions of freedom and pleasure will help us understand the context of this incorporative struggle.

The origins of the libertarian left lay largely in the moment of the New Left, which coalesced in the late 1950s out of shared opposition to the weaknesses of Labourism and the brutalities and betrayals of Stalinism symbolised by the Soviet invasion of Hungary in 1956.[30] Indeed it may seem that the more recognisable historical term 'New Left' would be a clearer way of summarising the political tendency I refer to. I have chosen the term 'libertarian left', however, so as to include formations whose varied alignments either extended beyond the New Left, such as the women's movement, or whose alignment lay elsewhere, such as the Eurocommunist wing of the British Communist Party, but whose concerns had a degree of crossover.[31]

As Robin Blackburn has argued, the attempts of the New Left to challenge the 'paternalism' and 'philistinism' of postwar Labourism were extended over the following two decades by student revolt, the resurgence of feminism and a host of other forces.[32] Dennis Dworkin, too, notes the way that 'handfuls of ... scattered individuals' developed into a diverse, substantial movement via the expansion of higher education, the emergence of the counterculture, and the beginnings in the late 1960s of the postwar economic and social crises that would culminate in the General Election of 1979.[33] Though by no means cohesive, what brought this movement together was opposition to the old left's integration into capitalist institutions, its top-down bureaucracy, and its hesitancy to question cultural and social mores.[34]

What positively defined the libertarian left? Its understanding of freedom usually emphasised public ownership combined with a healthy level of decentralised independence. Crucially, though, this was not usually an economistic position, but rather a left humanistic one comparable to the previous chapter's discussion of Williams and Marcuse's shared rooting of human agency in the young Marx's theory of 'species being'.[35] If we are social and creative creatures, then a socialist economic system that shares both resources and decision making would seem to be the most appropriate one.

The frequent humanism of the libertarian left also meant that, as Sheila Rowbotham puts it, 'capitalism was seen as claiming your whole being', echoing Williams' 'structures of feeling' and Marcuse's concern with the 'biological'. It had thus to be contested at the level of the personal and everyday life. This was to be achieved by 'living your politics', meaning that 'the attack against capitalist society should carry the future within the present'.[36] The strategy took various forms, including what Williams might have called 'systematic utopianism': the prefigurative building of alternative institutions based on principles of shared ownership and democratic control. These took the form of the 'whole variety of industrial, community and cultural organisations' described by Hilary Wainwright[37]—co-ops, left trades councils, women's and community centres, independent printing presses, radical bookshops and so on.

Wainwright's mention of the cultural is indicative of the other key prefigurative element of the libertarian left, which was its attempt to search for qualitatively different pleasures than those advocated by consumer capitalism. This was often conveyed through cultural production, for example in the Women's Theatre movement, and more generally through the examination of lived feelings and values.[38] Such examination had its roots in the work of the early New Left journal *Universities and Left Review* (later *New Left Review*), edited by figures including Williams and Hall, which made comparable links to cultural production like the Free Cinema movement.[39] Recalling Marcuse's hopes for a 'new sensibility' and Williams' 'heuristic utopias', Rowbotham was wary of the puritanical outlook of Leninist sects, wondering 'why should the ruling class have the monopoly on cosiness?'[40]

Rowbotham also observes that it was this focus on culture and qualitative change which linked the libertarian left to 'movements concerned to change feelings and desires' such as the women's movement, gay liberation and the struggles of ethnic minorities.[41] Of these, I focus throughout the book on the women's movement for two reasons. Firstly, its influence on the libertarian left was so extensive that Rowbotham, Segal and Wainwright argued in *Beyond the Fragments* that the women's movement offered some of the most promising models for a renewal of leftist organisation and unity in the face of Thatcherism.[42] Secondly, the women's movement was also the most influential of the 'new social movements' on the politics of post-punk (though as we will see, ecologically motivated anti-consumerism also played a surprisingly neglected part).

By the first term of the Thatcher government, the libertarian left had built a strong institutional opposition, but it was about to run into serious difficulties. These 'closet Keynesians' may have dissented from paternalistic welfare-capitalism, but it had also left its imprint on them. Many shared the unconscious assumption concerning the state that 'if you made enough fuss they would take notice (like a child with kind parents)'.[43] A far sterner parent was now in power, with little tolerance for the disparate progressive advances of the 1960s and 1970s that right-wing media rhetoric had bundled together under the ideological banner of 'the permissive society'. By the second term of the Thatcher government, there was a concerted targeting of the institutional 'nooks and crannies' which the libertarian left had managed to occupy,[44] especially where these constituted a direct political challenge, as in the case of Ken Livingstone's tenure of the Greater London Council.

The libertarian left was not only winkled out at an institutional level. For some time, the right had been incorporating its claims on humanism, freedom and pleasure. Thatcher developed a canny anti-authoritarian rhetoric that presented the left as top-down, 'ideological' and doctrinal in contrast to Tory organicism,[45] stressing that what the Conservatives offered was 'vision, not blueprint'.[46] She made plain her support for the right-wing libertarian pressure group the National Association for Freedom, whilst keeping a public distance from unaccountable think-tanks like the Institute of Economic Affairs with which her party allies were associated.[47] Thatcher moved in on the personal politics of the left, too, famously claiming that 'economics are the method; the object is to change the heart and soul'.[48] Freedom and pleasure came to be equated with market choice, with Thatcher encapsulating the outlook of the New Right in her assertion that under capitalism, the consumer was 'free to take it or leave it, whatever it may be. Socialism says, "take it and lump it"'.[49]

This is not to discount the strength of what Hall referred to as 'authoritarian populism'[50]—what could be described in more concrete political terms as the conservative themes that have been contradictorily yet successfully articulated with economic neoliberalism since its inception. But even this ground was often discussed in terms of freedom: the moral campaigner Mary Whitehouse, who evolved from marginal figure of fun to figurehead of the 'silent majority' over the course of the 1960s and 1970s,[51] receiving a CBE from the Thatcher government in 1980,[52] railed against what she called media 'propaganda'.[53] This was in spite of her repeated advocacy of censorship. Meanwhile, the influential conservative intellectual Maurice Cowling openly claimed: 'What [conservatives] want is the sort of freedom that will maintain existing inequalities or restore lost ones.'[54] As we will see, though, post-punk's conflicted politics related less to the New Right's attempted revival of conservative values. Rather, they were more closely tied to its incorporative response to the qualitative disaffection of the libertarian left.

From the Counterculture to Post-Punk

So far I have situated the politics of the libertarian left within the context of the late 1970s and early 1980s. But what was the historical connection between these political movements and post-punk? It was the libertarian left's relationship with the counterculture of the 1960s and 1970s, and post-punk's evolution from this movement. The subculture that developed around the early New Left in Britain was, according to Raphael Samuel, 'a nursery of 1960s counterculture'.[55] These links are made clearest in Jeff Nuttall's seminal *Bomb Culture*, which includes a substantial account of New Left institutions such as the Campaign for Nuclear Disarmament and locations like the Partisan Coffee House.[56] Discussing the 1970s, Lynne Segal has argued that the countercultural message of 'hedonism without consumerism' complemented the libertarian left's commitment to radical change at an 'emotional' as well as an 'intellectual' level.[57]

The countercultural rock of the late 1960s and early 1970s captured movements and desires; both at a populist and now mythologised level in songs such as John Lennon's triptych 'Give Peace A Chance', 'Power To The People' and 'Imagine';[58] and in more 'underground' expressions like Hawkwind's ecological prophecy 'We Took The Wrong Step Years Ago'. Developments like glam mirrored similar moments of focus on the libertarian left, such as gay liberation. The counterculture and the libertarian left, then, were intimately intertwined, something that is often evident as a structure of feeling in photographs of radicals from this era; flares, paisley, leather jackets and wild hair abound.

There was no simple elision, however. Elizabeth Wilson notes that the counterculture was not always consciously politicised, despite having 'material similarities' to the libertarian left, including the building of alternative institutions.[59] In *Play Power*, a key countercultural text, co-editor of underground magazine *Oz* Richard Neville declared that 'grubby Marxist leaflets and hand-me-down rhetoric won't put an end to toil. It will be an irresistible, fun-possessed, play-powered counter-culture.'[60]

This association of leftist political allegiance with a puritanical outlook was representative of a wider strand of opinion within the counterculture. It was a key factor in the right's incorporation of hippie dissent, which was closely intertwined with its incorporation of the libertarian left; Richard Neville, for instance, is now a business consultant. Peter York pithily captures the evolving structure of feeling of countercultural hedonism on the London fashion scene over the course of the 1970s, highlighting its imbrication with the consumerism it ostensibly opposed:

> The kind of girls who five years before would have been up to their necks in the Monsoon Indian print three-piece ... were on to Roddy this and Di that ... *absolutely fixated* on the high society idea ... tinkering about with this very stylised interest in luxury as kitsch ... Then in a little while you found they were turning really Right—like those progressive rock groups who said they were voting Tory in 1979.[61]

Freedom, too, was sometimes narrowly understood in the terms of individual economic gain discussed earlier. David Stubbs observes that: 'Most of rock's aristocracy, the [Rolling] Stones included, were put out by what they saw as the punitively high level of income tax imposed by Harold Wilson.'[62] Sinfield highlights the transformation of '1960s buccaneers' into '1980s takeover wizards';[63] once again, McGuigan's 'cool capitalism' thesis comes to mind. Subculturally, Paul Willis observed a frequent distrust of the left and a self-centred, rather than mutual, understanding of freedom. Willis quoted a hippie who declared, 'there's no room for me in communism ... no room for me as an individual ... I'd have less freedom ... I couldn't work for the society, I could only ever work for me'.[64] The counterculture, after all, was determined not just by qualitative disaffection with postwar consumerism but also by the way that consumerism melted down tradition, deference and collective values in favour of individual gratification. Gorz notes that 'individuals socialised by consumerism ... are encouraged to "be themselves" by distinguishing themselves from others and who only resemble these others in their refusal...to assume responsibility for the common condition'.[65]

One of the most valuable elements of Simon Reynolds' history of post-punk is the consistent emphasis it places on the residual influence of the counterculture on punk and post-punk. It is a useful corrective in the face of continued clichés in the media and other popular historical accounts regarding the radical break between 'hippies' and 'punks' and 'Punk Myth #1: the early seventies as cultural wasteland';[66] a myth that even the old hands of punk can now usually be relied upon to reproduce.[67] Yet as Jess Baines, a radical print-shop worker involved in punk and post-punk, recalls: 'You discovered that there were these *old people* doing DIY too—blokes with long hair.'[68]

What this legacy meant for post-punk in political terms was not only an inheritance of the counterculture's ambiguous libertarianism but also its culturalism. Reynolds refers to post-punks trying 'to do something innovative and challenging' rather than pursuing 'a more commercial path'[69] and claims:

I do very much see punk and post-punk as a continuation of the sixties ... with punk, there's internecine warfare being conducted across generational lines, but that all takes place *within* a ... consensus that sees rock as a force for change, disruption, subversion. Post-punk, because it let back in ideas of complexity ... reconnects even more to all those sixties ideas about rock-as-art.[70]

Thus post-punk was also deeply preoccupied with themes of freedom and pleasure, which I argued in the previous chapter tend to arise when the production of culture occurs through institutional practices and in circumstances that encourage a culturalist understanding of the arts. In order to fully understand the politics of post-punk, it is important to emphasise this residually culturalist element against the overly schematic aspects of otherwise useful attempts to differentiate post-punk from related musical movements, such as Theodore Gracyk's portrayal of it as an 'anti-romantic strain of artistic modernism'.[71]

Gracyk's reference to modernism does shed some light, however. 'The entire period', Reynolds claims, 'looks like an attempt to replay virtually every modernist theme and technique via the medium of pop music'.[72] Through immersion in the world of art schools and the counterculture, the bohemian legacy of successive avant-gardes filtered through. Importantly, the attraction was often to movements like Dada, and figures such as Bertolt Brecht, where there had been a reaction against the rarefied status of culture even as this status was residually preserved. Post-punk, then, inherited not just the culturalism of the counterculture, its aesthetic anti-commercialism, but also its anti-culturalist suspicion of the separation of art from commerce and civilisation (see Chap. 2). This anti-culturalism helped to open up emergent political possibilities on the left of post-punk. These included self-reflection on creative practice, attention to gender, and a shift from an alternative to a fully oppositional attitude towards independence at the level of the institutions of the music industry.

However, the source of this anti-culturalism was not always modernism, which, after all, was by no means always critically reflective and was ideologically appropriated as representative of art in the free West in the immediate postwar context of the Cold War.[73] Nor was attendance at art school or university always the institutional origin, as Reynolds can tend to assume. Sometimes, anti-culturalism arose more straightforwardly from the diffusion of libertarian left concerns through the counterculture, a connection which could be direct (as with the links of The Raincoats, The Fall, and the Blue Orchids to the women's movement, and Scritti Politti's Communist Party membership) or more indirect and prone to greater tension (as in the case of The Slits' relationship with feminism). Furthermore, residual countercultural interests in the esoteric could be surprisingly reworked in ways that allowed for an anti-culturalist approach to the politics of popular musical production, as with the Blue Orchids. Finally, art school and university also introduced bands to more directly politicised theories of cultural production, as in the case of Gang of Four, Scritti Politti and The Raincoats.

POST-PUNK AS DISTINCTIVE FORMATION

It is undeniable that there was break as well as continuity between the counterculture, punk and its numerous offshoots. Largely this was generational; a younger demographic sensing stagnation, confusion and hypocrisy within the ranks of the counterculture that prevented it from fully grasping the overall structure of feeling of the late 1970s. Punk was early on characterised as a social realist and populist phenomenon capturing the disaffection of the 'kids'.[74] In formal terms, this translated initially into a reworking of diverse strands of countercultural rock sharing a more aggressive and cynical tone, including The Stooges, early Who and The Velvet Underground. The latter two bands also appealed because of their links to the Pop Art anti-culturalism that fed into punk via svengalis like Malcolm McLaren and The Clash's manager Bernie Rhodes, both of whom had come of age in the 1960s.

Fashion-wise, punk borrowed provocatively from subcultures hostile to the counterculture, masking continuities of generation and outlook. Jon Savage observes that Vivienne Westwood and Malcolm McLaren's harnessing of the ted revival was 'a useful polemic with which to crash through the detritus of hippie culture', but did not reflect 'the libertarian currents of the 1960s' that had formed and directed the pair's efforts. 'The teds', Savage claims, 'were as English as meat pies and racism: McLaren and Westwood ate vegetarian food and wouldn't buy South African oranges'.[75] The residual influence of the counterculture was not confined to the older figures responsible for fomenting the movement; for instance, a teenage punk penned an article for *Flicks* fanzine entitled 'Human Lib'.[76]

The Sex Pistols' John Lydon captured this conflicted punk sensibility succinctly in an interview with the impressively afro'ed Charles Shaar Murray. 'I can remember going to those concerts and seeing all those hippies ... *despising* me because I was about twenty years younger', Lydon claimed with characteristic exaggeration. 'Far out', he sneered in response to Murray's earnestness, before backtracking: 'It's hard not to run into those hippie phrases, because some of them were good, some of them actually meant something.' This was followed by an astute observation of one of the key faultlines in the counterculture: 'It's just a shame they ruined [things] with silly ideas about "I wanna be *free*", which meant fuck all.'[77]

Lydon's cynical tone, though, was indicative of the way in which the initial moment of punk was overwhelmed by a corrosive nihilism. Numerous commentators have attributed the nihilism that marked punk to its emergence at a moment of profound social anxiety and uncertainty during the final stage of the collapse of welfare-capitalist consensus.[78] This mood is perhaps captured best in Derek Jarman's 1978 film *Jubilee*. Punk's nihilism carried over into the early 1980s too, finding no shortage of focus as the Thatcher government set about its ruthless restructuring of the British economy, leading to spiralling unemployment and social unrest.[79] Matthew Worley has noted that numerous factions of punk's fallout developed a symbolic fixation on the prospect of nuclear armageddon in the wake of the renewed Cold War.[80]

A comparable bleakness could be detected in the attenuated production of post-punk bands such as Joy Division and other early Factory Records acts; *City Fun* writer Liz Naylor recalls the penchant for 1930s-referencing charity shop garb on the Manchester scene, observing that 'the whole ... population of Hulme seemed to be wearing the clothes of dead men'.[81] 'Both sides of the river, there are bacteria', Lydon caterwauled in 'Careering', a song by his post-Pistols band Public Image Limited, while the music of Cabaret Voltaire burbled with paranoid media collages. Gaunt, high-contrast photographs of bands stared out from the pages of the music weeklies. As times changed and countercultural optimism subsided, the dankness of its squatted and liminal infrastructure, upon which punk and post-punk had been built, seeped in.

Despite all this, the name of This Heat's rehearsal space seemed to capture the fate of countercultural and libertarian left utopianism in post-punk: 'Cold Storage'. 'Please', Mark Stewart of The Pop Group pleaded against a clangourous backdrop that portentously descended in pitch, 'don't sell your dreams'. Oliver Loewenstein's severe fanzine *Dangerous Logic*, meanwhile, described itself as 'a grey journal ... with a bit of vigour and hope'.[82]

As well as breaking with punk's 'no future' stance, this attitude stood at odds with the drift of mainstream politics; a drift that continued even after Conservative electoral victory in 1979 seemed superficially to resolve the tension. Noting that the piecemeal management of capitalist crises was becoming an ever-more determinate feature of government policy, distorting or overtaking any manifesto promises, Williams claimed that 'world-weary adaptation', 'sceptical resignation' and 'a willingness to leave matters to ... a strong leader' had come to predominate and that 'the most widely practised form of general thinking about the future, in political programmes and manifestos, carries with it disadvantages which often lead to the abandonment of any real thinking about the future'.[83]

By contrast, the fragile strand of hope detectable in post-punk resonated with the main oppositional response to this 'politics of temporary tactical advantage'. This was the renewal of utopianism 'against the disappointments of current politics ... but also against the incorporated and marketed versions of a libertarian capitalist cornucopia'.[84] Post-punk was often informed by the qualitative opposition of the libertarian left; its concern both with 'systematic utopias' through the building of alternative institutions, and with 'heuristic utopias' through a focus on qualitatively different understandings and practices of freedom and pleasure. One of the most important features of punk salvaged by post-punk was, 'following in the footsteps of the Situationists', the identification of:

> Boredom as *the* problem facing youth in the affluent West ... if punk was a destructive response to boredom, you could say that post-punk was a constructive response: it was literally about making up a whole bunch of reasons to be excited, a mesh of fevered activity and discussion that made the world seem more interesting and life seem more urgent.[85]

Two other features marked post-punk out from first-wave punk, both of which are central to an understanding of its politics. Each recalls the organising principles that Williams suggests bring cultural formations together. Firstly, post-punk broke away formally, a feature succinctly characterised by Reynolds: 'Groups that had been catalysed by punk but didn't sound "punk rock" in the classic ... sense ... they interpreted punk as an imperative to keep changing.'[86] In other words, there was 'the common pursuit of some specific artistic aim'.[87] Often, this innovation was consciously or unconsciously politicised. Jon Savage defended the electronic experimentation of Cabaret Voltaire against the 'new conservatives'.[88] Young Communists Scritti Politti advocated 'scratchy-collapsy ... enthusiastic' attempts at innovation, linking them to 'new ideas' and 'commitment',[89] whilst This Heat tied their 'all channels open' musical approach to a 'liberating' anti-hierarchical stance[90] and a desire to 'fight back against these bastards who were ruining the world'.[91]

Although post-punk's influences were wildly eclectic, a 'space of possibility' rather than the coalescence of one specific sound,[92] certain musical genres took on particular significance (see Chap. 2's discussion of form).

Vivien Goldman's captivating New Musick article on dub reggae, for instance, described its 'surrealist potential' and the 'fun' that could be had in producing its 'fevered dream' manipulations of sound. This emphasis on new experiences and perceptions resonated with the submerged utopianism of post-punk. Furthermore, Goldman's interview with Dennis Bovell of British reggae band Matumbi laid bare the technical processes behind dub production, building bridges with post-punk impulses to DIY demystification.[93]

It is important, however, not to elide this future-focused form with progressive politics. Like the counterculture from which it developed, post-punk as a whole was not always a leftist phenomenon. Nor even was it always politically committed, as Reynolds notes, for example, in the case of Howard Devoto of Magazine, describing the band's song 'Shot By Both Sides' as 'a defence of the bourgeois art-rock notion that the individual's struggle to be different is what really matters'.[94] 'It's not political … it's just life',[95] Siouxsie Sioux claimed of the Banshees' music, tiring too of journalists mentioning the band's middle-class background: 'There's nothing in class at all.'[96]

The left of post-punk was, however, influential enough to prompt Devoto to write the song, and for the Banshees' Steve Severin to declare a few years later that he was 'extremely left-wing', expressing puzzlement that anyone might interpret the band's politics otherwise.[97] Paul Morley, meanwhile, framed the interview in which Sioux dismissed class and politics with quotations from Erich Fromm and Bertholt Brecht. This tension between the alternative and the oppositional was as true of the institutions that supported post-punk as it was of the bands and their music, as I go on to explore in my analysis of key post-punk independent labels. In order to avoid the radical wish fulfilment so common to cultural studies, highlighted in the previous chapter, it makes sense to focus on bands with explicit links to the politics of the libertarian left, accounting for the selection of case studies in Chaps. 4–6.

Post-punk's second break was its close association with the independent label boom in the wake of punk,[98] distinguishing it from the abandonment of the DIY ideals often present in the first wave of punk as 'the top bands without exception followed the traditional rock route and looked for the best major label deal they could get'.[99] Few post-punk bands signed to established majors, and those that did so were often interrogated as to their reasons. I consider this issue in some detail in the following chapter on Gang of Four and Scritti Politti. This aspect of post-punk recalls

Williams' definition of alternative and oppositional formations, which develop 'alternative facilities' for cultural production.[100]

A focus on formal innovation and economic independence as key defining elements of post-punk helps to better clarify the ways its politics were expressed. Nevertheless, the debates in the music weeklies that marked its split did not always focus directly on these issues. They were also routed quite centrally through the themes of class and education, as the tensions arising from punk's initial, thrilling fusion of 'outcasts from every class'[101] began to bubble to the surface. Frequently, continued education was elided with a middle-class background, and its absence associated with a working class one. *Sounds'* Garry Bushell (himself a grammar school-educated working class boy and a former student) was an early adopter of this line; Bushell's interview with Sham 69 made much of the band's singer Jimmy Pursey's claim that 'the intelligentsia' were not in favour of 'commoners' like himself 'getting their hands' on punk.[102] A few weeks later, a letter indicated that Bushell was tapping something broader: the 'Middle Park Mafia' wrote to express their appreciation that Bushell liked 'real kids' bands' and was not an 'intellectual snob'.[103] One year on, and Bushell, enthused by lumpen bands like the Angelic Upstarts and the Cockney Rejects, began propagandising a 'New Punk' (later known as 'Oi!'): a 'working class rebellion' opposed to the apparent betrayal of Billy Idol revealing his 'nice middle class upbringing'[104] and lyrics that sounded 'like seminar rooms'.[105]

This elision of education and culture with the middle classes is of course commonplace. It derives from the mobility associated with education in an unequal society and the ideological attribution of manual, rather than mental, labour to the working class—as if these kinds of work could be separated easily.[106] The theme's pervasiveness in post-punk media was, however, ironic at a historical moment when Britain's primary industries, which had been so closely associated with 'manual' labour and working class identity, were in severe decline and education meanwhile was continuing to expand. It reflects broader anxieties and uncertainties at this time regarding changing class composition, captured on the left, for instance, in Eric Hobsbawm's 'The Forward March of Labour Halted?'[107]

Repeated often enough, this discourse became tenacious. Numerous influential accounts of punk and post-punk, both academic and popular, have reproduced it.[108] It appears in the opening pages of *Rip It Up and Start Again*, where Reynolds claims that post-punk marked the point at which 'punk's fragile unity between working-class kids and arty, middle-class bohemians began to fracture'.[109] Yet post-punk's class make-up was variable, as subsequent chapters of Reynolds' book valuably go on to illustrate. This was true of the broader subculture too, hinted at by a pair of letters to *Sounds* objecting to journalist Dave McCullough's elision of students with the middle classes and questioning his claim that their involvement was inauthentic. 'More and more working class kids are becoming students', wrote 'a lost, lonely, extremely depressed little girl'. 'We're still kids, we still hate (and right now we hate YOU!) ... We know ... that punk has disintegrated and we've modernised.'[110]

The continued elision of education with being middle class in accounts of post-punk means that working class post-punks' negotiations of educational experience, crucial to an understanding of their politics, have so far been neglected. One example of this is that Reynolds, though acknowledging that 'not everybody in post-punk attended art school or ... university', assimilates working class autodidacts The Fall into a now largely institutionalised tradition of avant-garde anti-art.[111] Mark E. Smith's 'invective' is further characterised as coming from 'somewhere outside the class system'.[112] As we will see, Smith's politics were profoundly rooted in his working class background, his attendance at a grammar school, and his autodidactic stance thereafter. After moving away from association with radicalism, Smith's critique was most often directed at a perceived middle-class fraction within and outside post-punk with which he identified the politics of the libertarian left. Similarly, because three of Gang of Four attended university, it has long been assumed that their background was solidly middle class. In reality, the two key songwriters and strategists of the band were from working or lower middle-class backgrounds, and their experience of grammar school and university as class mobility strongly shaped their political development.

The polarising rhetoric of journalists also had implications for post-punk as a potentially populist force. The argument often went that post-punk, with its difficult formal experiment and its 'squattage industry',[113] was a marginal middle-class fraction, memorably satirised in a Ray Lowry cartoon strip as 'pale, anaemic music played by pale anaemic individuals ... written about by pale, anaemic journalists—to rampant apathy'.[114] The discourse had taken hold as early as January 1979; Dave McCullough, interviewing Scritti Politti, presumptively assumed he was writing to an everyman readership that would automatically be dissuaded by the band's art school background.[115] As with class and education, this slightly misleading portrayal has proven influential, even among those who were rightly dubious of it at the time. Jon Savage writes retrospectively of punk's division into 'arties' and 'social realists',[116] describing the former as having 'lost contact with the social mix which had given the original Sex Pistols so much of their bite … the result was laboratory pop'.[117]

Yet post-punk attempted to touch a populist pulse too. Siouxsie Sioux linked the Banshees' attitude to broader events in a New Musick feature by Vivien Goldman, speculating 'maybe there is a new ice age coming'.[118] Less than a year later, the band would appear on Top of the Pops. Savage portrayed Cabaret Voltaire's sound as inextricably linked with the industrial/post-industrial north, capturing 'the grey air, thick with moisture, revealing vistas of factories, tower blocks, endless tightly patterned semis', and tapping what lay 'under the bland homogenised façade of our present mesmerisation'.[119] Ian Wood saw The Fall as a contemporary L.S. Lowry canvas, explicitly concerned with everyday life. Mark E. Smith claimed that they existed outside the false divide between 'intellectual' bands and 'headbanger bands for ordinary people'.[120] Bob Last of record label Fast Product wanted to do 'something interesting without it being labelled as avant-gardist',[121] while Rough Trade's Geoff Travis opposed the 'small funnel towards stardom' and aimed to 'include as many people and ideas as possible'.[122] In numerous cases, this desire for impact was fulfilled: though sales figures are a partial and instrumentalist definition of populism, the fact that bands such as The Slits and Gang of Four made the Top 40, whilst Joy Division featured in the Top 10 on the independent Factory, showed that something was going on.[123]

Nevertheless, the influential debates of the weeklies, combined with the undeniable difficulties faced by post-punk's fledgling independent infrastructure, provoked two responses. From without came Oi!, encapsulated in Bushell's claim that the 'teenage warning' of 'working class hero[es]' the Angelic Upstarts had 'more relevance' than any of the 'New Musick'.[124] From within came the new pop, articulated by those who had once helped formulate and champion post-punk. Scritti Politti's Green Gartside, for example, began declaring his desire to move away from 'marginality' and the pursuit of a 'mythical alternative'.[125]

Significantly, Oi! and new pop polemics on class and populism often encompassed the politics of the post-punk left too. Bushell wrote of Gang of Four's 'middle class leftism'[126] and, in a direct appeal to media satire of the libertarian left, opposed the 'regular … working class following' of the UK Subs to 'pretentious pseudo-intellectual points about the Tooting Popular Front'.[127] The construction of Oi! as macho and homophobic—'hard' working class men versus 'disco queens'—betrayed an association of the radical gender and sexual politics that sometimes characterised post-punk with an effete, overeducated middle class parodied as wasting time with obscure 'meeting(s) on the sexuality of Argentinian … revisionists'.[128]

Oi! would evolve beyond Bushell's definitions in contradictory political directions, which nevertheless tended to share an emphasis on collective working class identity and experience in opposition to the perceived detachment of post-punk's 'middle class' radicalism. And it was true that the culture of the libertarian left had long generated a sense of exclusion among those who had not learned its lexicon or mixed in its circles.[129] Oi!'s defining feature was its partial fulfilment of punk's initial claim to have given voice to working class disaffection.[130] This, though, was the disaffection of a specific, largely male, fraction, often rendered newly lumpen by the crises and transformations of the British economy during this era.

The crossover between Oi! and the skinhead revival of the late 1970s and early 1980s was significant; it evoked John Clarke's characterisation of first-wave skinheads as the 'dispossessed inheritors' of a disappearing culture.[131] By the second time around, skinhead was rendered even more nostalgic by the way in which, as Peter York notes, the meaning of subcultural accoutrements had become jumbled, complexified and sometimes even depthless by the increasing prominence of popular cultural analysis and the widening consumer availability of fashion styles throughout the 1970s.[132] Post-punk bands like The Fall and the Blue Orchids would give voice to somewhat different forms of working class dissent, as we will see in Chap. 5.

Meanwhile, Paul Morley claimed that The Pop Group's second album, unambiguously titled *For How Much Longer Do We Tolerate Mass Murder?*, gave a 'bad-drab' name to 'post-punk' and portrayed their political commitment as 'elitist'.[133] The politics of new pop were complex; they could appear similar to those of left post-punk, at times advocating economic independence[134] and using the terms 'post-punk' and 'new pop' interchangeably.[135] There were two key differences, however. Firstly, there was an impatience regarding populist impact, resulting in the advocacy of 'operat[ing] from within'[136] that would eventually lead to the dismissal of the independent sector. Secondly, left post-punk's political critique, and the shrouding of its residual utopianism in the gloom and anxiety of early Thatcherism, allowed it to be portrayed in similar terms to media and popular cultural satire of the left—as po-faced, puritan and hypocritical. A common strategy of new pop ideologues on this front was the implicit elision of post-punk with burgeoning anarcho-punk. It was fairly easy to frame as dour and self-righteous the statements of figures like Penny Rimbaud of Crass, who fulminated against 'the system', 'parasitic' journalists and a life that was not 'much fun'.[137]

In place of oppositional pleasures, new pop tended to advocate a qualified and/or ironic appropriation of consumerist, status-seeking hedonism often filtered through the encroaching postmodern turn of the intellectual left, echoing the New Right's move in on the libertarian left's dreams of fulfilment. Steve Singleton of ABC declared, 'we want it so that everybody can go to places like The Embassy ... not just the London club aristocracy',[138] while Green Gartside began speaking about 'jam today' rather than 'the golden tomorrow'.[139] This tendency would turn increasingly critical of its roots and, as the implicit careerism of wishing to succeed on existing terms set in, openly divisive: ABC's Martin Fry mocked 'anti-image groups' who 'never smile',[140] while Ian Penman's attention-seeking journalism laid into the 'precious' Slits and the 'contemptible' Pop Group.[141]

Because new pop was a direct outgrowth of post-punk, and because the political differences between the two tendencies focused the era's hegemonic struggle over freedom and pleasure, the case studies of subsequent chapters often engage with the positions of new pop figures. Before moving on to those case studies, it is important to get beyond the largely parodic descriptions of left post-punk's politics discussed so far. The following section specifies post-punk's connections with the libertarian left in more detail and highlights the issues and complications they provoked.

THE POLITICS OF LEFT POST-PUNK

New Sensibilities

Though themes of freedom and pleasure mediated most political concerns of the post-punk left, there was a particular focus on their implications at the level of the senses. Leftist post-punk's countercultural inheritance meant that such 'new sensibilities' were often articulated in ways comparable to the interplay between the counterculture and the libertarian left. These included the pursuit of a sensuous reason placing human fulfilment above the instrumentalist pursuit of profit, sexual liberation, and a revaluation of the natural environment motivated by anti-productivist and anti-consumerist critique. The expression of these impulses ran the gamut; they ranged from the precocity of the teenage Pop Group, who saw themselves as 'experimental primitives'[142] decrying the artificiality of urban life,[143] to the lush, playful feminist eroticism of The Raincoats' later work. Reynolds illuminates this point from time to time; however, he largely concentrates on the interrogation of dominant sensuous freedoms and pleasures by leftist post-punk bands, presenting, at one point, 'puritanical zeal, coupled with anxiety and guilt' as the definitive features that distinguished punks and post-punks from their countercultural antecedents.[144] As the phrasing suggests, the very act of interrogation is considered destructive of freedom and pleasure per se. In this, Reynolds re-treads an established position in histories of punk and post-punk: Jon Savage, for instance, claims of bands like Scritti Politti and The Raincoats that 'despite the apparent liberation of their rhetoric ... there were so many things you could not be—sexist, racist, entryist, Rockist—that the negatives overpowered any potential *jouissance*',[145] a view Savage re-iterates in a more recent oral history of Rough Trade.[146]

What this means is that, despite a youthful critique of new pop,[147] there is a degree of sympathy in Reynolds' later work for two of its features: the way new pop discourse mocked the puritanical tendencies of post-punk (Ian Penman lamented that 'no-one is allowed to have FUN anymore')[148] and new pop's unwillingness to conceive of freedoms and pleasures not directly bound up with the dominant. Discussing the evolution of label Fast Product, Reynolds claims that its 'signature balancing act' of 'celebrating consumer desire while simultaneously exposing the manipulative mechanisms of capitalism' anticipated 'a new kind of left-wing sensibility ... that would flourish in the eighties: a "designer socialism" purged of its puritanical austerity and pleasure-fear, attracted to stylishly-made things yet determined not to be hoodwinked or exploited'.[149] This is an astute point, and one that is explored in more depth in the following chapter. But it is also important to stress the counterweight: the exploration and celebration of potentially oppositional sensuous freedoms and pleasures by leftist post-punk bands.

The Politics of the Personal

Given left post-punk's politicised concern with the senses, it is no surprise that there was also a broader preoccupation with the political implications of everyday actions. Reynolds identifies one source of this 'acute self-consciousness' in the exposure of many post-punks to conceptualist art theories at art school and university.[150] It was also, we should add, framed by the counterculture's sometime crossover with the libertarian left's position that 'the lived relation of subordination is to be contested wherever it is to be found'.[151] As with the anti-culturalist politics of leftist post-punk more generally, 'the politics of the personal' was encountered in a variety of different ways, each with their own determinate influence. In the case of the Blue Orchids, for example, the key factor was a habitus that found common ground between the counterculture's emphasis on the personal and what Martin Bramah referred to as 'working class solidarity'. Bramah's claim hints towards older traditions of British socialism, which Sheila Rowbotham has identified as a central residual source of the libertarian left. She notes, for example, the stressing of 'the transformation of values and relationships' and an understanding of 'the personal meaning of socialism' in movements such as Chartism.[152]

The politics of the personal also took numerous forms within leftist post-punk. The most common was a conscious recognition of the political potential of a particular feature of institutional autonomy in the music industry. Toynbee's argument that the self-managing band form has been historically influential in the production of popular music informs his point that music making can often be 'structurally democratic'.[153] Toynbee's extension of this point to the often 'decentralised' nature of the means of musical production hints towards the possibility that the making of popular music may, in some cases, prefigure the libertarian left framing of freedom in economic terms as comprising the sharing of resources and decisions. Internal democracy was a political issue for all of the bands I focus on, especially Gang of Four and Scritti Politti, but it was not the only manifestation of the politics of the personal. Bands such as the Blue Orchids, for example, also understood the personal in a manner comparable to their concern with new sensibilities as a crucial political battleground over what counted as individual fulfilment.

The democratising personal politics of leftist post-punk, however, were soon challenged and undermined by the re-emergence of a countervailing historical tendency identified by Toynbee: the expression of romantic individualism in the context of the capitalist marketplace as the vainglory of the pop star.[154] Coming from within post-punk, yet sharing close parallels to the entrepreneurial and consumerist individualism promoted by Thatcherism, this was the dominant position of new pop. An awareness of the politics of the personal sometimes co-existed uneasily with a desire for freedom and fulfilment within the terms of commercial success, something we will see with Scritti Politti.

Feminism

Another feature which post-punk shared with the libertarian left was the significance of gender and feminism. Punk had marked an emergent step forward in countercultural rock; although, as Segal argues, the counterculture and the women's movement had both been concerned to redefine freedom and pleasure, with women not only 'the passive prey of men in the sixties' but active agents themselves,[155] countercultural sexism remained a persistent problem. At a subcultural level, Rowbotham has noted numerous examples.[156] Paul Willis observed a 'far from progressive' perspective on women amongst the male and female hippies he interacted with, who 'distrusted the women's movement and contrasted its ideals with their notion of the *natural* female and her organic role'.[157] In terms of music, Peter Doggett describes the 'groupie' phenomenon and the sexism of many rock lyrics.[158] Mavis Bayton, a British feminist, punk musician and historian of women in rock, recalls dancing to the Rolling Stones at a women-only social and suddenly thinking, 'hold on... "Under My Thumb" ... the contradictions of dancing to those lyrics!'[159] Sheila Whiteley, meanwhile, argues that the few women performers in countercultural rock were positioned 'as romanticised fantasy figures, subservient earth mothers or easy lays'.[160] The assessment is generalised, but it is true that the growing influence of the women's movement by the late 1970s clearly affected a new generation of musicians more than it had those involved in countercultural rock.

This was also a situation determined by the specific character of punk: Helen Reddington's much-needed and valuable interviews with women punk and post-punk musicians reveal that many had little or no prior musical experience but were inspired to participate and develop by the populist, democratising 'do it yourself' rhetoric of punk. By doing so, they defied the sexist assumption that proficiency in rock musicianship was the property of men.[161]

Though women who had played a central part in the first wave of punk challenged gendered expectations of female popular musicians—Siouxsie and the Banshees, for example, 'played off Siouxsie's dominatrix-style hauteur against three pretty-boy musicians'—and though the 'inner circle' punk groups were often animated by an inchoate concern with 'sexual politics',[162] there was a fairly swift counter-revolution. 'I hated ... the bully-boy aspect of punk which began to emerge in later 1977', recalls Jon Savage. 'Being a lad was not what punk was initially about.'[163] Viv

Albertine of The Slits, meanwhile, remembers: 'punk became more macho as people's rock'n'roll tendencies started to sneak back out again'.[164] It was here that post-punk came in, as Savage recalls.[165] Reynolds, too, notes that post-punks often upheld 'progressive sexual politics' against the sexism of other formations that had emerged from punk, including Oi![166] This frequently shared commitment accounts for my analysis of the gender politics not only of women post-punks but also of bands that throughout their history were fully or largely made up of men, such as Gang of Four.

The relationship between leftist post-punk and feminism was not, however, unproblematic. The difficulties that arose can often be considered in terms of freedom and pleasure. Though many bands shared the transformative aims of the women's movement, there was sometimes a wariness of direct alignment. Lucy Toothpaste (now Whitman) wrote the feminist fanzine *Jolt* with its arresting cover images, including a naked Mary Whitehouse in bed with another woman. She claims that despite early punk and post-punk making 'women feel they could compete on equal terms to men ... I never got one woman in any of my interviews to say she was a feminist'.[167] Whilst this is rhetorical—in *Jolt* 2, Palmolive of The Slits (and later The Raincoats) stated, 'we are feminists, in a way'[168]—substantively, the records corroborate with Whitman's memory. Music journalist and feminist Caroline Coon recalls having to 'take a deep breath' after The Slits told her, 'we have nothing to do with Women's Liberation'.[169] Meanwhile, Liz Naylor once wrote a short feature for *City Fun* opining that sexists should be lobotomised on the NHS but went on to claim that this was 'not so much feminism as reasonable personism'.[170] Naylor, who now considers herself a feminist, has recalled that 'I remember going to see The Raincoats ... and me and Cath [Carroll, Naylor's co-editor and partner at the time] were at the back going "pah, pah, these feminists"'.[171]

This wariness had its roots in a variety of sources. To begin with, the residual counterculturalism of post-punk meant that freedom was sometimes defined in an individualistic manner unwilling to compromise with feminist critiques of certain social and cultural practices as reproductive of sexism. The growth of New Right media backlash against the women's movement was also clearly influential. Its portrayal of organised feminism as extremist, dogmatic and misguided would likely have been lurking in the consciousness of post-punks even if they had had some experience of the women's movement. 'Women's Lib Lost Me My Children', a *Daily Express* article wailed in 1978, in which civil servant Colin Frier blamed feminism for his wife leaving him and taking their two children to live in a commune. 'She was an ordinary housewife before she joined Women's Lib. It turned her into a man-hater. I have heard her say all men are pigs.'[172] Part of this stereotype was the imagery of feminism as a solely middle-class preoccupation; Naylor, from a working class background, recalls that this was one aspect which contributed to her hostility.[173] In response to this, Chap. 5 considers the feminist contribution of Una Baines to The Fall and the Blue Orchids, reflecting on the interplay between her working class background, her experience of the women's movement, and the influence of countercultural mysticism.

A third reason for suspicion of feminism was that during the period of post-punk, the women's movement itself was suffering from internal tensions. They came partly from the inevitable divergences of any initially unified social movement and partly from the pressure of the incipient shift to the right in the broader culture. The response of one faction was undeniably puritanical; following the expression of her exasperation with bands like The Slits for rejecting Women's Lib, Caroline Coon admits that 'I understood it, because the way feminism was presenting itself was, even to me, pretty horrendous. I remember going with a girlfriend … to a feminist benefit, and they weren't allowed in because they were wearing … lipstick.'[174] Again, the tabloids exploited this to the hilt. The *Daily Express* gloated that the only significant opposition to 'beefcake' US model John Carvallo appearing naked on television came from 'Women's Lib'.[175] The *Daily Mirror* was more subtle and incorporative, enlisting 'glamorous' Germaine Greer as representative of a previous era in which women 'began talking about their right to an orgasm' and contrasting her with the 'furious feminists' of the early 1980s.[176]

I thus consider, for example, the feminist commitments and contributions of Gang of Four in relation to critiques that claimed the band's conceptualism and incorporation of leftist theory into their lyrics risked blocking a pleasurable engagement with their work. I also contrast The Slits' individualist approach to gender politics and its sometime pre-emergent suggestion of 'post-feminism' with The Raincoats' closer association with the women's movement and its resultant influence on their often unflattering portrayal in the music press and subsequent popular history.

Politics

Gender was not the only topic addressed in directly politicised terms by leftist post-punk. Dave Laing has argued that one of punk's strengths was not 'a flawless ideological argument', but simply its re-introduction of overt political commentary in hits like 'God Save the Queen' and 'White Riot', 'something which the mainstream of popular music had success-fully resisted for a decade',[177] and which had also become less prominent in countercultural rock. This was no small achievement considering the strength of the hegemonic attitude, noted in the introduction, that poli-tics and popular music should not mix. Rock Against Racism was symbolic in the development of punk and post-punk, diffusing not just anti-racism but other libertarian left concerns such as gender and sexuality by way of localised activism and its fanzine *Temporary Hoarding*.[178] RAR also dis-interred familiar debates over art and commitment on the left:[179] Mark Perry of post-punk band Alternative TV was suspicious of the backing given to RAR by the Socialist Workers Party, claiming, 'I don't need to be told by a commie organisation to love blacks'.[180] I have opted, however, to discuss RAR only incidentally, given the substantial amount of existing material on it.[181]

Reynolds raises the issue of post-punk and politics, although his ten-dency to portray post-punk's radicalism in formalist terms means that he differentiates between the politics of punk and post-punk in the following manner: 'Punk's approach to politics—raw rage or agit-prop protest—seemed too blunt or too preachy to the post-punk vanguard, so they tried to develop more ... oblique techniques.'[182] Elsewhere, for exam-ple, Reynolds associates the 'protest aspect' of reggae with punk and its influence as a 'sonic revolution' with post-punk.[183] Yet Mark Stewart of The Pop Group claimed that 'going to sound systems with black mates ... that kind of yearning for a better world, that questioning of the system—it just made my hairs stand on end'.[184] As Stewart's recollection suggests, there was no simple division between radical form and radical content when it came to the emergence of post-punk from punk. Rather, leftist post-punk maintained and developed political themes first articulated by punk, often in fairly straightforward ways. In line with a libertarian left focus on qualitatively different definitions of freedom and pleasure, anti-consumerist critique was a particularly common topic.

Reynolds also makes a distinction in the introduction of *Rip It Up and Start Again* between punk and post-punk on the basis of political commitment, claiming that 'as bohemian nonconformists, [post-punks] were usually made uncomfortable by calls to solidarity or toeing the party line'.[185] As we have seen, this is an accurate description of certain bands. Yet as Reynolds goes on to note, others were directly involved with political groups, including Scritti Politti's membership of the Communist Party. Along with the implications of leftist post-punk's politicised commentary and form, then, the complexity of such commitments also deserves further investigation.

The Music Industry

Alex Ogg's recent history of independent labels in the UK usefully summarises the economic context of the music industry in the late 1970s. It helps to account for the success of the many independent labels associated with post-punk by observing that in contrast to the sales slump experienced by majors during this period,[186] 'the advent of cheaper technology and manufacturing capabilities, a ready audience primed by punk for almost anything released ... by an independent record label and the majors' sloth in responding are all contributory factors'.[187]

This proliferation was not an entirely new development; as Ogg's book illustrates, there had been a long history of independent labels in Britain prior to punk. None, however, had consistently understood their activity in oppositional terms, with the exception of the still-flourishing folk label Topic, which had begun as an offshoot of the Communist Party affiliated Workers' Music Association in 1936.[188] Many simply viewed themselves as upholding a free market by challenging major label concentration or using their small size to respond more quickly to demand.[189] David Hesmondhalgh has also noted that pre-punk independents were often no less likely than major labels to engage in especially exploitative treatment of the musicians who had signed to them.[190]

The conflicted politics of the counterculture tended to confuse matters when it came to the politics of independent labels. The cult solo artist and Communist Party member Robert Wyatt began as the drummer of psychedelic band The Soft Machine and experienced renewed popularity in the post-punk period after signing to Rough Trade. Wyatt noted that in the early 1970s, it was easy to be taken in by the adoption of countercultural signifiers by the newly founded Virgin: 'For example, Richard Branson grew his hair—that was a new one!'[191] Branson's 'humane management' of his immediate staff, however, 'didn't extend to the musicians ... who were treated as stock to be bought and sold'[192] and placed on contracts which claimed the bulk of their earnings.[193] Astutely recognising how such individualist elements of the counterculture came to be incorporated by the New Right, Wyatt describes Branson as 'a Thatcherite before

Thatcherism existed'.[194] Numerous post-punk labels were similarly uncon-
nected to the libertarian left politics of one strand of the counterculture,
though they have had less subsequent commercial success than Branson
and usually displayed more of a culturalist distaste for the exigencies of
business: Ivo Watts-Russell, founder of 4AD, for example, has defined his
motivation as a love of music in contrast to a solely instrumental pursuit of
profit.[195] Yet he has also remarked: 'I'm no socialist.'[196]

Nonetheless, post-punk contained emergent elements which directly
politicised economic independence as an egalitarian and democratising
challenge to major labels and made a principle of avoiding reliance on
services controlled by the majors, such as distribution.[197] Reynolds has
reflected that even with hindsight, it is difficult to understand the novelty
and excitement surrounding post-punk independence.[198] One explanatory
factor, however, may well be the influence of the libertarian left's focus in
this era on the necessity of oppositional, prefigurative institutions as part
of socialist struggle.

Of the more significant labels that consciously referenced leftist influences, though, only Rough Trade managed to substantially and practically
implement its ideals during the post-punk era. Bob Last, founder of Fast
Product, displayed his Situationist influences by releasing 'items of consumer detritus' such as collages of the Red Army Faction packaged with
rotting orange peel[199] and was involved in the Cartel, the independent
distribution network set up by Rough Trade.[200] He was also, however,
part of the foment of new pop, encouraging the artists he signed to move
on to major labels[201] and claiming 'if you're working within a capitalist
economic system, they're all on a continuum ... we wanted to change people's lives, but we never, ever claimed any ethical superiority over anyone
on EMI or whatever'. Last's art direction of Fast Product's releases was
also an example of postmodernist recuperation of Situationist *détournement*, evident in the puzzling claim that 'we liked the world of branding,
marketing and capitalism, because it was oppositional'.[202] His presumed
opposition was the apparently dour, puritanical, 'hippyish' Rough Trade
milieu,[203] but the evidence is somewhat thin; Rough Trade record covers
were rarely pedestrian and often displayed similar avant-garde influences
to Last's, as in the case of Scritti Politti detailing their recording processes
and costs, just as Fast Product band The Mekons had done. The influence
of Last on Gang of Four and Scritti Politti is discussed in more detail in
the following chapter.

Tony Wilson's much-mythologised Factory Records, meanwhile, represents a still exemplary challenge. Where Rough Trade's strength was in the steady building of oppositional networks, Factory excelled in idiosyncratic pranksterism rooted in regionalist pride. Nevertheless, the label's legacy has been heavily co-opted by the 'municipal entrepreneurialism'[204] adopted by Manchester City Council from the late 1980s onwards. Liz Naylor has argued that although this has been most evident in recent years, Factory's interventions in the late 1970s and early 1980s were in part a pre-emergent indicator of the council's proto-New Labour turn, despite the label's simultaneously oppositional features and its links to the left.[205] James Nice's recent history of Factory highlights Wilson's use of Situationist ideas and imagery as a 'pseudo-radical marketing tool' comparable to Last's tactics.[206]

By contrast, Rough Trade was, and largely remained, a libertarian left institution in various ways. It was also, with its distribution wing, the central node of post-punk independence; accounting for the centrality I accord it in subsequent chapters. Neil Taylor's recent oral history of Rough Trade opens with a quote from one of its early contributors, Steve Montgomery, which encapsulates the label's understanding of itself as a prefigurative, oppositional force: 'We figured we could change the world, or at least our little corner of it, and in so doing we would take one step forward for everybody.'[207] Rough Trade attempted to share profits by offering 50:50 deals rather than single figure royalty rates, and signings were based on personal trust rather than long-term contracts. In a male-dominated industry, the label's staff was often predominantly made up of women and it made a point of signing numerous all-female bands such as The Raincoats, Kleenex and the Mo-Dettes.[208] Within four years of existence, it had helped create an alternative, principled nationwide distribution network linking together smaller labels and independent record shops. It was at one point directly supported by Ken Livingstone's Greater London Council and would close in solidarity with striking nurses and miners.[209]

Rough Trade owed its politics to key figures having been involved in politicised manifestations of the counterculture. Its founder Geoff Travis worked on a kibbutz as a teenager, attended the anti-Vietnam war demonstration at Grosvenor Square in 1968, was involved in political protest at university, travelled America, and set up the record shop from which the label grew in Notting Hill due to the area's countercultural connections.[210] Travis also read Marx, the Beats and feminist texts, was inspired by the working methods of women's theatre, watched speakers such as Daniel Cohn-Bendit and Tariq Ali, lived communally, and read the countercultural press.[211] Key to Travis' outlook was a view of culture as potentially liberating; another Rough Trade figure, Mayo Thompson, recalls that F.R. Leavis had taught Travis at Cambridge, and it is entirely possible that he encountered Raymond Williams there too.

Certainly, the way that Travis' politicised, residual culturalism co-existed with an anti-culturalist desire to 'de-mystify' the music industry suggested that this may have been the case, as did his description of Rough Trade as neither 'the record business' nor 'art' but 'a space of cultural production'.[212] Band members would sometimes perform label work or serve customers in the record shop, staff democratically approved or rejected the release and stocking of records and fanzines, refusing, for example, to deal with material considered sexist or racist,[213] and the label produced a do it yourself guide to making a record.[214]

With parallels to the position first advanced by Williams in 'Culture is Ordinary', which broke from the elitist, Leavisite conception of minority culture and mass-market civilisation, Rough Trade also adopted a kind of oppositional populism. In its early years, the label aimed to circumvent the ideological division between the association of major labels with large audiences and independents with minority tastes, hoping to reach a substantial audience with the innovative music released. This attitude encompassed the sphere of production as well as consumption: David Hesmondhalgh has argued that the label had a long-term democratising effect on the British music industry which encouraged broader participation by those often excluded from cultural production due to 'gender, ethnic and class inequalities', partly decentralised the means of production, and fostered 'collectivism, collaboration and co-operation'.[215]

The Rough Trade milieu, however, came in for the same criticism from emerging new pop in terms of freedom and pleasure as that directed at leftist post-punk more broadly. Bob Last, for example, has claimed that post-punk independents were actually 'dependents', denied the freedom of highly capitalised businesses,[216] whilst parodies of the label as sanctimonious were rife; Kate Korus of the Mo-Dettes recalls: 'I have to confess we considered them very old-fashioned "up-the-rebels" hippies at the time. We tried to distance ourselves from their "worthy", serious image. We were all about injecting some humour and fun back into the business.'[217] It is in this context that I situate my analysis of the relationship between the bands I consider and their attitude towards Rough Trade. I assess how far bands were representative of the label's early ideals, how far they diverged, and the political implications in each case. In doing so, I draw on cultural materialism to advance debate by moving on from accounts which have analysed the economics of post-punk independence separately from post-punk cultural production.

By 1983, even Rough Trade had begun to make concessions in order to survive, partly under pressure from the turn to new pop, partly due to financial difficulties experienced the previous year and partly due to the effects of recession in the British economy catching up with the label.[218] Travis, for example, helped set up Blanco y Negro, an independent with major label support which ostensibly challenged the perception that bands had to move to a major once they had achieved a certain level of commercial success. In reality, though, it replicated similar arrangements from the 1970s, reneged on the ideal of oppositional independence and gave Travis a large salary and the ability to promote music he favoured without the consensus of Rough Trade's democratic structures.[219] Though The Smiths were signed to Rough Trade and achieved significant commercial success, this had partly been achieved through paying the sales force of London Records with money from Blanco y Negro.[220] Neatly for the purposes of historical analysis, these and various other moves on the part of Rough Trade coincided with the beginning of the second term Thatcher government's concerted targeting of the 'nooks and crannies' which the libertarian left had managed to occupy[221] and with the point at which five out of the six bands I focus on had either broken up or moved to major labels, as the post-punk moment came to a close.

NOTES

1. Alwyn W. Turner, *Crisis? What Crisis? Britain in the 1970s* (London: Aurum, 2008), p. 271.
2. The Thatcher government's provocation and ruthless suppression of the 1984–85 miners' strike, exposed by Seumas Milne in *The Enemy Within: The Secret War Against the Miners* (London: Verso, 1994), was only the most dramatic and symbolic instance of over a decade of class struggle culminating in the Poll Tax protests which drove Thatcher from office.
3. Dominic Sandbrook, *Seasons in the Sun: The Battle for Britain, 1974–1979* (London: Allen Lane, 2012), p. 26.
4. Sandbrook, *Seasons in the Sun*, pp.298–306.
5. Turner, *Crisis? What Crisis?*, p. 270.
6. Turner, *Crisis? What Crisis?*, pp. 230–240.

7. Stuart Hall, 'The Great Moving Right Show', in *The Politics of Thatcherism*, ed. Stuart Hall and Martin Jacques (London: Lawrence and Wishart, 1983), pp. 19–39 (p. 19).

8. Stuart Hall and Martin Jacques, 'Introduction', in *The Politics of Thatcherism*, pp. 9–16 (p. 13).

9. Raymond Williams, 'Problems of the Coming Period' [1983], in *Resources of Hope: Culture, Democracy, Socialism*, ed. Robin Gable (London: Verso, 1989), pp. 161–174 (p. 165).

10. Hall, 'The Great Moving Right Show', p. 27.

11. Ben Jackson and Robert Saunders note that 'Survey evidence does not support the emergence of more individualist popular attitudes, and the Conservative share of the vote actually declined in each election from 1979 to 1992...the British electorate was not significantly "Thatcherised"; nor was it persuaded of the Thatcher governments' ideological claims in relation to full employment and the welfare state. The political success of Thatcherism owed a considerable debt to the electoral system, and to a constitution that permitted radical policy change on the basis of 42–44 per cent of the popular vote.' Ben Jackson and Robert Saunders, 'Introduction: Varieties of Thatcherism', in *Making Thatcher's Britain*, ed. Jackson and Saunders (Cambridge: Cambridge University Press, 2012), pp. 1–21 (p. 16).

12. Raymond Williams interviewed by Terry Eagleton, 'The Practice of Possibility', in *Resources of Hope*, p. 320.

13. Ben Jackson, 'The Think-tank Archipelago', in *Making Thatcher's Britain*, ed. Jackson and Saunders (Cambridge: Cambridge University Press, 2012), pp. 43–61 (p. 53).

14. 'Mirror Comment—The Lunatic Fringes', *Daily Mirror*, 1 June 1976, p. 2.

15. Julian Petley, 'Hit and Myth', in *Culture Wars: The Media and the British Left*, ed. James Curran, Ivor Gabor and Julian Petley (Edinburgh: Edinburgh University Press, 2005), pp. 85–107 (p. 85).

16. BBC, *Till Death Us Do Part*, Series 7, Episode 4: 'The Window', originally broadcast 26 November 1975. Available online at: https://www.youtube.com/watch?v=gA0-fnOsZeo, accessed 29 April 2015.

17. For example, see Charles Shaar Murray, ''Ullo Alexei! Gotta New Audience?', *NME*, 6 March 1982, pp. 14–15.

18. Ann Leslie, 'Femail—Another Middle Class Rebel Hits the Headlines—But How Much Is It a Case of Getting Back at Daddy?', *Daily Mail*, 7 September 1976, p. 10.

19. Hilary Wainwright, 'Moving Beyond the Fragments', in Sheila Rowbotham, Lynne Segal and Hilary Wainwright, *Beyond the Fragments: Feminism and the Making of Socialism* (London: Merlin, 1979), pp. 211–253 (p. 224).

20. Alan Sinfield, 'Sexuality and Subcultures in the Wake of Welfare Capitalism', *Radical Philosophy* 66 (Spring 1994), pp. 40–43.

21. John Medhurst, *That Option No Longer Exists: Britain 1974–76* (Alresford: Zero, 2014), pp. 88–89.
22. Raymond Williams, *The Long Revolution* [1961] (Harmondsworth: Pelican, 1965), pp. 328–334.
23. Peter Taylor-Gooby, *Public Opinion, Ideology and State Welfare* (London: Routledge, 1985), pp. 112–114.
24. Hall, 'The Great Moving Right Show', p. 31.
25. Conservative Party Election Broadcast, 'The International Prosperity Race', 19 April 1979, www.politicsresources.net/area/uk/pebs/con79.htm, accessed 5 October 2015.
26. Margaret Thatcher quoted in Peter Golding and Graham Murdock, 'Privatising Pleasure', *Marxism Today*, October 1983.
27. Williams, 'Problems of the Coming Period', p. 171.
28. Williams, 'Problems of the Coming Period', pp. 172–173.
29. André Gorz, *Critique of Economic Reason* (London: Verso, 1989), p. 45.
30. Sheila Rowbotham, 'The Women's Movement and Organising for Socialism', in *Beyond the Fragments*, pp. 21–155 (p. 22).
31. Rowbotham, 'The Women's Movement and Organising for Socialism', p. 98.
32. Robin Blackburn, 'Introduction', in Williams, *Resources of Hope*, p. xi.
33. Dennis Dworkin, *Cultural Marxism in Postwar Britain* (Durham: Duke University Press, 1997), p. 125.
34. Dworkin, *Cultural Marxism*, p. 133.
35. Lynne Segal, 'A Local Experience', in *Beyond the Fragments*, pp. 157–209 (pp. 159–160).
36. Rowbotham, 'The Women's Movement and Organising for Socialism', p. 30.
37. Wainwright, 'Moving Beyond the Fragments', p. 224.
38. Rowbotham, 'The Women's Movement and Organising for Socialism', p. 118.
39. Dworkin, *Cultural Marxism*, p. 58.
40. Rowbotham, 'The Women's Movement and Organising for Socialism', p. 68.
41. Rowbotham, 'The Women's Movement and Organising for Socialism', p. 118.
42. Hilary Wainwright, 'Introduction', in *Beyond the Fragments*, pp. 1–20 (p. 2).
43. Alan Sinfield, *Literature, Politics and Culture in Postwar Britain*, 3rd ed. (London: Continuum, 2004), p. 282.
44. Lynne Segal, *Why Feminism? Gender, Psychology, Politics* (Cambridge: Polity, 1999), p. 21.
45. Robert Saunders, 'Crisis? What Crisis? Thatcherism and the Seventies', in *Making Thatcher's Britain*, ed. Jackson and Saunders, pp. 25–42 (p. 29).
46. Margaret Thatcher, Iain Macleod lecture entitled 'Dimensions of Conservatism', 4 July 1977, http://www.margaretthatcher.org/document/103411, accessed 5 October 2015.
47. Saunders, 'Crisis? What Crisis? Thatcherism and the Seventies', p. 34.

48. Ronald Butt, 'Mrs Thatcher: The First Two Years', *The Sunday Times*, 3 May 1981.
49. 'It's Your Freedom They Hate', *Sunday Express*, 23 November 1975.
50. Hall, 'The Great Moving Right Show', p. 22.
51. Turner, *Crisis? What Crisis?*, p. 138.
52. Matthew Grimley, 'Thatcherism, Morality and Religion', in *Making Thatcher's Britain*, ed. Jackson and Saunders, pp. 78–94 (p. 86).
53. 'Mary Whitehouse—Obituary', *The Telegraph*, 24 November 2001,http://www.telegraph.co.uk/news/obituaries/culture-obituaries/tv-radio-obituaries/6605110/Mary-Whitehouse.html, accessed 5 October 2015.
54. Maurice Cowling, 'The Present Position', in *Conservative Essays*, ed. Cowling (London: Cassell, 1978), p. 9.
55. Raphael Samuel, 'Born-Again Socialism', in *Out of Apathy: Voices of the New Left 30 Years On*, ed. Oxford University Socialist Discussion Group (London: Verso, 1989), pp. 39–59 (p. 42).
56. Jeff Nuttall, *Bomb Culture* (London: Paladin, 1970).
57. Lynne Segal, *Straight Sex: Rethinking the Politics of Pleasure* (Berkeley: University of California Press, 1994), pp. 18–20.
58. Lennon also wrote for *Black Dwarf*, a countercultural magazine featuring contributions by New Leftists, anarchists and dissident Trotskyists alongside pop cultural figures such as David Hockney. See Dworkin, *Cultural Marxism*, p. 128.
59. Elizabeth Wilson with Angela Weir, *Hidden Agendas: Theory, Politics and Experience in the Women's Movement* (London: Tavistock, 1986), p. 48.
60. Richard Neville, *Play Power* (London: Jonathan Cape, 1970), p. 258.
61. Peter York, *Style Wars* (London: Sidgwick and Jackson, 1980), p. 17.
62. David Stubbs, 'Join The Chant? Pop's Endlessly Problematic Relationship with Politics', *The Quietus*, 21 April 2015, http://thequietus.com/articles/17715-politics-pop-music-general-election, accessed 29 April 2015.
63. Sinfield, *Literature, Politics and Culture in Postwar Britain*, pp. 315–316.
64. Paul Willis, *Profane Culture* (London: Routledge, 1978), p. 132.
65. André Gorz, *Critique of Economic Reason*, p. 47.
66. Simon Reynolds, *Rip It Up and Start Again: Postpunk 1978–1984* (London: Faber, 2005), p. 4.
67. Glen Matlock interviewed on the Shaun Keaveny breakfast show, BBC 6Music, 5 May 2011.
68. Jess Baines, speaking at the working seminar '1979 Revisited—The Cultural Production of Structures of Feeling under Thatcherism' held at Birkbeck University, London, 21 November 2014.
69. Simon Reynolds, *Totally Wired: Post-Punk Interviews and Overviews* (London: Faber and Faber, 2009), p. 413.
70. Reynolds, *Totally Wired*, p. 410.

71. Theodore Gracyk, 'Kids're Forming Bands: Making Meaning in Post-Punk', in *Punk & Post-Punk* 1, no. 1 (Sept. 2011), 73–85 (p. 83).
72. Reynolds, *Rip It Up*, p. xviii.
73. Sinfield, *Literature, Politics and Culture in Postwar Britain*, pp. 213–217.
74. Tony Parsons, 'Go Johnny Go', *NME*, 3 October 1976, p. 29.
75. Savage, *England's Dreaming*, pp. 36, 50.
76. Jon Herlihy, 'Human Lib', *Flicks* 1 (January 1977).
77. Charles Shaar Murray, 'John, Paul, Steve and Sidney: The Social Rehabilitation of the Sex Pistols', *NME*, 6 August 1977, pp. 23–26.
78. Dick Hebdige, *Subculture: The Meaning of Style* (London: Methuen, 1979), p. 65; Savage, *England's Dreaming*, p. 516; Barry Miles, *London Calling: A Countercultural History of London since 1945* (London: Atlantic Books, 2010), p. 352; Sheila Rowbotham, *A Century of Women: The Story of Women in Britain and the United States* (London: Penguin, 1999), p. 426.
79. Jackson and Saunders, 'Introduction: Varieties of Thatcherism', pp. 5–6.
80. Matthew Worley, 'One Nation under the Bomb: The Cold War and British Punk to 1984', *Journal for the Study of Radicalism* 5, no. 2 (2011), 65–83.
81. Liz Naylor, *Various Times*—unpublished MA thesis quoted in Owen Hatherley, *A Guide to the New Ruins of Great Britain* (London: Verso, 2010), pp. 126–127.
82. Oliver Lowenstein, *Dangerous Logic*, no. 1, 1978.
83. Raymond Williams, *Towards 2000* (London: Chatto & Windus, 1983), pp. 10–11.
84. Williams, *Towards 2000*, p. 14.
85. Reynolds, *Totally Wired*, p. 415.
86. Reynolds, *Totally Wired*, p. 408.
87. Williams, *Culture*, p. 62.
88. Jon Savage, 'Cabaret Voltaire', *Sounds*, 15 April 1978, pp. 16–17.
89. 'From the Pressing Plants to the Concert Halls, We Want Some Control', *After Hours* fanzine, 1979.
90. Oliver Lowenstein, 'A Question of Identity', *Sounds*, 19 August 1978, p. 21.
91. Reynolds, *Rip It Up*, p. 212.
92. Reynolds, *Totally Wired*, p. 408.
93. Vivien Goldman, 'New Musick: Dub', *Sounds*, 3 December 1977, pp. 22–24.
94. Reynolds, *Rip It Up*, p. 21.
95. Adrian Thrills, 'Siouxsie in Wonderland', *NME*, 24 June 1978, pp. 18–19.
96. Paul Morley, 'In Defence of Siouxsie and the Banshees', *NME*, 23 December 1978, p. 39.
97. Lynn Hanna, 'Into the Valley of the Voodoo Doll', *NME*, 15 August 1981, p. 44.

98. Reynolds, *Totally Wired*, p. 408.
99. Reynolds, *Rip It Up*, p. 93.
100. Williams, *Culture*, p. 70.
101. Savage, *England's Dreaming*, p. xiv.
102. Garry Bushell, 'Will Jim Take the Money?', *Sounds*, 5 August 1978, p. 19.
103. Letters, *Sounds*, 26 August 1978, pp. 50–51.
104. Garry Bushell and Dave McCullough, 'Cockney Rejects and the Rise of the New Punk', *Sounds*, 4 August 1979, pp. 16–17.
105. Garry Bushell, review of Gang of Four, *Entertainment!*, *Sounds*, 6 October 1979, p. 43.
106. Sinfield, *Literature, Politics and Culture in Postwar Britain*, p. 179.
107. Eric Hobsbawm, 'The Forward March of Labour Halted?', *Marxism Today*, September 1978.
108. Savage, *England's Dreaming*, pp. 70–71, p. 114; Dave Laing, *One Chord Wonders: Power and Meaning in Punk Rock* (Milton Keynes: Open University Press, 1985), p. 108; Simon Frith and Howard Horne, *Art Into Pop* (London: Methuen, 1987), pp. 124–129 who write disparagingly of 'the provincial proletariat' and Paul Fryer, 'Punk and the New Wave of British Rock: Working Class Heroes and Art School Attitudes', *Popular Music and Society* 10, no. 4 (1986), 1–15 (p. 2) who writes even more disparagingly of 'barely literate…class conflict', opposing this to a middle-class tendency that was apparently 'highly educated and self-conscious'.
109. Reynolds, *Rip It Up*, p. xvii.
110. Letters, *Sounds*, 24 February 1979, p. 59.
111. Reynolds, *Rip It Up*, p. xviii.
112. Reynolds, *Rip It Up*, p. 178.
113. Green Gartside of Scritti Politti quoted in Simon Dwyer, 'The Politics of Ecstasy', *Sounds*, 29 May 1982, pp. 26, 29.
114. Ray Lowry, *City Fun* 2, no.14 (1981).
115. Dave McCullough, 'The Nitty Gritty on Scritti Politti', *Sounds*, 13 January 1979, p. 11.
116. Savage, *England's Dreaming*, p. 396.
117. Savage, *England's Dreaming*, p. 488.
118. Vivien Goldman, 'Siouxsie and the Banshees', *Sounds*, 3 December 1977, pp. 26–27.
119. Savage, 'Cabaret Voltaire'.
120. Ian Wood, 'The Fall Stumble into the Void', *Sounds*, 8 April 1978, p. 26.
121. Ian Cranna, 'Product, Packaging and Rebel Music', *NME*, 13 January 1979, pp. 22–24.
122. Ian Birch, 'Rough Trade Records: The Humane Sell', *Melody Maker*, 10 February 1979, p. 19.

123. Official Charts, available online at http://www.officialcharts.com/home/, accessed 27 May 2015.
124. Garry Bushell, live review of the Angelic Upstarts at the Rainbow, *Sounds*, 14 June 1980, p. 50.
125. Barney Hoskyns, 'Where Radical Meets Chic', *NME*, 31 October 1981, pp. 30–31.
126. Bushell, review of *Entertainment!*
127. Garry Bushell, 'UK Subs', *Sounds*, 12 August 1978, pp. 12–13.
128. Bushell and McCullough, 'Cockney Rejects and the Rise of the New Punk'.
129. Dworkin, *Cultural Marxism*, p. 126.
130. Matthew Worley, 'Hey Little Rich Boy, Take a Good Look at Me': Punk, Class and British Oi!', *Punk & Post-Punk* 3, no. 1 (2014), 5–20.
131. John Clarke, 'Skinheads and the Magical Recovery of Community', in *Resistance Through Rituals: Youth Subcultures in Postwar Britain*, ed. Stuart Hall and Tony Jefferson (London: Hutchinson, 1977), p. 100.
132. York, *Style Wars*, p. 46.
133. Paul Morley, review of The Pop Group—*For How Much Longer Do We Tolerate Mass Murder?*, *NME*, 22 March 1980, p. 39.
134. Paul Morley, 'Pink Military: Post-Modernist Pop Music', *NME*, 12 January 1980, pp. 6–7.
135. Paul Morley, review of Scars—*Author! Author!*, *NME*, 11 April 1981, p. 33.
136. Paul Morley, 'In Defence of Siouxsie and the Banshees'.
137. Letters, *Sounds*, 5 June 1982, pp. 62–63.
138. Adrian Thrills, 'ABC', *NME*, 18 July 1981, pp. 14–15.
139. Dave McCullough, 'Turn of the Scrits', *Sounds*, 8 December 1979, p. 18.
140. Adrian Thrills, 'ABC'.
141. Ian Penman, review of The Slits and The Pop Group split single 'In the Beginning There was Rhythm/Where There's a Will', *NME*, 15 March 1980, p. 21.
142. Steve Walsh, 'Pop Group Mania', *NME*, 18 February 1978, p. 19.
143. Max Bell, 'Idealists in Distress', *NME*, 30 June 1979, pp. 24–27.
144. Reynolds, *Totally Wired*, p. 426.
145. Savage, *England's Dreaming*, p. 516.
146. Neil Taylor, *Document and Eyewitness: An Intimate History of Rough Trade* (London: Orion, 2010), p. 126.
147. Simon Reynolds, 'New Pop and its Aftermath' [1985], in *On Record: Rock, Pop and the Written Word*, ed. Simon Frith and Andrew Goodwin (London: Routledge, 1990), pp. 466–471.
148. Ian Penman, 'Political Conscience Every Now and Then, Pub Every Night', *NME*, 27 June 1981, pp. 21–22.
149. Reynolds, *Rip It Up*, p. 94.
150. Reynolds, *Rip It Up*, p. xxvi.

151. Rowbotham, 'The Women's Movement and Organising for Socialism', p. 119.
152. Rowbotham, 'The Women's Movement and Organising for Socialism', pp. 120–122.
153. Jason Toynbee, *Making Popular Music: Musicians, Creativity and Institutions* (London: Arnold, 2000), p. xi.
154. Toynbee, *Making Popular Music*, p. xi.
155. Segal, *Straight Sex*, p. 9.
156. Rowbotham, *A Century of Women*, p. 364.
157. Willis, *Profane Culture*, p. 128.
158. Peter Doggett, *There's a Riot Going on: Revolutionaries, Rock Stars and the Rise and Fall of '60s Counter-culture* (Edinburgh: Canongate, 2008), p. 280.
159. Helen Reddington, *The Lost Women of Rock Music: Female Musicians of the Punk Era* (Bristol: Equinox, 2012), p. 112.
160. Sheila Whiteley, *Women and Popular Music: Sexuality, Identity and Subjectivity* (London: Routledge, 2000), p. 23.
161. Reddington, *The Lost Women of Rock Music*, p. 24.
162. Savage, *England's Dreaming*, p. 418.
163. Paul Gorman, *In Their Own Write: Adventures in the Music Press* (London: Sanctuary, 2001), p. 256.
164. Savage, *England's Dreaming*, p. 418.
165. Savage, *England's Dreaming*, p. 418.
166. Reynolds, *Totally Wired*, p. 422.
167. Savage, *England's Dreaming*, p. 418.
168. The Slits interviewed by Lucy Toothpaste, in *Jolt* 2, 1977.
169. Reddington, *The Lost Women of Rock Music*, p. 177.
170. *City Fun* 3, no.3 (1982).
171. Reddington, *The Lost Women of Rock Music*, p. 187.
172. Express Staff Reporter, 'Women's Lib Lost Me My Children', *Daily Express*, 6 December 1978, p. 4.
173. Reddington, *The Lost Women of Rock Music*, p. 187.
174. Reddington, *The Lost Women of Rock Music*, p. 177.
175. Jean Rook, 'Carvallo's Body Blow to Women's Lib', *Daily Express*, 1 July 1978.
176. 'Mirror Woman Meets Germaine Greer', *Daily Mirror*, 27 May 1982, p. 9.
177. Laing, *One Chord Wonders*, p. 31.
178. David Widgery, *Beating Time* (London: Chatto and Windus, 1986).
179. Coincidentally, Williams was exploring this issue concurrently in a literary context—see Raymond Williams, 'The Writer: Alignment and Commitment', *Marxism Today*, June 1980.
180. Lindsey Boyd, 'Alternativevision', *Sounds*, 24 December 1977, p. 12.

181. As well as Widgery's account, there is Ian Goodyer's *Crisis Music: The Cultural Politics of Rock Against Racism* (Manchester: Manchester University Press, 2009) and Dave Renton's *When We Touched the Sky: The Anti-Nazi League 1977–1981* (Cheltenham: New Clarion Press, 2006).
182. Reynolds, *Rip It Up*, p. xxii.
183. Reynolds, *Rip It Up*, p. 6.
184. Reynolds, *Rip It Up*, p. 88.
185. Reynolds, *Rip It Up*, p. xxiii.
186. Alex Ogg, *Independence Days: The Story of UK Independent Record Labels* (London: Cherry Red, 2009), p. 487.
187. Ogg, *Independence Days*, p. 573.
188. Ogg, *Independence Days*, p. 5.
189. Ogg, *Independence Days*, pp. 24–26.
190. David Hesmondhalgh, 'Post-Punk's Attempt to Democratise the Music Industry: The Success and Failure of Rough Trade', in *Popular Music 16*, no. 3 (1997), 255–274 (p. 256).
191. Ogg, *Independence Days*, p. 191.
192. Taylor, *Document and Eyewitness*, p. 147.
193. Ogg, *Independence Days*, p. 191.
194. Taylor, *Document and Eyewitness*, p. 147.
195. Ogg, *Independence Days*, p. 226.
196. Ogg, *Independence Days*, p. 242.
197. Reynolds, *Rip It Up*, p. 93.
198. Reynolds, *Rip It Up*, p. 92.
199. Reynolds, *Rip It Up*, p. 95.
200. Taylor, *Document and Eyewitness*, p. 210.
201. Taylor, *Document and Eyewitness*, p. 215.
202. Taylor, *Document and Eyewitness*, p. 210.
203. Taylor, *Document and Eyewitness*, p. 221.
204. Steve Quilley, 'Entrepreneurial Turns: Municipal Socialism and After', in *City of Revolution: Restructuring Manchester*, ed. Jamie Peck and Kevin Ward (Manchester: Manchester University Press, 2002), pp. 76–94.
205. Liz Naylor, *Various Times* (unpublished MA thesis) and 'Must the Haçienda Be Built?', in *New Perspectives in British Cultural History*, ed. Rosalind Crone, David Gange and Katy Jones (Newcastle: Cambridge Scholars Publishing, 2007), pp. 255–265.
206. James Nice, *Shadowplayers: The Rise and Fall of Factory Records* (London: Aurum, 2010), p. 29.
207. Taylor, *Document and Eyewitness*, p. 3.
208. Ogg, *Independence Days*, pp. 196–197.
209. Taylor, *Document and Eyewitness*, pp. 204, 207, 252, 271.
210. Ogg, *Independence Days*, pp. 174–175.

211. Taylor, *Document and Eyewitness*, pp. 25–36.
212. Reynolds, *Rip It Up*, p. 106.
213. Reynolds, *Rip It Up*, pp. 106–107.
214. Taylor, *Document and Eyewitness*, p. 19.
215. Hesmondhalgh, 'Post-Punk's Attempt to Democratise the Music Industry', p. 258.
216. Taylor, *Document and Eyewitness*, p. 215.
217. Ogg, *Independence Days*, p. 197.
218. Hesmondhalgh, 'Post-Punk's Attempt to Democratise the Music Industry', p. 263.
219. Ogg, *Independence Days*, p. 206.
220. Taylor, *Document and Eyewitness*, p. 244.
221. Segal, *Why Feminism?*, p. 21.

CHAPTER 4

Is Natural in It? Radical Theory and Educational Capital

Gang of Four and Scritti Politti were not the first British popular musicians to be significantly influenced by Marxist theory. But they were the first to take such a fusion deep into the charts; Scritti Politti's Green Gartside, in particular, became a transatlantic star, scoring numerous Top 10 hits. The trajectory from speed-frazzled, squat-dwelling former art school students subjecting each and every personal action to political scrutiny to major label career players is a captivating one. Many of the themes raised in the previous chapters can be focused by taking time to investigate, in the context of emerging Thatcherism, where these bands came from and what shaped their work; how they have been received; the way their commercial successes (and failures) played out; and the broader resonances of what might initially seem to be instances of the perennial 'artistic differences' that tear groups apart.

Existing writing on the two bands offers a further way of focusing in on how they were politically situated and why this might matter today. One common claim that has long dogged both Gang of Four and Scritti Politti is that their influence by the leftist conceptual art formation Art and Language, and each band's utilisation of Marxist and post-structuralist theory, risked denuding their work of the emotive and pleasurable effect often considered central to popular music. Another oft-covered theme is the decision of both bands to adopt either a prototypical or fully fledged new pop strategy. When it comes to this point, evaluations tend to be

© The Editor(s) (if applicable) and The Author(s) 2016
D. Wilkinson, *Post-Punk, Politics and Pleasure in Britain*,
DOI 10.1057/978-1-137-49780-2_4

far less critical, usually accepting the rationale of each band for having done so. My own perspective, as will become clear, is almost the reverse. Though I question the way in which the two bands handled radical theory, I also argue that at times they successfully drew on a Marcusean 'sensuous reason'. Meanwhile, Gang of Four and Scritti Politti's new pop moves are subjected to greater scrutiny than they have so far received. Other issues dealt with include each band's negotiation of the politics of the personal, the significance of Scritti Politti's Eurocommunist commitments, and the feminist consciousness of Gang of Four.

The argument is unified by a concern that has so far gone undiscussed. This is the class background and education of Gang of Four and Scritti Politti and its ambiguous political consequences. The particular educational background of key members from each band strongly influenced their cultural production, which often overcame the hegemonic division between radical theory and feeling. Gang of Four and Scritti Politti's education also contributed to the manner in which their cultural production addressed issues of gender, the personal politics of popular musical production and the music industry in progressive terms. However, vocalist Jon King and guitarist Andy Gill of Gang of Four and vocalist and guitarist Green Gartside of Scritti Politti also inherited the dominant understanding of education as class mobility. This contradictory process took place during the rise of the New Right and the pessimistic response of one section of the left to this development. Therefore, I also look at the ways in which the educational and political experience of each band bore on the fact that their development of qualitatively oppositional understandings of freedom and pleasure was less pronounced than in the work of fellow left post-punks. Furthermore, I consider how such experience shaped the bands' involvement in the moment of new pop.

'But That Was Once I Got out of Wales...'[1]

The influence of Art and Language on both bands cannot be underestimated. Former member of Art and Language Terry Atkinson taught Gill and King at Leeds University, whilst Gartside met drummer Tom Morley on his art degree at Leeds Polytechnic and 'started a sort of counter-curriculum. I'd got in with some members of the Art and Language group, and I'd organised visiting lectures ... it got very popular.'[2] The future members of Gang of Four and Scritti Politti attended university in the mid- to late 1970s at just the point when many who had taken part in the libertarian left revolts of the late 1960s were becoming institution-alised. (Gartside claims in an early interview that 'Leeds ... was toted [sic] as a very trendy place to go, as you had lecturers there that made names for themselves in the sixties'.)[3] But there was a further reason for this common encounter. Members of Art and Language had discovered teach-ing was their only route to economic survival given that there was little market interest in the austere, often textual and philosophically influenced works they produced.[4] The issues of pleasurable engagement, populism and market appeal faced by both bands, then, have fairly direct roots.

John A. Walker has noted that the catalogue for a 1970 exhibition by Art and Language sharply contrasted with the predominantly 'colourful, ornamental, psychedelic style' of the countercultural underground press.[5] Furthermore, a didactic poster produced by the group in 1975, ostensibly addressed to school children and students, declared that 'cultural revolu-tion is not associated with the mindless "counter-culture" of pop/rock festivals'.[6] Suspicious of the potential of countercultural romanticism to detach consideration of cultural production from the social conditions in which it was made, the group rejected it altogether. Atkinson gave a talk at an Institute of Contemporary Arts conference in early 1978 that pitilessly played up the links between John Locke's theory of possessive individualism, free market capitalism, and the culturalist understandings of freedom which preponderated in art schools and which, as noted in the previous chapter, had significantly influenced the character of coun-tercultural dissent.[7] When he returned to figurative drawing and painting, Atkinson's logic derived not from the romantic notion of self-expression often associated with this style, but from a desire to appropriate images from the past in order to politically problematise and re-signify them.[8] This was a technique familiar from previous radical avant-gardes, such as Dadaist collage and the Situationist technique of détournement, or 'diversion' of 'pre-existing aesthetic elements'.[9]

Indeed, Atkinson had first been appointed at Leeds University thanks to the influence of former Situationist-turned art historian T.J. Clark.[10] Michael Hoover and Lisa Stokes note the concurrent and in some ways complementary anti-culturalist influence on Gang of Four of fellow depart-mental figures, such as structuralist Marxist Fred Orton and feminist Griselda Pollock.[11] Gartside, meanwhile, recalls his interest in what he views as the 'seamlessly contiguous areas' of Gramscian Marxism and 'the politi-cal dimension of the linguistic turn in philosophy', having begun to acquire works of post-structuralist theory from university bookshops in Leeds.[12]

The effect on the habitus of key band members was pronounced. Gill, for example, views first-wave punk as naively romantic: 'I always think of Liberty leading the people over the barricade with the wind blowing in her hair, which is definitely where The Clash were coming from.' He contrasts this to Gang of Four by referring to the arch avant-garde humour displayed on the sleeve of their debut single 'Damaged Goods'. It featured a reproduction of their letter to Bob Last of Fast Product requesting that the cover show a photo of a matador and a bull having a conversation in speech bubbles about their implication in the entertainment industry.[13]

In a fanzine interview, Gartside similarly critiqued what he viewed as the 'silly, over-romanticised notion' of The Clash's claim that 'they felt like the Magnificent 7—a bunch of outlaws that would come into town to put everything to rights'.[14] Instead, members of Scritti Politti sat up for days on amphetamine in the Camden squat they had moved to after graduating, discussing critical theory in relation to gigs and records.[15] In interviews for the weekly music papers, they would grill journalists about the role of the music press in the popular music industry, leading *Sounds* journalist Dave McCullough to conclude that the band possessed a 'fastidious CONSCIOUS sense of alternative reasoning'.[16] Asked about Scritti Politti's aims, Gartside disrupted the common-sense distinction of culture from questions of production and everyday life, claiming that 'a lot of … problems aren't actually encountered at the stage of writing or performing a song per se', referring to 'the interface between making music and the rest of your life' and insisting that the band wanted to create an effect with their 'general practice, not just the music'.[17]

Though the theoretical approach of both bands meant they were consciously aware of the processes and implications of cultural production beyond questions of form, they applied the same approach to musical concerns. Gill recalls beginning to write the song 'Anthrax' with King by sketching out a diagram 'like a scientific formula'[18] and that 'jamming was the J-word … the idea of just sitting around and "let's just see what happens"—it seemed to relate to some older ethos that was basically alien to us'.[19] Furthermore, the musical 'possibles' which the band adopted and developed from their various influences were consciously deployed in order to contribute to the political themes explored in songs. For example, the simultaneous spoken and sung vocal parts of 'The Murder Mystery' by The Velvet Underground inspired the monologue featured in 'Anthrax' which overlays the sung lyrics, questioning the theme of mystified love as ultimate fulfilment in popular song.[20] The band adopted the 'rhythmic, stripped down' sound of rock band Free, though Gill claims, 'you loved Free and yet were aware of the utter idiocy of the lyrics ... Paul Rodgers would be singing about his car and his woman'.[21]

These dominant notions of freedom and pleasure, including libidinal investment in consumer goods and romantic partners viewed in the same reified terms, survived in Gang of Four's songs too, but were instead subjected to doubt and scrutiny. Dub reggae, meanwhile, which Gill claimed was what he and King 'loved above all ... [it's] all about space and things disappearing and coming back',[22] provided the band with a structural understanding of their songs as constructed from discrete yet mutually supportive elements. Each had their own significance, rather than a rhythm section acting as the unobtrusive backdrop for romantic, expressive solos. Such an understanding, as will become clear, was linked with Gang of Four's handling of the politics of the personal at the level of form.

Scritti Politti adopted a similar position, with bassist Nial Jinks commenting in an early interview that 'it wouldn't make a lot of sense for us to be doing 12 bar things 'cos that wouldn't communicate the ideas and thoughts we're trying to convey ... that's sealed, that's not dynamic'.[23] Gartside concurs with Reynolds when asked if he and Jinks' incorporation of British folk and countercultural folk rock elements into early Scritti Politti songs consciously correlated with their membership of the Communist Party and its history of viewing folk as 'the people's music'.[24] He recalls having 'sat down for months and months and wrote screeds of justification'[25] upon deciding in 1980 that the band should pursue a musical direction influenced by black American popular music in order to increase its appeal.

It may seem, then, as if both bands were at some distance from the culturalism which I argued in the previous chapter was the residual source of leftist post-punk's political concern with issues of freedom and pleasure. This, however, was not the case. Gill and King first experienced dissent in the late 1960s whilst at secondary school in their hometown of Sevenoaks, Kent. Its source was their art teacher Bob White. Gill remembers that in contrast to the 'pointless repression' of official school policy, White was representative of 'a certain Sixties cultural and political openness ... he had this little world going on [and] would speak to us like intelligent human beings ... it was the first time we had adult conversations ... on the same level as the teacher'.[26]

The atmosphere evoked in this vignette is highly similar to that satirised by Art and Language: discussing the 'art rip-off' of mystified cultural production under capitalism, they claimed that it was 'the more poignant for those students who ... are stuck in various harmless corners, of which "the art room" is usually the saddest. These students are being trained to be hopeless: their teachers have let down the system in failing to produce the tidy individuals it requires', before going on to mock idealistic art teachers as 'trendy young bores'.[27] Yet Gill and King, remembering their experience of pursuing art through to A-Level at school, associate it with their discovery of countercultural rock and the radical cultural and political activity of groups such as the Yippies,[28] therefore inheriting the libertarian left focus on culture as potentially utopian. The band's drama student drummer Hugo Burnham shared a similar structure of feeling, attempting to set up a radical theatre group whilst at Leeds.[29]

In a lengthy article on Gang of Four for *Melody Maker*, Mary Harron linked them residually to the point in the mid- to late 1960s where rock became dominated by romantic, culturalist understandings of art. Harron perceptively pointed out that countercultural rock was marked by both romantic authenticity and a rapid dynamic of formal change, so that paradoxically, what was considered authentic was often subject to alteration. She argued that conceptualism and demystification, despite their challenge to culturalist romanticism, had become popular within post-punk, and therefore constituted the latest measure of authenticity.[30] This peculiar blend of culturalist and anti-culturalist opposition on the part of the band led to a complex, unusual and sometimes highly effective strategy of critique regarding dominant understandings of freedom and pleasure, something I explore most fully in connection with their attitude towards new sensibilities. It also had similarly complex implications for their political negotiation of the music industry; though fully aware of their position within a capitalist market, members of Gang of Four tended to fall back occasionally on the culturalist distinction of culture from commerce in terms of creative freedom.

Gartside, meanwhile, recalls that in addition to Scritti Politti's intensely questioning stance, motivated by 'what was happening politically at the time, and also because of what had seeped out to us from academia ... beyond those things was just something we'd grown up with: the power of pop ... we all knew about that latent utopian possibility in the music'.[31] Remembering his upbringing in the Welsh new town of Cwmbran, Gartside described listening to the countercultural music played by John Peel as a lifeline. Scritti Politti, he acknowledges, was 'a massively *romantic* project'.[32] Furthermore, the band did not only encounter representatives of Art and Language and post-structuralist theory whilst at Leeds Polytechnic. They were also taught by none other than the 'wonderfully entertaining, rude and often very drunk' Jeff Nuttall,[33] who had thoroughly explored the links between the culturalism of romantic and post-romantic art movements, the libertarian left and the counterculture in *Bomb Culture*. Initially, this fusion informed the politics of the band's cultural production in a similar manner to Gang of Four. Gartside, though, increasingly came to view non-linguistic elements of musical form as the locus of an irrational rebellion in opposition to Marxist theory. I explore the reasons for this move, and its ambiguous political consequences, in subsequent sections.

This shift on Gartside's part hints at the issue of class and education raised earlier, and its connection with the changing political directions pursued by each band. Andy Gill and Jon King came from lower middle-class and working class backgrounds respectively and went to Sevenoaks School, a Direct Grant grammar school where places were paid for partly with public funds and partly by private pupils. The former kind of place was offered as a scholarship based on educational merit assessed via the 11-plus exam. It was passing this exam that secured both future band members a place there.[34] Alan Sinfield has noted how the Education Acts of the 1940s perpetuated a stratified class system, despite having been presented as egalitarian advance.[35] Certain comments made by King in particular seem to indicate that he understood his education and his acquisition of cultural capital in terms of class mobility. King recognised that his ambition to be an artist was aided by 'being in this ... little clique at school' (one which also produced the documentary maker Adam Curtis and the director Paul Greengrass). He associated his working class background with 'tedium' in contrast to 'going to a school with very rich kids ... it was amazing being exposed to books for the first time'.[36]

Though the educational background of Scritti Politti prior to Leeds Polytechnic is less clear, the band's key (and later sole remaining) member Green Gartside shared a similar experience and understanding of education to Gang of Four. It was, however, more overtly politicised in nature. He described his family background as 'working-class Tory' in interview with Reynolds.[37] Gartside's stepfather was a travelling sales representative for the food company Batchelors.[38] After meeting future Scritti Politti bassist Nial Jinks, whose family were involved with the Communist Party, the pair attempted to set up a local branch of the Young Communist League. Gartside recalls that it 'got into the local newspaper' and 'heralded the beginning of a decline in my relationship with my parents. I didn't see them for years and years.' Asked by Reynolds if being a Communist 'was simply a normal, acceptable thing' in South Wales in the early 1970s, Gartside responded that it was not; he associated meeting other members of the YCL with attending university and Marxist summer schools in London 'once I got out of Wales'.[39] For Gartside, it seems, education was contradictorily bound up with both radical politics and escape from a provincial working class background associated with reaction and limitation.

Bourdieu has argued that prolonged institutional education is a key factor in the unequal class distribution of cultural capital, producing a disposition[40] that can be advantageously transposed to various cultural fields.[41] The cultural capital acquired by Gartside through his education is evident in the claim that other post-punks regarded him as a figure of authority.[42] Meanwhile, Reynolds notes that Gang of Four strongly influenced other contemporaneous post-punk acts.[43]

Bourdieu's theory of what he calls the 'new petit bourgeoisie' also resonates with the background of Gang of Four and Scritti Politti. For Bourdieu, this fraction is a combination of those from middle-class backgrounds 'to whom the educational system has not given the means of pursuing the trajectory most likely for their class'[44] and those, like key members of Gang of Four and Scritti Politti, from working or lower middle-class backgrounds whose aspirations, inculcated by educational success, have not been immediately realised due to the 'overproduction of qualifications and [their] consequent devaluation'.[45] It is characterised by 'a refusal of the most typically "bourgeois" configurations and by a concern to go against common judgements, in which aesthetic commitments feature prominently',[46] and is associated with the countercultural popularisation of the avant-garde.[47] Bourdieu distinguishes between the formerly working or lower middle-class 'parvenu' component of this class fraction, who 'owe their capital to an acquisitive effort directed by the education system',[48] and those from a middle- or upper-class family background which tends to produce a falsely naturalised faith in one's distinction.[49] Parvenus usually have a 'more serious, more severe, often tense'[50] relationship with their cultural capital than their 'mondain' class superiors. This observation is evocative of the intensely critical, anti-culturalist aspect of each band's approach to their cultural production. It also chimes with *NME* journalist and member of Scritti Politti's squat collective Ian Penman's recollection that 'everyone was *brittle* with ... sincerity'.[51]

Meanwhile, Raymond Williams observed that in relation to education, class, and the British left's predicament in the face of Thatcherism, 'some of our worst enemies are now working class boys who've made it'.[52] It would be inaccurate and unfair to apply this claim to Gang of Four and Scritti Politti, given the leftist commitments of each band. Nevertheless, Williams' insight does reveal the way in which the welfare-capitalist expansion of education in terms of 'equality of opportunity' sometimes acted as an unfortunate complementary precursor to Thatcherism's aggressive ideological promotion of individual aspiration within an unequal society. This is an issue that continues to resonate: recently, Jo Littler has traced the history of the term 'meritocracy' through its usage under welfare-capitalism, on to its take-up by right-wing think-tanks and its centrality in the discourse of New Labour, arguing that under the Conservatives, it now forms a central 'plank of neoliberal political rhetoric and public discourse' under the banner of 'aspiration'.[53]

It was not only their experience and understanding of education as class mobility that positioned Gill, King and Gartside in relation to a structure of feeling that the New Right capitalised on. It was also the specific content of this education. This might seem surprising, given its frequently radical content. However, Walker has noted that the 'questioning' attitude of leftist conceptual artists in the 1970s could sometimes manifest itself as a sense of superiority over their peers.[54] An echo of this can be detected in each band's assessment of The Clash discussed above. With regard to the structuralist Marxism that influenced Gang of Four and Scritti Politti, it is worth remembering that Louis Althusser regarded the libertarian left revolt of May 1968 in France as 'infantile leftism' and formulated some of his most influential work (such as the anti-humanism of 'Ideology and Ideological State Apparatuses') as an apparently more sophisticated response to these events.[55]

On a related theme, it is necessary to trace post-structuralism further back than the beginning of its dissemination in Anglophone academies to its moment of emergence amongst the Parisian intelligentsia. Perry Anderson has argued convincingly that the often pessimistic implications of such work regarding radical change can be partially traced to the one-time support of key post-structuralist figures for the French Communist Party, which squandered an historic opportunity to increase its already significant influence and whose support began to fall behind the moderate Socialist Party in the 1970s.[56]

It's worth noting that it was not only Communist failure that led post-structuralist thinkers along the paths of 'clamourous transfers to the right to mute exits from politics altogether'.[57] The 1960s and 1970s also wit-nessed, as in Britain, the re-emergence and gradual retreat of the liber-tarian left in France. Derrida, Deleuze, Guattari and Foucault expressed support for this kind of politics at certain points, though they came to be increasingly critical of it; for example, Foucault's profoundly influen-tial travestying of radical sexual politics in *The History of Sexuality*,[58] and Derrida's telling doubt about even the possibility of freedom when recall-ing his involvement in May 1968: 'I was on my guard ... in the face of the enthusiasm of a finally "freed" speech ... and so forth.'[59] The loss of faith in the left engendered amongst post-structuralist thinkers is also connected to another feature of their thought identified by Anderson: 'the extraordinary *lability* of the political connotations [it has] succes-sively assumed'.[60] The particular political connotations of the work of such figures within the specific conjuncture I discuss will be further explored throughout the chapter.

'IF ALL THE TIME YOU REACT TO THINGS ON AN EMOTIONAL LEVEL, YOU'LL NEVER GET ANYWHERE'[61]

Throughout the course of Gang of Four's existence, the band has been critiqued by otherwise sympathetic commentators from a broadly cultur-alist position. The argument has either been that the theoretical critique embodied in their cultural production threatened its political effectiveness by overshadowing its emotive, and thus pleasurable qualities, or that these qualities were present in the band's music in spite of the theoretical content of the lyrics. Some, including Reynolds, have even wondered if the value of the band's music was threatened by the fact that it was consciously con-ceptualised. In his review of the band's debut album, Jon Savage claimed that 'the price you pay for your entertainment is a series of descriptive, exhortatory and ... overtly didactic vignettes'.[62] Gary Bushell, meanwhile, opined that 'I suggest you check 'em out ... for the sheer quality of their music, and then make your own mind up about the lyrics, ok?'[63] Mary Harron claimed that 'if there is one thing to be learnt [from listening to Gang of Four] it is that a group can have the most complex theories and still play music that makes you jump up and down'.[64] Subsequent reflections have adopted similar positions: Hoover and Stokes argue that 'more than anything else, Gang of Four was a dance band trapped in a prison-house of leftist-intellectual language'.[65] Reynolds, though celebratory of *Entertainment!* as one of the masterpieces of post-punk, goes on to claim that 'the trouble with demystification is that it takes the mystery out of everything'.[66]

What all of these positions have in common is the assumption that the rational critique of the band was automatically devoid of emotional or pleasurable content, needing in some way to be balanced by 'pure', unmediated musical pleasure and disagreeing only on the extent to which the band succeeded in doing so. But, as shown in Chap. 2's discussion of musical form, such a division of words and music is untenable, something which Gang of Four's Jon King would also concur with: 'Music and lyrics, the one always analogous to the other, impossible to separate sound and meaning.'[67]

A different way of considering the theme of sensuous pleasure in Gang of Four's songs is to focus on one of their persistent lyrical preoccupations: characters whose understandings and experiences of freedom and pleasure are bound to the dominant culture, but who begin to question these notions. Greil Marcus has nicely characterised this process as 'false consciousness in rebellion against itself', calling it 'a shocking little drama'.[68] Marcus' use of the words 'shocking' and 'drama' point towards the way that the critical content of many of these songs is also capable of provoking an engaging emotional response in concert with the rest of the music.

Such songs operated in accord with the notion of a sensuous reason explored by Herbert Marcuse. For Marcuse, the dominant application of reason was as an instrumentalist tool of capitalism, which denied individual freedom and self-fulfilment understood in libertarian left terms.[69] In opposition to this, Marcuse argued with reference to the young Marx that socialists must develop an understanding of reason guided by the senses.[70] Marcuse's influence was visible in the commonly shared attitude of the counterculture that work must become pleasurable[71] and in its critique of the paradoxically maddening effects of the apparently rational routine of wage labour and 'leisure time'. This was captured in an iconic graffito, which appeared in Notting Hill in 1968: 'Same thing Day after day—

Tube-Work-Dinner-Work-Tube-Armchair-TV-Sleep-Work. How Much More Can You Take. One in Five Go Mad, One in Ten Cracks Up.'[72]

At their most powerful, then, Gang of Four's 'shocking little dramas' undo framings of their work as marked by a sterile intellectualism by conveying complex leftist critique in experiential, deeply felt and frequently enjoyable terms. Punk musician and music writer Lucy O'Brien hints at this, quoting King's claim that 'making trouble is entertaining'. She recalls the 'riotous' mood created by Gang of Four's performance on the back of a lorry during an abortion rights protest, arguing that 'the band have been criticised as sounding cold and unemotional, but in contrast there is an intense passion to their delivery. Their world is combative yet engaging.'[73] Furthermore, humour was often deployed to make points; the anti-arms trade song 'Armalite Rifle', for example, contained a droll reference to the band's bassist in the line 'I disapprove of it, so does Dave.'

At the root of this was the band's recognition that there was no divide between their reasoning and their everyday experience as students taking in the theories that they had been exposed to. Gill describes the structure of feeling which animated them in the claims that 'as far as we were concerned, it was just telling it like it is, from our point of view and in our language'[74] and 'we had a greater clarity of thought [than punk bands such as the Sex Pistols]' but 'what we were doing ... was from the gut'.[75] To be fair, it could be claimed that it was precisely this art school experience that distanced Gang of Four from the possibility of populist connection—a position taken up by critics such as Garry Bushell, as we saw in the previous chapter. Yet the band's commercial success belies such an attitude to some extent.

Gang of Four, then, more than likely did not struggle to connect at the level of emotion and pleasure as much as has been supposed. The sensuous reason of their songs, though, usually tends to halt at critique, rather than simultaneously prefiguring qualitatively different understandings and practices of freedom and pleasure, a path also formulated by Marcuse: 'Emancipation of the senses implies that the senses become "practical" in the reconstruction of society, that they generate new (socialist) relationships between man and man, man and things, man and nature.'[76] The relative absence of such utopianism in the band's songs distinguished them from peers such as the Blue Orchids and The Raincoats, as we will see in the next two chapters.

The song 'Natural's Not In It' from the band's debut album is a good example of these issues, offering a critique of the leisure industry and the commodification of the body. Its lyrics implicate both band and listener in these processes by noting our inescapable social interaction in an unequal system and the way that even well intentioned actions, therefore, usually come with 'strings attached'. Despite the ostensibly puritanical tone, the lyrics also sensitively explore the conflicted desires of the song's protagonist, seeing leisure as a 'problem' and recognising the pain and alienation that come with commodification of pleasure, love and the senses. In doing so, the song powerfully conveys the notion that it is consumer capitalism that is responsible for the oscillation between the puritan work ethic and the constant incitement to gratification through consumption. This is best summed up in the contrast between a biblical reference to Lot's wife recommending the renunciation of 'vice' and the observation that the body is 'good business'. This line manages to condense Marx's theory of the exploitative circuit of capital via the body of the wage labourer[77] into five words, somewhat giving the lie to Savage's claim that the band did not have the 'knack' of making complex political theory accessible and compelling.[78]

Furthermore, the music of the song actually complements the sensuous reason of the lyrics rather than offering pleasurable respite or being stripped of enjoyment value through its prior conceptualisation. It features many of the techniques identified by Gill when asked by Reynolds how the band's music was consciously thought-through in order to achieve an estranging effect from rock conventions. These include 'anti-solos' in place of a standard verse, chorus and middle-eight structure, whereby various instrumentalists would simply stop playing temporarily; a drum part with jarring rhythmic emphases;[79] a melodious bass part that has more in common with funk and disco than with rock; and the re-signification of a musical 'possible' which in a former context signified romantic authenticity: Gill's guitar part is highly reminiscent of the style of Wilko Johnson, guitarist for mid-1970s Essex pub rock band Dr Feelgood, who mythologised their Canvey Island home as the 'Thames Delta' after their blues influences.[80] The 'sober' production of the album noted by Reynolds is particularly evident too; guitar, bass, drums and vocals sound brittle and claustrophobic. Rather than being 'cold-blooded' though, as Reynolds describes it,[81] the combination of this production with the scything guitar and the recurrent stop–start of instruments magnifies the emotional tension in the lyrics, making their politicised theme seem compelling. One example is the point at which the song suggests the endless fascination of 'repackaged' sex by repeating a lyrical phrase accompanied at first only by guitar, followed by bass, the melody of each part mirroring that of the lyrics. The immersive panning effect on this line also highlights the partial nature of the band's deployment of sensuous reason, hinting as it does that stepping outside the dominance of commodified pleasure is impossible. Though the subject of the song comes to recognise their 'coercion' and makes a collective identification with others against this process, there is no suggestion of what qualitatively different pleasures might look like.

This might not be of particular note were it only the case in 'Natural's Not In It'. However, it is a consistent feature of much of Gang of Four's cultural production throughout the post-punk era. On *Entertainment!* alone, the narrator of 'Damaged Goods' recognises the connections between a romantic relationship and commodity exchange, leading him to end it; 'I Found That Essence Rare' finishes with the fatalistic declaration 'I knew I'd get what I asked for'; and 'Return the Gift' concludes with the repeated, ironic request for time off from a worker whose labour is 'on the price list'. 'To Hell With Poverty', from the time of the band's second album *Solid Gold*, can only advocate—admittedly thrillingly—the compensation of spending the dole money on the temporary oblivion of 'cheap wine'. The ironically titled third album *Songs of the Free* features 'Call Me Up', which evokes infantile consumers 'grateful' for their pleasures. *Hard*, the band's final album prior to breaking up, concludes with 'Independence', a slow, mournful track which focuses on the dismal let-down of embracing Thatcherite understandings of freedom. Though Gang of Four successfully challenged understandings of radical theory as unpleasurable, then, their steadfast avoidance of prefigurative understandings of liberation hinted at the way their habitus and intellectual influences played out, as I go on to consider.

WANTING BETTER?

In the early work of Scritti Politti, too, there is a comparable inseparability between the pleasure of music and lyrics and the critique embodied in them. Yet the band faced similar criticisms to Gang of Four on this front: Dave McCullough followed a description of the band's conceptualism and politics with the rhetorical question 'yes, but is it rock and roll? I hear you scream',[82] Ian Birch described their first releases as 'achingly intellectual',[83] and Barney Hoskyns questioned whether the original Scritti Politti line-up's 'hearts were in their music or in their minds'.[84] Gartside, however, has claimed that thinking through the band's aims and standpoint was 'part of the pleasure'[85] and that their live improvisation, which was 'ideologically in keeping' with the desire to demystify,[86] was also enjoyable.[87] McCullough perhaps unconsciously concurred with this view in his description of a 1979 gig by the band as the best of the year which 'seemed to attack you with ... emotional force'.[88]

With regard to the political content of this conceptualism, Gartside had recognised as a teenager that Marxist theory could be successfully incorporated into popular music, having been a fan of the progressive rock band Henry Cow whose work he describes as 'frightening' but attractive. Henry Cow was the most notable British group prior to Gang of Four and Scritti Politti to have attempted such a strategy, and their residual influence stretched to Gartside organising gigs for them after having made their acquaintance via the Communist Party.[89] When faced with Reynolds' speculation that 'hardline socialist politics' were 'normal, everyday, even mundane' for those from certain backgrounds in the 1970s, and thus may have prompted alternative, aesthetic forms of rebellion, Gartside counters the suggestion with the claim that 'there was nothing about the sense of communism I got from Nial that wasn't wholly comfortable about it sitting alongside surrealism. I didn't feel at that point that there was any impediment to the imagination involved in ... learning about Marxism.'[90] This situation was not to last, however, and nowadays, Gartside claims that 'Marxist analysis gave shape to whatever dissatisfactions I had at the time ... be it industrial South Wales, my family or anything else'.[91] Though, like Gang of Four, this statement shows that the band's use of theory was rooted in experience rather than abstraction, it does suggest that a point was reached where it was no longer a pleasurable, aesthetically charged experience.

What prompted this shift? In *Rip It Up and Start Again*, Reynolds notes that 'the stern regime of questioning everything and constant ideological wariness' combined with the band's 'self-neglect', including living in a squat without a functioning bathroom, wore them down and resulted in a tense, fractious and 'paranoid' collective mindset.[92] For Gartside, this resulted in becoming 'properly depressed and completely inert'[93] from late 1979 and on into 1980. The historical events of this period more than likely negatively affected the mood of Scritti Politti too as the effects of the first year of the Thatcher government's policies made themselves felt, despite the band's claim in 'P.A.s' that 'the dole-drums roll us into battle'. There was, however, another factor in the despair. This was the increasing prevalence of post-structuralism over Marxism in Gartside's thought. His understanding of these theories was marked by their tendency to a view of language that risked minimising its enabling capacities: 'I was not well … There was that whole thing of making a music that was trying to be expressive of the stresses of being … spoken by the language that we were being spoken by.'[94]

As this position became more entrenched, so language was progressively abandoned to 'power'. The possibility of a sensuous reason, through which words and music could work together to pleasurably convey critique and oppositional possibilities, gradually receded. The cover of the band's *Peel Sessions* EP featured a page from an essay by Gartside entitled 'Scritto's Republic' which stated that 'the axioms of Marxism were not those of science but those of discourse […] the nexus and operative of much of repression was understood to be Language […] The rules of a society are embodied in the rules of its language […] Language pre-exists our entry into it and defines what is normal.' Crucially, the piece displays an early formulation of Gartside's developing thought that would later become more prominent. This was his hesitant hope for the possibility of political opposition in the 'semiotic instability' of 'beat music' (the term the band used in interviews in an attempt to break with the conventions of rock).

The lively and chaotic introduction of 'Doubt Beat', from the band's *4 A-Sides* EP, seems to express such a hope for music as pleasurably subversive. Coinciding with the beginning of the vocals, however, the instruments begin playing more settled and clearly structured melodies and rhythms, illustrating from a post-structuralist position the capacity of language to organise and regulate according to the norms of power. It is more than likely a deliberate irony that the reassurance of the lyrical melody, accompanied by a rhythm section influenced by the ska and dub reggae popular with fans of punk and post-punk, is also the element which demonstrates Gartside's view of the repressive regulation of sensuous pleasure by language; 'Scritto's Republic' had declared that 'drives meet the external organisation of language and either structure accordingly or get repressed. To leave speech and language uninterrupted is to submit to the cultural order by which sexuality, thought etc. is regulated.' Gang of Four may have avoided articulating oppositional notions of pleasure, but their work did allow for the possibility of hegemonic complexity and collective dissent from the dominant. In 'Doubt Beat', however, there can be no opposition at all at the level of language, and its lyrics even reveal an uncertainty about the ability of music to undo the coherence of power, with Gartside singing ironically of a 'heart breaking mess'.

The position was untenable, and after the onset of ill health and a serious anxiety attack followed by a period of recuperative isolation back in rural Wales, Gartside emerged with a new direction for the band. Despite having written an almost book-length theoretical framing of this new direction,[95] his ostensible position regarding the location of subversive pleasure had not altered significantly from the 'Scritto's Republic' essay and the lyrics of 'Doubt Beat'; all that had changed was that the uncertainty over whether music disrupted language had been replaced with a 'metaphysical' faith that this was so.[96]

What did make itself newly felt, however, was an active opposition between Marxism and sensuous pleasure, recalling Perry Anderson's observation that post-structuralism had supplanted Marxism not only amongst many of those who had previously espoused the latter but also on the same theoretical terrain of social structure and subjectivity.[97] 'You grow up as a good, almost Catholic-leftist boy, and you learn to be scared of your sexuality, to be scared of your power', Gartside claimed, going on to state that the group's politics had 'moved from an essentialist and reductionist position in which we believed in a history of science which could make sense of the future to one that realised that what you've got is needs, demands and desires, and you go out and you fight for them'.[98]

Gartside's newly romanticised view of music came with unintended political implications. In the post-structuralist inspired descriptions of his Marxist past as joyless and limiting and his pragmatic approach to a competitive field of individualist desires, there was a faint suggestion of the ideological strategies of the New Right discussed in the previous chapter: firstly its denigration of the left as puritanical and secondly its claims on freedom and pleasure. Of course, this was presumably the last thing Gartside wished to advocate; his evocation of struggles for fulfilment was more than likely still conceived of in leftist terms. The crossover of rhetoric was more an indication of the indirect but growing ideological influence of Thatcherism than it was of any political about-face on Gartside's part.

'Jacques Derrida', from Scritti Politti's debut full-length album *Songs to Remember*, provides a snapshot of this complex structure of feeling in its lyrical association of revolutionary politics with reason and bad weather. Lines that claim the singer used to be like a depressed industry link Gartside's previously poor mental health with his fading interest in Marxism, which he now viewed as outmoded in its concerns. By contrast,

some very Derridean word-play (*'bossanova'*, 'cashanova') links the pleasures of music, monetary wealth, love and identification with the interests
of the ruling class. There is clearly an ironic intent to such lines and the lyrics go on to proclaim the singer's revolutionary affiliation. This, though, is
delivered in a muted, incidental fashion and is followed by an affirmation
of individualistic desire sung by female backing singers in a euphoric, soulful style, thus connecting such desire with pleasurable musical sensations.

Similarly, the singer announces his love for an Italian leftist, though he
also implies that his love for Derrida's work gives him an anti-humanist
suspicion of such feelings. The singer wants better than this: the claims that
his desires cannot be fully satisfied as things stand and that a 'living wage'
is not enough both seem to evoke the qualitative critique of the libertarian left. Yet he is prepared to settle for 'whatever you've got'. What seems
like compromise is laced with an insatiable desire that will 'overthrow' and
devour the 'nation-state'. Along with an implied leftist internationalism,
however, these lines simultaneously evoke a notion of 'desire', which, as
Reynolds has noted, 'fits the tenor of the hip crit of the day ... but ...
sounds a lot like how globalisation works: flows of capital ... that make a
nonsense of national borders'.[99]

'Jacques Derrida', then, is an appropriately ambiguous song, capturing
as it does the struggle between the New Right and the libertarian left over
understandings of freedom and pleasure. The delivery of part of the lyrics in
rap form, moreover, undermines Gartside's hope that the subversive power
of pop could transcend its historical conditions.[100] As discussed in Chap. 2,
all musical 'possibles' carry socially and historically rooted meanings and
associations. In this instance, the assertive delivery of rap is clearly being
drawn on to counteract the pronounced multiaccentuality of the lyrics.

Sweet and Sour

There were similar ambiguities in Gang of Four's approach to gender.
A significant number of songs by Gang of Four deal with relationships
between men and women, consciously situating them within capitalist
social relations. Andy Gill has claimed that his father having left the family
when Gill was ten was directly connected to the band's lyrical preoccupation with such themes.[101] For Reynolds, Gang of Four's handling of gender
issues is bound up with his critique of their anti-culturalist, 'demystifying'
approach quoted earlier in relation to sensuous reason. Characterising the
band as overly masculine in terms of their adherence to 'hardness and

unyielding reason', Reynolds argues: 'the "unisex" brand of feminism in vogue on the Leeds scene meant that women [in bands such as Delta 5] became tough, assertive and "dry". The men, however, didn't become any "moister".'[102] This, though, was not always the case; just as Gang of Four invoked a sensuous reason in their critique of dominant notions of freedom and pleasure in terms of consumerism, so they often applied the same approach in relation to gender.

One reason for this strategy may well have been the fact that Gill and King had been taught by the leftist feminist art scholar Griselda Pollock. Pollock's work in the 1970s and early 1980s was concerned with ways in which feminist artistic production might encompass 'the aesthetic dimension of knowing' in a manner directly comparable to Marcuse, which in the context of feminism had the added benefit of breaking down gendered distinctions between masculine reason and feminine emotion. Pollock also advocated the exploration of 'emancipatory pleasures ... based on rigorous understanding of and active participation in a world of our collective remaking' in contrast to the puritanical direction increasingly being pursued by certain fragments of the women's movement at this point.[103]

In a similar manner to the way they handled sensuous reason, however, Gang of Four showed more interest in the first of Pollock's suggestions in relation to gender. Their feminist critique is often aestheticised, but usually unconcerned with 'emancipatory pleasures'. In the 1982 single 'I Love A Man in Uniform', for example, the subject of the song is a man who expresses his lack of fulfilment in terms related to both gender and capitalism. He believes that joining the army has solved his unemployment, lack of self-respect and lack of a partner, punning that women 'love to see you shoot'. The song displays sensuous reason in its puncturing of the man's illusions by dramatising the emotional tension between him and his girlfriend. His claims that he is the stronger partner and his belief that becoming a soldier has increased his allure are shattered by the female backing singers' mocking rejoinder—'you must be joking'—and the ironic tone of the chorus's titular phrase. The camp humour present in the sexual connotations of firing a gun and the implication of military role-play, complemented by a pop melody and the dance-oriented disco influence of the instrumental and backing vocal parts, all add to the pleasure of the song's critique.

Nowhere, however, is there an indication of how the problems explored might be resolved more positively. This is consistent throughout the band's output: 'Contract', from *Entertainment!*, explores marriage as a business arrangement and a couple's mutual inability to live up to social expectations in domestic space. 'Woman Town', from *Hard*, asserts women's autonomy and personhood in the face of objectification, mocking the insensitivity of the song's male character and its relationship to commodity fetishism. Yet it perpetuates an individualist understanding of freedom and fulfilment—'I don't need you'—rather than raising the possibility of equal, reciprocal personal relations.

This outlook of conscious critique that nevertheless does not often point clearly beyond dominant gender relations could also be seen in the mixed experience of Sara Lee, the bassist who replaced Dave Allen from Gang of Four's third album *Songs of the Free* onwards. Lee occupied a role then considered unusual for a woman in rock and 'on the whole ... had a good working relationship' with Gill and King. Yet she also considers their creative control to have been 'distinctly unfeminist' at times, including their decision to overdub some of her parts on *Songs of the Free* and *Hard* with those of a male session musician without having consulted her first.[104] Lee's time in Gang of Four was sometimes made difficult by finding herself in the middle of the clashing egos of her male counterparts.[105] These observations are not intended as personal critique of Gill and King; rather, they highlight the frequent difficulties of libertarian left and feminist injunctions to 'live your politics' within a hegemony that is hostile to them.

'Whatever You Do Is Political with a Small "p"'[106]

Considering that this was the case, it would be easy to assume that the personal politics of Gang of Four's internal democracy were also fragile. Initially, this was not so: Reynolds notes that the band's 'collectivist ideals ... permeated every aspect of [their] existence, from the way their music was jointly composed to the four-way split of publishing rights ... every member of the group and its entourage was paid the same wage ... except for the roadies, who got *double* during tours'.[107] Reynolds also astutely relates this ethos to Gill's reflection that in the band's recorded output, the different instruments 'coexisted' and were 'on the same level'.[108] The song 'Not Great Men', from *Entertainment!*, is a good example due to the complementary concerns of its lyrical theme, which sketch the dominant 'great men' approach to history, with its implied values of individualism, hierarchy and patriarchy, the opposite of those the band were attempting to live by. Numerous references to the domestic sphere emphasise the hegemonic reproduction of such attitudes. The one line chorus consists of the simple realisation that history is not made in this way—another example of 'false consciousness in rebellion against itself'.

Though the lyrics highlight the contradictions of dominant attitudes and a rejection of them, they do not indicate a radical alternative perspective, for example, the Marxist 'history from below' position exemplified in the work of E.P. Thompson and Eric Hobsbawm. The music, however, could be interpreted as an oppositional, libertarian left perspective in action; its funk influences mean that each part is tightly synchronised, a well-functioning collective effort that is nevertheless composed of recognisably discrete elements. The lack of dynamic variation, a conventional rock technique that appears in other songs on the album, including 'Ether', 'Damaged Goods' and '5.45', maintains the volume and intensity at an unremarkable level throughout. This could suggest both the everyday nature of historical production by the majority of people, and egalitarian co-operation without tension. Additionally, the vocal doubling in the chorus undermines the individualism of the 'great men' theory and suggests that no action can be undertaken without a relation to the actions of others.

The band's efforts set a standard; a positive example for others who would follow. Yet as with the aim of following feminist principles within a patriarchal hegemony, things were not always easy. Paul Lester's recent biography of the band complicates the harmonious portrayal of the band's internal democracy (though it is worth contextualising this by observing that the book's interviews with band members are coloured by more recent fallings-out between them). Even during the recording of *Entertainment!*, tensions apparently arose regarding the greater input of Gill and King into the album's production.[109] By the time of the band's third album, bassist Dave Allen had left and Gill and King ousted drummer Hugo Burnham prior to the recording of *Hard*.

Despite the claims of Allen and King that class was not an issue in the intra-band tensions which developed (Allen was from a working class family), Allen's recognition that 'I would always argue that I missed out on the education'[110] reveals that social differences may have played a part. Allen now attributes having left the band to feelings of insecurity arising from being unable to keep pace with the rest of the band's theoretical discussions and the issues they were asked about in interviews.[111] This difference in experience of class and education may not seem to account for the removal of Burnham, which Sara Lee attributes simply to 'personality clashes',[112] though class was more than likely a background pressure: Burnham was from an established middle-class family and went to prep and boarding school,[113] in contrast to the background of Gill and King discussed earlier. It is possible that Gill and King's long friendship and shared experience of education as class mobility had a bearing on events. It meant that the band's early and unavoidably abstract ideals of freedom as egalitarian democracy were gradually supplanted by the pair's closer affinity with one another than with Allen or Burnham, which manifested itself in their desire for control over the project. Even by the band's third album, Gill claims that he and King were writing all songs in full together.[114]

When quizzed about this gradual move away from democratic ideals, Gill's explanation was 'the one thing about Gang of Four that marks us out from other people with a very political bent is that we've never suggested that we're not "collaborators"'.[115] Gill is likely referring here to King owning a Vichy coin whilst at university, which read 'work, family, country' in place of 'liberty, equality, fraternity'. The coin fascinated him due to the political process of hegemonic normalisation it symbolised, replacing the slogan of the French Revolution with the right-wing values of the Vichy regime.[116]

One broader determinant of this fascination may well have been the influence of structuralist Marxism on the pair. Its exaggeration of the extent to which subjectivity is an effect of the dominant allowed them to adopt a position that made them appear more sophisticated from a leftist perspective in their recognition of the pervasiveness of hegemony. This position became a justification for yielding to hegemonic pressure, as we are all undoubtedly compelled to at times. Such a focus on constraints and 'collaboration' also accounted for the frequent absence of qualitatively oppositional visions of pleasure and freedom in the band's cultural production, and would have implications for their negotiation of the music industry, as I go on to examine.

Born to Lead?

Like Gang of Four, Scritti Politti began with a libertarian left commitment to freedom as democratic control over cultural production. In their case, this was semi-formalised and extended to the collective with whom they shared their squat.[117] Gartside claimed that initially, despite being the main musical contributor, 'I genuinely didn't think of myself as the leader'.[118] The band would promote co-operation in interviews, significantly linking it to the ethos of Rough Trade, to which they were signed.[119] Reynolds, however, has noted that even early on, Gartside would oscillate between this position and 'a battle to "win space" that translated as barging rivals like The Pop Group out of the way by discrediting them ideologically'. For Reynolds, this was not just motivated by the band's attempt to question taken-for-granted notions on all fronts, but by 'a hefty component of pure ego' on the part of Gartside.[120]

Being fair to Gartside, it is possible that this ego was not so much 'pure' as it was an element of his habitus, marked as it was by the insecurity of the parvenu; Sue Gogan of leftist post-punk band pragVEC recalls that before one Scritti Politti gig, 'he was in hysterics and needed to have a substantial ego massage before he could be persuaded to go on and do a stunning ... set',[121] whilst Gina Birch of The Raincoats claims 'he was ... a fragile character ... He had a group of people who would kind of run around him.'[122] A reviewer for Rock Against Racism fanzine *Temporary Hoarding*, meanwhile, accused Gartside of throwing 'a classic rock star moody' at a RAR benefit gig.[123]

Aided by a new pop structure of feeling promoting straightforward ambition that was concurrently developing amongst key writers for the music press and various other bands such as ABC,[124] Gartside moved to take full control of Scritti Politti. Along with his new definition of musical pleasure in opposition to the band's Marxist past, it seemed that personal autonomy was now framed in a manner that was similar in its hostility to consciously collective and co-operative practices as means of self-realisation. In a pun on the title of a New Order single, *Melody Maker* journalist Lynden Barber noted that 'everything's gone Green'. The interview featured Gartside claiming of the band's drummer Tom Morley that 'he doesn't really do anything at all' and rejecting 'all the old claims to pseudo-collectivism ... in retrospect a lot of it was hot air ... this is where we are now, just down to me. Which it always was.'[125] Unsurprisingly, Gartside was soon the sole remaining member of the original group.

Just as Andy Gill has hinted at Gang of Four's theoretical influences as justification for he and King's takeover of the band, so Gartside's individualist new direction was framed in post-structuralist terms in 'Lions After Slumber' from *Songs to Remember*. Ironically, Gartside has described the song as 'a little relativistic hymn. It's anti-singularity. It ... mean[s] that I am made up of a million ... intersections.'[126] Yet this does not seem to be a song about the supposed fiction of a singular identity, and certainly not one about ego-dissolution: the many 'intersections' that constitute the mantra-like lyrics are all preceded by the endlessly repeated possessive pronoun 'my'. There are also only a scant few references to the singer's dependence on other people for his sense of identity, each of which are presented as possessions (including, possibly, Tom Morley: 'my drummer').

As in 'Jacques Derrida', 'Lions After Slumber' contains a reference to Gartside's leftist political convictions, with similarly ambiguous connotations. The song's title refers to its final line, 'like lions after slumber in unvanquishable number', a quotation from Shelley's 'The Masque of Anarchy'. In retrospective interview with Reynolds, Gartside stated: 'I think it's the slumbering proletariat—that's basically what he was writing about.'[127] However, within the context of the song's lyrics, the phrase is the conclusion to the listing of 'intersections' that make up the protagonist, possibly referring to him as well as a collective and collectivist progressive political force. It thus aligns a revolutionary outlook with Gartside's self-conscious ambition for market success by way of his new strategy—'my ownership, my formula … my customer … my hunger'. Again like 'Jacques Derrida', a sense of irony and internal conflict is present, however—this time in lines such as 'my uncertainty … my limit'.

Excepting the introduction, the song remains in a locked funk groove. This complements the consistently self-scrutinising lyrical focus,[128] and once again re-signifies black popular musical form in accordance with Gartside's new vision. Occasional dramatic surges composed of rises in pitch in the lyrical melody and a more insistent delivery, as well as a swaggering saxophone solo midway through, are evocative of Gartside's newfound sensibility in their self-conscious and probably self-critical suggestion of ambition and overconfidence.

HAMMER AND POPSICLE[129]

One aspect of Gartside's background that might initially seem antithetical to the direction he later pursued is his activism on behalf of the British Communist Party. Yet Gartside's development of Scritti Politti could well have been an early indication of the dominant tendency which was to develop within the party throughout the 1980s and which was most visible on the pages of its journal *Marxism Today*. Gartside reflected that having discovered post-structuralism, 'I presumed those conversations would be had within the party and the ground would shift. I was working in the same building as the *Marxism Today* people ... some of whom were very bright and interesting. But that didn't happen ... So I just stopped going.'[130] The shift did not occur immediately, but there are parallels between Gartside as new pop star and the political evolution of former Eurocommunists and their fellow travellers.

From the early 1980s, the journal's dominant position shifted from a Gramscian perspective paralleled in Scritti Politti songs such as 'Hegemony' to one which involved commentators drawing on structuralism and post-structuralism to a more or less open degree in order to argue for a pessimistic, incorporative leftist strategy in the face of Thatcherism, one which was influential in the foment that later produced New Labour.[131] In 1981, the journal published an article by Ernesto Laclau and Chantal Mouffe espousing relativism, which parodied Marxist thought as consisting of its most dogmatically positivistic articulations.[132]

By 1984, instead of considering the scope for building an oppositional counter-hegemonic force, Stuart Hall claimed that 'the question is whether the Left can operate on the same ground' as Thatcherism.[133] Hall was at first non-specific about what such a project would entail, but by 1988, this ambiguity had disappeared. 'Thatcher's Lessons' for Hall turned out to be that the left needed to operate on the ground of the market and appeals to apparently undetermined individual choice,[134] and he now shared column inches with figures such as the Tory MP Edwina Currie.[135] Frank Mort and Nicholas Green's article 'You've Never Had It So Good—Again!', with its Harold Macmillan referencing title, argued that because of the recent economic boom, the left should speak the language of consumerist marketing to appeal to 'desire, pleasure and personal fulfilment'. This demonstrated not only the assumption that consumerist marketing was the only way to appeal to 'desire, pleasure and fulfilment', but also an acceptance of the short-term logic of capitalism.[136] Their buoyant tone must have rung hollow when recession struck two years after the article was published. By the late 1980s, the journal began to carry adverts for wine offers and clothing made by 'Central Committee Outfitters',[137] an ironic postmodern in-joke which echoed the pastiches on Scritti Politti record covers of luxury goods such as Dior perfume and Courvoisier brandy.

Though the parallels between the direction of *Marxism Today* and Gartside's steering of Scritti Politti are more evident in the band's later material, it is worth reflecting, in line with my argument that Gartside's position was a pre-emergent form of this structure of feeling, that the signs were present even in early Scritti Politti songs. One such example is 'Hegemony', from the band's second *Peel Sessions* EP. Ostensibly written from a Gramscian Marxist perspective, the song reveals the fact that throughout the 1970s, the concept of hegemony had been framed in somewhat different terms by humanists such as Williams, and structuralists such as Hall. As Andrew Milner has argued, significantly in relation to Hall's theorising of Thatcherism:

> Hall's Gramsci was not Williams's. The difference between their respective readings of Gramsci [was] that of whether to understand hegemony as culture or as structure, and of what relative weights to attach to the hegemonic and counter-hegemonic respectively. If hegemony is a culture, then it is materially produced by the practices of conscious agents, and may be countered by alternative, counter-hegemonic practices; if hegemony is a structure of ideology, then it will determine the subjectivity of its subjects in ways which radically diminish the prospects for counter-hegemonic practice, except in the characteristically attenuated form of a plurality of post-structuralist resistant readings ... Hall progressively assimilated [Gramsci's work] to a developing structuralist—and post-structuralist—paradigm.[138]

'Hegemony' is written in the form of a love song, with the concept itself presented as the singer's alternately adored and loathed object of desire. At first sight, this seems an effective gesture in that it conveys the experiential, everyday and emotive content of the hegemonic, and its connection with pleasure, as opposed to the conceptual limitations of ideology, and draws attention to one of the most common hegemonic themes of popular song. However, the song also demonstrates exactly the two problems with the structuralist understanding of hegemony as argued by Milner. Firstly, the anthropomorphic presentation of the concept reifies it, making it a seemingly unassailable 'thing' rather than a potentially controllable process. Secondly and consequently, its power is overestimated to the point that all that remains possible is to parody the hegemonic by speaking its language in a mocking tone in-between verses rather than presenting any kind of alternative.

A similar position prevails musically: the song features an introduction and a coda that sound like the band warming up. Both are more or less the same length, suggesting that they have been deliberately included in order to convey the constructed character of cultural production as against spontaneous romantic creativity. They also seem to fall outside the song's lyrical focus, and though this may indicate the possibility of counter-hegemony, their discordance suggests that anything outside the hegemonic can only be senseless and unpleasurable, in contrast to the compelling lyrical melody and its rhythmic accompaniment. Furthermore, the musical 'possibles' of rock form are directly commented on in the lyrics—one of the ironic recitals of stock phrases enquires, 'can you dance to it?' In the case of 'Hegemony', the answer would most likely be 'no', leading Gartside from its 'scratchy-collapsy'[139] deconstruction straight to the self-aware pop of *Songs to Remember* with no allowance for a genuinely oppositional stance, and eventually to the decision to leave Rough Trade.

'IF ONLY THE CLASH HAD MADE SWIPING THE SWAG SOUND SO DAMN COMPELLING'[140]

Gang of Four's first release, the *Damaged Goods* EP, was on the post-punk independent label Fast Product. Rather than their decision to sign with EMI for *Entertainment!* indicating a significant change of attitude, however, the two choices were actually congruent. As detailed in the previous chapter, Bob Last of Fast Product claimed no superiority over major labels and was happy for his signings to move to them, directly encouraging Gang of Four to do so with the argument that a major could more easily provide a bigger audience for the band to communicate its politics to.[141] Thus the band pursued a pre-emergent new pop strategy almost from its professional beginnings with little internal division.

Numerous commentators on the band largely concur with Gill's explanation—'the point for us was not to be "pure"—Gang of Four songs were so often about the inability to have clean hands'—and his dismissal of other leftist contemporaries' concerns about connections with major labels as 'bollocks hand wringing'.[142] Reynolds claims that 'it was much more provocative to intensify the contradictions and operate right at the heart of the leisure-rock industry'.[143] Hoover and Stokes argue of the band that 'obviously they wanted their music to be heard' and agree with King, who, they write, 'takes issue with those who would claim the "do it yourself" decentralisation of small independent firms spawned by the "punk revolution" represented an alternative to the established music business. After all, a rock band is a capitalist enterprise.'[144] At the time, Gary Bushell questioned them on the decision whilst simultaneously suggesting he did not find it a problem and was only doing so under pressure from the post-punk consensus regarding independence: 'Out of some vague sense of duty I raise the hoary old cul-de-sac of isn't it contradictory for them to attach themselves to such a powerful capitalist machine', accepting the band's response that 'any record company, big or small, is concerned with the same thing'.[145] Savage's only criticism was that the rationale for signing to EMI was not made clear enough in the band's lyrics.[146]

Once again, Gang of Four's theoretical influences are central when ascertaining why they pursued such a direction despite belonging to a formation that often developed independent labels as oppositional responses to majors. The limitation of structuralist Marxism regarding counter-hegemonic possibilities has already been discussed. There may well have been a precedent from Art and Language too, given that the group had mocked as naive leftist attempts in the art world to ameliorate the effects of capitalist relations of production or suggest ways beyond them, such as the community arts movement.[147] Art and Language also saw attempts to connect with potentially oppositional public tendencies as sentimental, given that they did not believe any significant oppositional public tendencies existed.[148] These influences alone do not explain the decision, though. They were rooted in the experience of educational capital common to Gill and King, which they have consistently drawn upon to make a convincing case that signing to a major was politically expedient.

Signing to EMI did mean that the band initially received greater exposure and sales than some of their peers, though the strategy eventually backfired. Burnham recalls that after 'I Love A Man In Uniform' was banned by the BBC prior to the outbreak of the Falklands War, EMI began to neglect Gang of Four, 'shifting allegiances' to the new pop band Duran Duran.[149] The label's move revealed the limits of the strategy's political expediency. Just as Williams had observed of the commercial press that freedom was limited to 'what can profitably be said',[150] so in the case of EMI, it was limited to what could most profitably be released. *NME* journalist Mat Snow observed of Gang of Four's final album *Hard* that throughout the LP 'a dynamic beat, a gleaming surface, some brilliantly choreographed and textured hooks and effects, but precious little substance' prevailed. Snow perceptively argued in somewhat unforgiving terms that this was bound up with the industry position the band had adopted: 'So what to do if you've got no real ideas yet your career demands more product? You bastardise other people's licks in the hope of reselling the market something you know it's bought before', going on to note the record's creative debts to new pop bands, such as ABC and the Human League.[151]

MAKING MONEY AND BEING THE BEATLES

At the point Gang of Four signed to EMI, Scritti Politti were still, in the words of *Melody Maker* journalist Lynden Barber, 'an almost archetypal Rough Trade recording group'.[152] The band possessed a conception of freedom centred on grassroots democratic control of production, having been inspired by the Desperate Bicycles' punk single 'The Medium Was Tedium' with its rambunctious chorus of 'it was easy, it was cheap, go and do it!' They compiled their own information pamphlet on 'DIY'[153] and discussed their conception of the progressive potential of the independent sector in interviews. Gartside differentiated the emergent post-punk focus on control of production from the vagaries of the counterculture, claiming the band stood for 'self determination ... [but] not in any silly hippy ... way'. He also brought to bear his Eurocommunist influences, referencing Gramsci's concept of 'war of position', or the gradual struggle which must precede the revolutionary action of a 'war of manoeuvre', when he stated that 'we are interested in ... DIY records, co-operation with other groups, seeing how ... large an alternative can be built, a positional alternative rather than a run-away-and-hide alternative'.[154] This is a distinction which could also be framed as that made by Williams between alternative and oppositional, 'that is to say between someone who simply finds a different way to live and wishes to be left alone with it, and someone who ... wants to change the society in its light',[155] with the band advocating the latter.

The song 'Scritlock's Door' from the band's second *Peel Sessions* EP crystallises the band's stance in this era. Its lyrics illustrate the lack of freedom on the part of producers and listeners of popular music when it is made and distributed through straightforwardly capitalist market relations. Pleasure is also central in the song's critique, observing as it does the link between what is considered attractive and the capitalist privileging of exchange value over use value: 'Fashion is fab when the product is made without necessity.' The word 'fab' was most likely chosen due to its association with the popular culture of over a decade before, to illustrate the rapid and fickle shifts of the market. Musically, the song is skeletal, consisting largely of a jarring drumbeat in a gesture perhaps meant both to disturb complacency and draw attention to the critique made by the lyrics. In line with the band's capacity for pleasurable theoretical critique, 'Scritlock's Door' is delivered in a fragile yet insistent tone with occasional incongruously soulful flourishes. There is also a sporadic, low-frequency bass rumble which perhaps symbolises the determinate influence of market relations; it begins as the singer wonders about the music of those that such relations have silenced, sometimes obscuring the words and significantly outlasting the unfinished final line of the lyrics.

Predictably, given the ambition which motivated Gartside's shifts on issues of sensibility, personal politics and Marxism, none of this was to last. It is unsurprising that although the band advocated DIY in interviews, the same hopes are absent from the content of their early songs beyond the slightly desperate sounding declaration of 'Scritlock's Door' for a 'harder' critique. Interestingly, Gartside's rejection of the independent sector came to be framed in similar terms to his rejection of Marxism, with pleasure as the key factor. This was directly in line with the rhetorical character of new pop music journalism: Paul Morley, for example, expresses pride in having upset *NME's* leftist cartoonist Ray Lowry with he and Ian Penman's gossip column about London club-land which hovered between irony and seriousness in its hymning of 'strawberry daiquiris' and 'trousers that cost more than a month's unemployment benefit', plus their slogan 'dance, don't riot'.[156] Gartside, meanwhile, began to elide pleasure with major label-supported music, describing the DIY cassette band network of music supported by Rough Trade's distribution wing as 'irritating'[157] and opining that 'what sells ... finds its way into people's hearts in a way that independent music never did', claiming to be 'sick to death of the ghetto of the independent scene'.[158] In the song 'Rock-A-Boy Blue' from *Songs To Remember*, the singer appears to question a perceived bad faith on the part of his contemporaries, disbelieving their supposed claims not to want to make money or 'be the Beatles', advocating dominant motivations of wealth and status and implying hypocrisy on the part of those who reject them.

At the time such statements were made, the band was still signed to Rough Trade. The label had spent a disproportionate amount of money on the production of *Songs to Remember* before sensing where Gartside's ambitions lay and making alternative arrangements. Geoff Travis pointed Gartside in the direction of Bob Last, who became his manager and signed Scritti Politti to Virgin for subsequent albums,[159] by this stage a public limited company with no 'pretence to independence'.[160] The publishing company set up by the pair for Scritti Politti's songs was, significantly, named Jouissance.[161] 'Jouissance' is a key term in the work of figures such as Jacques Lacan and Roland Barthes, which refers to excessive pleasure bound up with an absence or excess of signification.[162] Once more, Gartside's post-structuralist influences lay behind his part-ironic, part-serious explorations of freedom and pleasure in dominant terms. As in the instance of sensibility, this was partially obscured by the distracting frisson of the undefined, indeed indefinable, 'radicalism' of the transgression of meaning supposedly inherent in pop.

'WE WERE SEEN AS ANTI-CAPITALIST BUT WE WEREN'T'[163]

The lasting achievement of Gang of Four was not, as has been consistently argued, that the band set difficult truths about our implication in dominant notions of freedom and pleasure alongside enjoyable music. Rather, it was the rare ability to make those difficult truths part of the pleasurable overall experience of their cultural production, something achieved by Scritti Politti too. In the light of this, it may seem that I have scrutinised the bands too harshly; after all, Jon King has reflected accurately that Gang of Four has been and continues to act as an oppositional reference point for successive leftist bands.[164] Indeed, we could extend King's point to encompass listeners of both Gang of Four and Scritti Politti; each band certainly played such an important and valued role in my own case, priming me for further discovery of the theories and concepts referred to in their work and extending my understanding of how radicalism and countercultural popular music might be brought together. Gang of Four's participation in movements such as Rock Against Racism has further cemented their work as operating within an oppositional tradition of leftist popular cultural production and consumption.

Nevertheless, it has been worth exploring the two bands' conflicted trajectories, though not out of any sense of moralistic condemnation; part of my argument has been that complex issues of class, education, and the political conjuncture of Britain played a determining role in the way Gang of Four and Scritti Politti evolved. This renders any straightforward assessment of whether they made the 'right' decisions both sanctimonious and overly simplistic. Rather, what the analysis has shown is that in spite of their progressive intentions, the two bands were subject to pressures that placed them directly on the faultline of struggles between the libertarian left and the New Right over freedom and pleasure.

With this in mind, it is notable that Gang of Four's contradictory stance has now become more resigned since neoliberalism has achieved hegemonic purchase. In the same interview in which King highlighted the band's oppositional legacy, Gill declared that 'in no sense are we interested in banging the drum for socialism', despite also drawing attention to the current injustice of the ruling class's political response to global recession. At the level of popular music, King has admitted: 'I can't imagine a system in which you make music ... [where] you didn't want the music to be sold'[165] and Gill has claimed: 'being in a band is by its very nature an entrepreneurial thing'.[166] In 2011, Gill and King, accompanied by two new members, released a new Gang of Four album, *Content*. The title was typically Gang of Four in its demystifying gesture to the album as product and commodity. Read another way, though, it could be a further reference to the pair's 'collaborator' status, hinting perhaps ironically at a degree of comfort with such status.

Gartside, by contrast, has expressed regret about the direction he pursued, recognising that his treatment of fellow band members was 'badly ... handled'[167] and observing the alienation of his phase of pop stardom which led to a decade-long withdrawal from professional music making: 'I realised that sitting on couches in TV studios, talking to people who don't know who you are, about some record they don't care about—it eats away, perhaps irretrievably, at your sense of self-worth.'[168] Symbolically, Gartside accepted Geoff Travis' offer of re-signing to Rough Trade in the mid-2000s. All the same, Gartside's doubt regarding his decisions in the 1980s may well be motivated partly by the anxiety of the parvenu as well as by hindsight about their personal and political implications; he attributes much of the discomfort of his pop period to feeling inadequate in the presence of more experienced session musicians.[169]

NOTES

1. Green Gartside quoted in Simon Reynolds, *Totally Wired: Post-Punk Interviews and Overviews* (London: Faber, 2009), p. 177.
2. Reynolds, *Totally Wired*, p. 180.
3. Dave McCullough, 'The Nitty Gritty on Scritti Politti', *Sounds*, January 1979.
4. John A. Walker, *Left Shift: Radical Art in 1970s Britain* (London: I.B. Tauris, 2002), pp. 32–34.
5. Walker, *Left Shift*, p. 32.
6. Walker, *Left Shift*, pp. 140–141.
7. Walker, *Left Shift*, p. 214.
8. Walker, *Left Shift*, p. 170.

9. Anon, 'Definitions', in *Internationale Situationniste*, no. 1, June 1958 (trans. Ken Knabb), available online at Situationist International Online: http://www.cddc.vt.edu/sionline///si/definitions.html, accessed 16 June 2015.

10. Walker, *Left Shift*, p. 170.

11. Michael Hoover and Lisa Stokes, 'Pop Music and the Limits of Cultural Critique: Gang of Four Shrinkwraps Entertainment', *Popular Music and Society* 22, no. 3 (1998), 21–38 (pp. 22–23).

12. Reynolds, *Totally Wired*, pp. 182–187.

13. Paul Lester, *Gang of Four: Damaged Gods* (London: Omnibus, 2008), pp. 51–53.

14. 'From the Pressing Plants to the Concert Halls We Want Some Control', *After Hours*, fanzine June 1979.

15. Simon Reynolds, *Rip It Up and Start Again* (London: Faber, 2005), p. 203.

16. Dave McCullough, 'Turn of the Scrits', *Sounds*, 8 December 1979.

17. 'From the Pressing Plants...'.

18. Lester, *Damaged Gods*, p. 23.

19. Reynolds, *Totally Wired*, p. 112.

20. Lester, *Damaged Gods*, p. 48.

21. Reynolds, *Totally Wired*, p. 109.

22. Clinton Heylin, *Babylon's Burning: From Punk to Grunge* (London: Penguin, 2007), p. 340.

23. McCullough, 'The Nitty Gritty'.

24. Reynolds, *Totally Wired*, pp. 177–178.

25. Reynolds, *Totally Wired*, p. 189.

26. Lester, *Damaged Gods*, pp. 2–3.

27. Walker, *Left Shift*, p. 141.

28. Lester, *Damaged Gods*, pp. 8–11.

29. Reynolds, *Rip It Up*, p. 112.

30. Mary Harron, 'Dialectics Meet Disco', *Melody Maker*, 26 May 1979.

31. Reynolds, *Totally Wired*, p. 187.

32. Reynolds, *Totally Wired*, pp. 178, 187.

33. Gartside quoted in Neil Taylor, *Document and Eyewitness: An Intimate History of Rough Trade* (London: Orion, 2010), p. 105.

34. Lester, *Damaged Gods*, p. 1.

35. Alan Sinfield, *Literature, Politics and Culture in Postwar Britain*, 3rd ed. (London: Continuum, 2004), p. 63.

36. Lester, *Damaged Gods*, pp. 7–9.

37. Reynolds, *Totally Wired*, p. 177.

38. Pete Paphides, 'Kind of Green', *Mojo*, March 2011.

39. Reynolds, *Totally Wired*, pp. 177–178.

40. Pierre Bourdieu, *Distinction: A Social Critique of the Judgement of Taste*, trans. Richard Nice (London: Routledge & Kegan Paul, 1984), p. 28.
41. Bourdieu, *Distinction*, p. 112.
42. Richard Boon quoted in Reynolds, *Rip It Up*, p. 205.
43. Reynolds, *Rip It Up*, p. 128.
44. Bourdieu, *Distinction*, p. 150.
45. Bourdieu, *Distinction*, p. 147.
46. Bourdieu, *Distinction*, p. 63.
47. Bourdieu, *Distinction*, pp. 84–85.
48. Bourdieu, *Distinction*, p. 265.
49. Bourdieu, *Distinction*, pp. 69–74.
50. Bourdieu, *Distinction*, p. 265.
51. Reynolds, *Totally Wired*, p. 415.
52. Raymond Williams, 'Ideas and the Labour Movement' [1981], in *Resources of Hope: Culture, Democracy, Socialism*, ed. Robin Gable (London: Verso, 1989), p. 145.
53. Jo Littler, 'Meritocracy as Plutocracy: The Marketising of Equality under Neoliberalism', *New Formations*, 80–81, special double issue on 'Neoliberal Culture' (2013), 52–72.
54. Walker, *Left Shift*, p. 33.
55. Anon., 'Louis Althusser', available online at http://www.marxists.org/glossary/people/a/l.htm, accessed 8 October 2015.
56. Perry Anderson, *In the Tracks of Historical Materialism* (London: Verso, 1983), p. 76.
57. Anderson, *In the Tracks of Historical Materialism*, p. 77.
58. Michel Foucault, *The History of Sexuality: Volume One—The Will to Knowledge*, trans. Robert Hurley [1976] (London: Penguin, 1998). W. Mark Cobb has offered a convincing critique of Foucault's position on this issue, which makes specific reference to Marcuse. See W. Mark Cobb, 'Diatribes and Distortions: Marcuse's Academic Reception', in *Herbert Marcuse: A Critical Reader*, ed. John Abromeit and W. Mark Cobb (London: Routledge, 2004).
59. Jacques Derrida, 'A 'Madness' Must Watch over Thinking', interview with Francois Ewald, *Le Magazine Litteraire*, March 1991, in Elizabeth Weber (ed.), *Points...: Interviews 1974–1994*, trans. Peggy Kamuf (Stanford: Stanford University Press, 1995).
60. Anderson, *In the Tracks of Historical Materialism*, p. 56.
61. Jon King quoted in Chris Brazier, 'The Gang That Tries to Talk Straight', *Melody Maker*, 3 November 1979.
62. Jon Savage, review of Gang of Four—*Entertainment!*, *NME*, 6 October 1979.
63. Gary Bushell, 'The Gang's All Here', *Sounds*, 2 June 1979.
64. Harron, 'Dialectics Meets Disco'.

65. Hoover and Stokes, 'Gang of Four Shrinkwraps Entertainment', p. 31.
66. Hoover and Stokes, 'Gang of Four Shrinkwraps Entertainment', pp. 126–127.
67. Jon King interviewed by Hoover and Stokes, 'Gang of Four Shrinkwraps Entertainment', p. 23.
68. Greil Marcus, 'It's Fab, It's Passionate, It's Intelligent! It's the Hot New Sound of England Today!' [1980], in *In the Fascist Bathroom: Writings on Punk 1977–1992* (London: Penguin, 1994), pp. 128–129.
69. Herbert Marcuse, *Counterrevolution and Revolt* (Boston: Beacon Press, 1972), p. 64.
70. Marcuse, *Counterrevolution and Revolt*, p. 63.
71. Richard Neville, *Play Power* (London: Jonathan Cape, 1970), p. 263.
72. Neville, *Play Power*, p. 253.
73. Lucy O'Brien, 'Can I Have a Taste of Your Ice Cream?', in *Punk and Post-Punk* 1, no. 1 (Sept. 2011), 27–40.
74. Reynolds, *Totally Wired*, p. 109.
75. Lester, *Damaged Gods*, p. 76.
76. Marcuse, *Counterrevolution and Revolt*, p. 64.
77. Karl Marx, *Capital Volume 1*, trans. Ben Fowkes [1867] (Harmondsworth: Pelican, 1976), p. 716.
78. Savage, review of Gang of Four—*Entertainment!*.
79. Reynolds, *Totally Wired*, p. 110.
80. Michael Hann, 'It's Bloody Great Being Alive'—interview with Wilko Johnson, *The Guardian*, 2 February 2013, available online at http://www.guardian.co.uk/music/2013/feb/02/wilko-johnson-interview
81. Reynolds, *Rip It Up*, p. 121.
82. McCullough, 'The Nitty Gritty'.
83. Ian Birch, 'Scritti Politti', *Smash Hits*, 12 November 1981.
84. Barney Hoskyns, 'Where Radical Meets Chic', *NME*, 31 October 1981.
85. Reynolds, *Totally Wired*, p. 181.
86. Leroy Keene, interview with Scritti Politti, *Printed Noises*, fanzine 1979.
87. Reynolds, *Totally Wired*, p. 185.
88. McCullough, 'Turn of the Scrits'.
89. Reynolds, *Totally Wired*, p. 179.
90. Reynolds, *Totally Wired*, p. 178.
91. Pete Paphides, 'Kind of Green'.
92. Reynolds, *Rip It Up*, pp. 206–207.
93. Reynolds, *Totally Wired*, p. 186.
94. Reynolds, *Totally Wired*, p. 185.
95. Reynolds, *Totally Wired*, p. 189.
96. David Toop, interview with Green Gartside, *The Face*, June 1988.
97. Anderson, *In the Tracks of Historical Materialism*, p. 33.
98. Hoskyns, 'Where Radical Meets Chic'.

99. Reynolds, *Rip It Up*, p. 368.
100. Hoskyns, 'Where Radical Meets Chic'.
101. Lester, *Damaged Gods*, p. 1.
102. Reynolds, *Rip It Up*, pp. 126–127.
103. Griselda Pollock, 'Theory and Pleasure' [1982], in *Framing Feminism*, ed. Rozsika Parker and Griselda Pollock (London: Pandora, 1987), pp. 244–248.
104. Lester, *Damaged Gods*, p. 125.
105. Lester, *Damaged Gods*, p. 143.
106. Dave Allen quoted in Charles Shaar Murray, 'In New York They're Tourists', *NME*, 21 June 1980.
107. Reynolds, *Rip It Up*, p. 114.
108. Reynolds, *Totally Wired*, p. 111.
109. Lester, *Damaged Gods*, p. 70.
110. Lester, *Damaged Gods*, p. 30.
111. Lester, *Damaged Gods*, pp. 111–112.
112. Lester, *Damaged Gods*, p. 143.
113. Lester, *Damaged Gods*, p. 14.
114. Lester, *Damaged Gods*, p. 121.
115. Lester, *Damaged Gods*, p. 145.
116. Lester, *Damaged Gods*, p. 19.
117. Reynolds, *Rip It Up*, p. 198.
118. Reynolds, *Totally Wired*, p. 191.
119. Ian Penman, 'Reflections on In(ter)dependence', *NME*, 25 November 1978, p. 29.
120. Reynolds, *Rip It Up*, p. 207.
121. Reynolds, *Rip It Up*, p. 202.
122. Reynolds, *Totally Wired*, p. 199.
123. *Temporary Hoarding*, no 10, December 1979.
124. Reynolds, *Totally Wired*, p. 364.
125. Lynden Barber, 'The Sweetest Groove', *Melody Maker*, 29 May 1982.
126. Reynolds, *Totally Wired*, p. 190.
127. Reynolds, *Totally Wired*, p. 190.
128. Reynolds reflects that one reason why Gartside only achieved the massive sales he desired with the second Scritti Politti album *Cupid and Psyche* may have been the oblique, introspective preoccupations of *Songs to Remember*—Reynolds, *Rip It Up*, p. 369.
129. Scritti Politti, 'Asylums in Jerusalem', *Songs to Remember* (Rough Trade, 1982).
130. Reynolds, *Totally Wired*, p. 190.
131. Max Cotton, 'Where Did All the Comrades Go?', BBC Radio 4, 14 January 2013. The fact that Peter Mandelson was once a member of the Young Communist League (Owen Jones, 'Peter Hitchens Got Me Thinking: Do Lefties Always Have to Turn Right in Old Age?', *The Guardian*, 9 September

2015, available online at http://www.theguardian.com/commentis-free/2015/sep/09/peter-hitchens-tory-trotskyite-left-right, accessed 8 October 2015) is an indication of the level of dialogue that once existed between the Labour Party and the wider left. Ironically, it was a dialogue that would later be more or less wiped out by the actions of Mandelson and his fellow New Labour architects.

132. Ernesto Laclau and Chantal Mouffe, 'Socialist Strategy', *Marxism Today*, January 1981.

133. Stuart Hall, 'The Culture Gap', *Marxism Today*, January 1984.

134. Stuart Hall, 'Thatcher's Lessons', *Marxism Today*, March 1988.

135. Bea Campbell, interview with Edwina Currie, *Marxism Today*, March 1987.

136. Frank Mort and Nicholas Green, 'You've Never Had It So Good—Again!', *Marxism Today*, May 1988.

137. *Marxism Today*, April 1987.

138. Andrew Milner, *Re-Imagining Cultural Studies: The Promise of Cultural Materialism* (London: Sage, 2002), p. 115.

139. Reynolds, *Rip It Up*, p. 203.

140. Alex Ogg, *Independence Days: The Story of UK Independent Record Labels* (London: Cherry Red, 2009), p. 358.

141. Reynolds, *Rip It Up*, p. 118.

142. Reynolds, *Rip It Up*, p. 118.

143. Reynolds, *Rip It Up*, p. 118.

144. Hoover and Stokes, 'Gang of Four Shrinkwraps Entertainment', p. 26.

145. Bushell, 'The Gang's All Here'.

146. Savage, review of *Entertainment!*.

147. Walker, *Left Shift*, p. 132.

148. Walker, *Left Shift*, p. 167.

149. Lester, *Damaged Gods*, pp. 132–133.

150. Raymond Williams, 'Communications and Community' [1961], in *Resources of Hope: Culture, Democracy, Socialism*, pp. 19–31 (p. 25).

151. Mat Snow, review of Gang of Four—*Hard*, NME, 10 September 1983.

152. Barber, 'The Sweetest Groove'.

153. McCullough, 'The Nitty Gritty'.

154. Anon, 'From the Pressing Plants…'.

155. Raymond Williams, 'Base and Superstructure in Marxist Cultural Theory' [1973], in *Culture and Materialism* (London: Verso, 2005), pp. 41–42.

156. Reynolds, *Totally Wired*, p. 330. Lowry was not, however, humourless and puritanical, as the nature of his work should have indicated. He got his revenge in a comic strip for the post-punk fanzine *City Fun*. The strip satirised a clueless 'post-monetarist' music journalist spouting pseudo-post-modernist theory, showing an astute awareness of new pop's susceptibility to Thatcherite values. *City Fun* 2, no. 19 (Summer 1981).

157. Reynolds, *Rip It Up*, p. 366.
158. Birch, 'Scritti Politti'.
159. Reynolds, *Rip It Up*, p. 370.
160. Ogg, *Independence Days*, p. 49.
161. Reynolds, *Rip It Up*, p. 370.
162. See, for example, Roland Barthes, *The Pleasure of the Text*, trans. Richard Miller (New York: Hill and Wang, 1975).
163. Dave Allen quoted in Lester, *Damaged Gods*, p. 172.
164. Jon King interviewed on the *Today* programme, BBC Radio 4, 14 January 2011.
165. Hoover and Stokes, 'Gang of Four Shrinkwraps Entertainment', p. 26.
166. Lester, *Damaged Gods*, p. 134.
167. Reynolds, *Totally Wired*, p. 191.
168. Paphides, 'Kind of Green'.
169. Paphides, 'Kind of Green'.

CHAPTER 5

The Politics of the Post-Punk Working Class Autodidact

So far, the question of what we can learn from the way working class figures negotiated leftist post-punk has been little explored. This is due in part to the representations of class, education and post-punk discussed in Chap. 3. On this front, there is an especially compelling political comparison to be made between The Fall and the Blue Orchids. The latter band was an outgrowth of the former; they preserved and developed an outlook present in the original Fall, one which was lost when Mark E. Smith became its driving force. In this chapter, I examine how the two bands' conflicting political stances were shaped by residual countercultural and class-based influences, looking at the bands' attitudes towards pleasure and freedom within the context of post-punk and the broader conjuncture.

Another problem stands in the way of understanding The Fall in particular. In much writing on the band, both academic and popular, there is a persistent romantic myth of Mark E. Smith and The Fall as inscrutable.[1] Simon Reynolds registered his anxiety about writing on The Fall for *Rip It Up and Start Again*, feeling that they were 'kind of a mysterious band'.[2] The myth extends to the band's politics: Mick Middles claims that 'the politics of The Fall … remain splendidly locked in ambiguity',[3] whilst the music promoter and associate of the band Alan Wise summarises Smith's outlook as 'neither left nor right'.[4] Dick Witts, a key participant in Manchester's post-punk scene and now an academic, touches on Smith's politics by positioning them midway between 'old Labour' and Thatcherism, but offers no sustained analysis.[5]

© The Editor(s) (if applicable) and The Author(s) 2016
D. Wilkinson, *Post-Punk, Politics and Pleasure in Britain*,
DOI 10.1057/978-1-137-49780-2_5

One common motivation behind this view of The Fall as a mystery may well be an unwillingness to question Smith's distrust of institutionalised education. One of his perennial preoccupations, it is encapsulated in the lyrics of 'Fit And Working Again'. Analysis, for Smith, is 'academic', leading to 'nauseous' thoughts. The irony is that some reflection on this attitude towards education is central to any understanding of both The Fall and the Blue Orchids. Along with their working class background, their autodidactic immersion in countercultural texts and values shaped both their creative practice and political outlooks.

NORTHERN WHITE CRAP TALKING BACK

It is important to note of The Fall and the Blue Orchids that they did not share the influences of art school bands like Gang of Four, Scritti Politti, and The Raincoats. Marxist theory, post-structuralism, conceptual art and academic feminism were not the go-to sources for these inquisitive misfits. Instead they drew from an eclectic range of literary, artistic, philosophical and musical sources, which they discovered after having left secondary education. The early members of The Fall felt alienated not only from the world of higher education before the intensification of university expansion, but also from the determinations of their working class background. 'We were really just factory fodder ... totally wrapped up in music', Martin Bramah, The Fall's original guitarist and co-founder of the Blue Orchids, has said. 'It meant a lot to us. The bands we loved, we loved dearly; it was our escape from what the world was offering us.'[6] They thus reworked a residual, countercultural outlook long popular amongst working class youth because of the autodidactic way in which it was usually acquired; as Sinfield notes, countercultural rock 'ran purposefully counter to school culture'.[7] It was, along with complementary sources such as pulp fiction, a 'discourse of escape and a call to action', according to Keith Gildart.[8]

Simultaneously both bands retained some attachment to more conventional Northern working class traditions and identifications. They did so partly in reaction against fellow post-punks whose outlooks seemed to have little in common with the ways of life so central to The Fall and the Blue Orchids' experience. The bands' hostility towards this fraction of post-punk was understandable in the face of the patronising treatment they received early on from its representatives in the music press. One such example was Ian Penman. Though having passed up art school in favour of a job at *NME*, Penman was a member of Scritti Politti's

London squat collective. Absorbed in the deconstructionist rhetoric of post-structuralism, Penman simply assumed that The Fall's rebellion was less sophisticated than his own, describing it as 'just the exchange of one set of limitations for another'.[9]

Partly in response to this kind of provocation, Smith invented the alter-ego 'Roman Totale XVII', a fusion of amphetamine-fuelled post-punk outsider and autodidactic Northern working class plain-speaking, through which to voice his distinctive perspective. Smith also incorporated his love of the work of 'weird fiction' writers favoured by the counterculture into the character, putting Totale's Lovecraftian 'last testament' on the back of the 'Fiery Jack' single cover: 'I have not long left now but I urge the finder of this "master-tape" never to unleash it on humanity!—Ah! Already the evil Deit-y R-Kol is clawing at my brain!'[10] Smith's deployment of obvious signifiers of his class background merged with countercultural influences served a specific political purpose which I go on to examine: they acted as a marker of the supposedly authentic as against those who were viewed as dogmatic, joyless, naive and hypocritical and pointedly informed Smith's own view of freedom and pleasure. But they also lay behind The Fall's articulation of a potentially utopian structure of feeling that Martin Bramah has described as 'Coronation Street on acid'.[11]

Bramah, meanwhile, went on to sing the Blue Orchids' mystic manifes-tos in a strong Mancunian accent. Lines like 'threw my name in the bin' were delivered in a grounded, workaday social realist tone at odds with other Manchester post-punk contemporaries such as Howard Devoto's languidly ironic delivery or Ian Curtis' apocalyptic baritone. Baines' organ-playing, meanwhile, elicited the description of 'the Velvet Underground under the Blackpool illuminations'.[12] Bramah describes how the band got their name from John Cooper Clarke's story of 'The Blessed Orchids', 'a gang of haemophiliacs who are brought up on a council tip in Salford', saying 'the whole idea had this bizarre working-class Gormenghast feel'.[13] The mention of Mervyn Peake's fantasy trilogy is significant; Ballantyne republished it in the 1970s with countercultural graphics on the cover to capitalise on the popularity of fantasy novels with hippies.[14] As with Smith, the fusion of countercultural sources and the traditions of a working class background had a political resonance. In this case, it was the Blue Orchids' development of an oppositional ethos of freedom and pleasure that was equal parts G.I. Gurdjieff and the Workers Educational Association.

Although this process of socialisation and the experience of post-punk did result in similarities of habitus, it would produce quite different political attitudes in Smith on the one hand and Bramah and Baines on the other. Initially, however, it seemed the band was politically unified. Early Fall songs were informed by libertarian left causes such as anti-fascism, anti-psychiatry, feminism, and a critique of dehumanising capitalist industry. An early live review by Paul Morley noted that many of the audience's reaction to the band was 'I thought The Clash were political until I saw [The Fall]'.[15] The band's first gig was put on by the Manchester Musicians Collective, a venture which provided shared equipment, rehearsal and performance space to new bands. It was initiated by Dick Witts and Trevor Wishart, two classical musicians with 'New Left sympathies' who had access to Arts Council funding and a desire to re-direct it away from an 'elitist contemporary [classical] music scene'.[16] The Fall also played Rock Against Racism events and gigs at The Squat, a derelict university building which had been occupied by students.[17]

Baines claims that Smith was initially receptive to progressive causes, recounting that as a teenage couple they would 'check out women's groups and opinions across the political left'.[18] The claim is backed up by Smith's performance of songs with such themes; it is difficult to imagine such a stubborn individualist doing so if he did not have any conviction in their content. Smith also showed interest early on in the issues of form, content and populism that preoccupied many leftist post-punk bands: 'I don't agree with Tom Robinson playing anti-sexist songs against stale old Chuck Berry riffs … but I also don't agree with Henry Cow singing political tracts in front of quasi-classical avant-garde music, even though I enjoy it. It's very obscurist.'[19]

Yet these concerns and values co-existed awkwardly with Smith's more reactionary leanings. When Bramah and Baines formed the Blue Orchids in 1979 after becoming a couple and leaving The Fall within a year of one another, Smith's internal political conflict was largely resolved. Smith claims that Bramah and Baines 'were never really part of The Fall. They were part of some other group. Blue Orchids was just about right. That's where their heads were at.'[20] For this reason, the chapter concentrates on Fall songs which post-date the departure of Bramah and Baines in order to highlight the contrast in outlook between the bands.

Smith's outlook may well have been influenced in part by his family background. They were from working class Higher Broughton in Salford, moving to the north Manchester suburb of Prestwich after Smith's father inherited his own father's plumbing business. Both Smith's father and grandfather had served in the army, and the former was culturally conservative, forbidding the presence of a record player or popular music in the family home until Smith was 14.[21] There are suggestions of familial loyalty to the armed forces in Smith's semi-ironic defence of the Falklands war, apparently finding the fact that 'every bloody group was bringing out anti-war singles' to be 'fucking disgraceful'.[22]

Such working class conservatism was a major component of Thatcherism's construction of an authoritarian populism,[23] and its contradictory articulation in British popular music was not new. For instance, Gildart highlights the political 'ambiguity' of The Kinks' Ray Davies, whose amalgam of socialism and conservatism 'was rooted in a particular strand of British working class identity'.[24] Notably, The Fall would score a hit single with their cover of The Kinks' 'Victoria'. Smith's mother, Irene, has claimed, 'I was always a great believer in ... giving my children freedom',[25] though as will become clear, Smith's interpretation of freedom was a highly specific one, sharing some degree of crossover with the New Right in its condemnation of the left on the basis of perceived authoritarianism. The shift was also coloured by class and educational difference, with Smith perpetuating stereotypes of the post-punk and broader libertarian left as a middle-class malaise.

Smith gradually developed an outlook with loose affinities to Thatcherism, though never, it should be stressed, actual support for it: despite provocatively claiming to have voted for a local Tory councillor,[26] Smith noted critically of Thatcher: 'People voted her in for their own greed.'[27] His conception of freedom, alloyed with individualistic, rather than libertarian left, countercultural values, also tended to overreach the Thatcher government's, which was always caught between the amoral market and authoritarian social conservatism; when in 1986 the band released the amphetamine-hymning garage rock cover 'Mr Pharmacist' during a government crackdown on drugs, Smith claimed that 'if someone wants to smoke themselves to death or drink themselves to death ... or whatever then it's their basic right'.[28]

There are also elements of The Fall's cultural production that continue to resonate from a left perspective. I concentrate here on two: the potential implications of qualitative social transformation in Smith's uncanny depictions of his local environment, and a desire for an alternative populism opposed to new pop and backed up by the belief that most people have the potential to enjoy more innovative and complex music than that which they are exposed to by a patronising popular culture industry.

Smith's former band-mates, meanwhile, undermined his class stereo-typing of the libertarian left. The Blue Orchids went on to adopt an out-look that was focused on the self whilst being simultaneously co-operative and democratic, initially in direct reaction against their experience of The Fall. Bramah recalls that 'we'd done a lot of work [yet] what was initially a collective became a dictatorship'.[29] The new band's approach was not informed by political theory as with Gang of Four and Scritti Politti—Bramah has stated that 'I wasn't interested in left wing political concepts that you might learn when you're taking a degree'[30]—though it was con-sciously politicised. The belief of the couple in working class solidarity played a significant part: 'The core of that left-wing attitude [from the early Fall] was working-class struggle and that's what we related to.'[31] Discussing politics now, Baines believes that leftist political change, if it occurs, 'is going to be grassroots … the bottom. The top's as corrupt as it can get.'[32]

Baines' early experience of the women's movement in Manchester was also significant, chiming with her rejection of a Catholic upbringing. She remembers: 'As a child I was very devout … until [I got] to an age of questioning. My best friend was very wise for her age, and our friendship, apart from a love of Elvis Presley when he wasn't cool, was based on phi-losophy … we'd looked at the Bible and found it appallingly anti-women.' Aged 16, Baines spotted a women's centre on her way home from school, went to a meeting there with her friend, and thus initiated a lifetime of feminist activism.[33]

Bramah and Baines also shared an interpretation of punk as an impera-tive to change the politics of rock, and, in so doing, continue the ideals of the countercultural libertarian left. Leftist *NME* journalist Lynn Hanna observed that 'Martin sees punk as essentially the same as 60s hippiedom'. Bramah believed that punk 'had the same values. It was based on love but hating the crap that had built up around the hippy philosophy. It was healthy because it was caring.'[34] Bramah's following claim, that 'punk doesn't mean anything now', further suggests that post-punk was more than an opportunity of musical progression for the Blue Orchids, but also the necessary rejection of nihilism in favour of developing the inchoate political aims of punk. Discussing the sexist values and practices of rock and noting that she 'met people [involved in post-punk] who thought they were the coolest thing on the planet [but] their views were like 1950s old blokes', Baines claims that such attitudes were 'a contradiction of the punk thing'.[35]

The dominant and unifying feature of the band's cultural production, however, was an interest in the esoteric. This encompassed the theories of the Russian mystics G.I. Gurdjieff and P.D. Ouspensky, Celtic legends, tarot, and Robert Graves' *The White Goddess*, a treatise on poetry influenced by ancient mythology.[36] There was a residual countercultural influence here: Bramah notes that although he did not 'seek out *The White Goddess* because I'd been told it was a worthy book', it was likely that 'some old hippie' had ordered it into the local library where he discovered it. Yet such bodies of knowledge could also be seen as part of post-punk as an emergent formation: 'For me it was about [taking] cultural references from the past and saying things in a new voice—"now, today, here" you know?'[37]

Bramah's belief that 'there were more interesting things to sing about than our business affairs' and the autodidactic distrust of formal education which he shared with Smith meant that the Blue Orchids leaned more to the culturalist end of the post-punk spectrum. Curiously, though, they often addressed the leftist political themes usually made possible by an anti-culturalist stance, for example, personal politics and the political economy of cultural production, filtering them instead through a mystical concern with spiritual development. The band thus brings to mind Jonathan Rose's argument that autodidactic reading has historically allowed those from working class backgrounds to develop their critical faculties, appropriating texts for their own purposes.[38] As will become clear, this was a strategy with consequences both complementary and conflicting.

'CORONATION STREET ON ACID'

There is a potentially transformative power to The Fall's cultural production at the level of sensibility in its fantastical transmutation of its Northern working class culture and environment. *Sounds* journalist Sandy Robertson succinctly identified this trait: 'The Fall are true alchemists in their recognition that shit masks gold, the apparently worthless can be the source of the thrill of it all.'[39] In line with Smith's drift from the causes embraced by the early Fall, there is no conscious desire for a specifically leftist change in sensibilities. The songs, however, occasionally escape intention in what they evoke.

It is possible to isolate a specific pleasure to be gained from engaging with such representations that is at odds with the sensibilities appealed to by Thatcherism. The nature of this distinction hinges around immediacy and difficulty. As I argued in Chap. 2, Thatcherism's tactic was to position itself as the representative and enabler of the dominant aspirations to wealth and status fostered by postwar consumer capitalism, which it framed as having been stifled by the limits of consensus politics. Due to their hegemonic nature, such desires are usually unexamined and therefore superficially straightforward. The Fall's depiction of 'Coronation Street on acid', however, was anything but. As the *NME* critic Barney Hoskyns persuasively argued: 'What [the band's cultural production] implied was that the whole bastion of comfortable working class traditions ... could be transformed, could even perhaps transform themselves into a deep cultural revolution.' This would not be an easy process, however: 'The Fall is the cultural catharsis we must undergo before beauty can be grasped ... real desire cannot be attained inside the insidious synaesthetico-cultural trick of Pop. The Fall may politically propel you outside it.'[40]

This propulsion came from Smith's application of the 'weird fiction' horror genre to his own environment, specifically its focus on the uncanny: 'The horror of the normal. I like that sort of stuff; with writers like M.R. James and Arthur Machen the stories are right there on your doorstep ... using the mundane everyday as a backdrop for great terror.'[41] The visions conjured up, then, were not idealised versions of Manchester, but were often warped and grotesque. They contradicted the assumption that what exists is all that is capable of doing so, without suggesting that a better world is already fully present if we know where to look for it.

There is a risk, however, that the uncanny depiction of the everyday can also encourage a lack of interest in, or repudiation of, transformation because it finds a fatalistic pleasure in what exists already. Mark Fisher argues that 'for Smith ... homesickness is a pathology ... there is little to recommend the ... class-ridden Britain of "sixty-hour weeks and stone toilet back gardens" [yet] there is a sense that, no matter how far he travels, Smith will in the end be overcome by a compulsion to return to his blighted homeland, which functions as his poison and remedy'.[42]

The difficulty is not only one of content, but also of form. In most of The Fall's cultural production from their post-punk period, Smith's diction and the production of the music are often deliberately obscure, unclear and lo-fidelity. Highlighting the way that he had adapted the rough and ready 'directness' of punk for different purposes, Smith claimed: 'everybody thought our production was bad because we want to be credible. But it's because I'm really into a rough production and you have to work hard to achieve that ... I want people to work at understanding the songs.'[43] Colin

Irwin observed in his review of *Hex Enduction Hour* that this difficulty was also an attraction: 'Smith's vocals are mixed so low that the task of deciphering his crumbs of lyrical genius becomes a job for MI5 codebreakers ... I doubt any Fall fan could describe what captivates them so. The challenge?'[44]

Smith's use of 'work' is a keyword, helping us understand one way in which these difficulties of form and content have political resonance. These awkward pleasures of content and form run counter to Thatcherism's stress on the work ethic as an essential and more or less failsafe means of class mobility, captured in the claim that 'I do not know anyone who has gotten to the top without hard work ... it will not always get you to the top, but it will get you pretty near'.[45] In contrast, the work required to comprehend the sensibility of The Fall's cultural production is not bound to a desire to occupy a higher class position in an unequal society. Instead it arises from an attempt on Smith's part to offer a complex and engaging experience to the listener and, underlying this, a belief that this should be the function of cultural production rather than an unchallenging, compensatory backdrop to a life of overwork. There are echoes here of Marcuse's argument that a truly qualitative socialist break from capitalism in the sphere of labour would not simply mean the re-organisation of production to put basic human needs before profit. It would also break down the division between labour and leisure, using 'the imagination' as a 'productive force'.[46] With these issues in mind, it is worth looking more closely at how they interact in a particular Fall song.

'Psykick Dance Hall', the opening song from the band's second album *Dragnet*, makes reference to Smith's repeated claims that he possessed psychic powers, at least until he expressed the belief that 'I drank my way out of it'.[47] More specifically, it refers to a location in Prestwich, as described in Simon Ford's biography of the band:

> [The supernatural] was an interest he shared with [Smith's girlfriend and manager of The Fall] Kay Carroll ... who attended séances at the Whitefield Spiritual Church with her mother. In the early seventies, Carroll's mother opened a psychic centre ... in Prestwich. 'It was over a row of shops that consisted of a bakery, hairdresser's and a shoe shop,' Carroll explained. 'It had originally been a dance studio, you know, tap, ballroom dancing, things of that nature. *Voilà* "Psykick Dancehall"! It's still open to my knowledge.'[48]

The song's theme thus humorously unites the mundanity of a row of local shops in a working class area with the strangeness of the supernatural.

It begins with Smith asking, 'Is there anybody there?' in the manner of a séance. The uncanny theme is established even before the band answer 'yeah!' by the technique of double-tracking two recordings of the same question delivered with varying intonation. The track that is higher in the mix is delivered playfully in Smith's distinctive speaking voice. The combination of mild amusement and regional accent creates an impression of unthreatening everyday life, and the dominance of the recording implies the prevalence of this mode of experience. The other recording, by contrast, is delivered in a rasping, sinister whisper. This juxtaposition is present throughout the song, in instances such as a vision of a monster on the other side of the road, the exaggeratedly banal description of the dancehall's location being round the corner, and the exhortation to step outside everyday routine and become aware of it, which is delivered in the commonplace Northern slang phrase for noticing something: 'Clock it, clock it!'

From the opening, Smith goes on to celebrate the psychic centre, using the associations of its former function as a dancehall to make the claim that it shares an affinity with rock music. What the affinity between the psykick dance hall and rock might be, however, needs making clearer, and becomes so when Smith describes it as an antidote to boredom, evoking Reynolds' claim that post-punk was a constructive response to the boredom generated by dominant expectations of fulfilment under postwar capitalism.[49] Here, Smith expresses this response through the metaphor of the dancehall, uniting thought, feeling and visceral experience in terms which collapse distinctions and describe the total sensory transformation that is its promise: the dancehall offers a 'mental orgasm'.

Nonetheless, Smith's description of the sensibility of those who attend the dancehall is not promising: they are in thrall to the waves of extra sensory perception, intuiting the wordless questions of others. There are distinct connotations here of a kind of intuitive, common-sense and unsystematised style of cognition with close parallels to the manner in which hegemonic assumptions are made. However, Smith's final lines suggest that his recorded 'vibrations' will outlive him, continuing to affect people after his death. This projects the listener into the future, making the mission of unmasking the 'gold' behind the 'shit' a long-term project and the psychic vibes of the Bury New Road a means to that end rather than the ultimate end itself.

How to Use Freedom?

Beginning with the departure of Bramah and Baines from The Fall, Smith increasingly began to characterise the means and aims of the libertarian left within post-punk and more broadly as naive, hypocritically authoritarian and puritanical and put forward his own vision of fulfilment in response. It was a vision somewhat at odds with the potentially progressive emphasis on the uncanny in songs like 'Psykick Dancehall'. Within it, freedom and pleasure intertwine once more in that Smith often advocated the freedom to pursue even pleasures with damaging consequences as a marker of authentic freedom.

This outlook coalesced first on the single 'Fiery Jack', sung from the imagined perspective of a hard-bitten, amphetamine-fuelled 45-year-old pub alcoholic who Smith claimed 'is the sort of guy I can see myself as in twenty years'.[50] It was an identification that was to prove significant in terms of the character's values and vices. We are first introduced to Jack in the song through his self-description—a 'slack' face and ruined kidneys. Whilst there is an acknowledgement of the negative effects of his lifestyle, the glee with which he describes his meat pie diet suggests that this kind of pleasure is only magnified by an awareness of its damaging side effects rather than troubled. Smith has recently reflected that 'Fiery Jack types 'are quite heartening in a way ... even though they're clearly doing themselves damage, there's a zest for life there ... they're not all boring cunts'.[51]

This kind of amoral freedom and pleasure, as Simon Reynolds and Joy Press have argued, is not without precedent in countercultural rock music. Their analysis highlights the continuity between the Romantics, de Sade, Dostoyevsky and the Beats through to countercultural rock such as The Doors and the punk self-destruction of Sid Vicious, on the basis of 'the cult of the criminal as amoral superman' and the privileging of 'desire over responsibility, aesthetics over ethics'.[52] In line with this tradition, Jack is associated with the demonic. The mention of a 'burning ring' also fuses the song's rockabilly musical form to its lyrics with its echo of Johnny Cash's hit 'Ring of Fire'. The single cover features a drawing of the character by Smith's sister Suzanne, in which Jack's shadow has acquired satanic horns and a tail, and he is depicted as a bedraggled Victorian villain, suggesting an association with Jack the Ripper. Smith initiates in 'Fiery Jack' what would become a long-running theme in The Fall's cultural production: a supposedly authentic working class worldview in opposition to all ethical and political frameworks, including Thatcherism: Jack is 'too fast to work', is opposed to 'free trade', and his speed habit and alcoholism might well have jarred with the petit bourgeois morality promoted by the government.

The fantasy that the amoral pursuit of pleasure transcends politics, however, has always been just that. The claim on the freedom to pursue pleasures without concern for the potentially negative effects on oneself and others (or even because of the satisfaction gained from such effects) has much in common with the amoral market freedoms of Thatcherite neoliberalism. It also disavows both social responsibility and egalitarianism. Thus it is inimical to the aims of the left, a fact made abundantly clear in a Fall interview soon after 'Fiery Jack's release. Smith claimed the song was about a variety of topics, including an 'anti-left-wing' stance and 'ageism … people go round and think they're smart when they're 21 but these old guys you see have been doing it for years'.[53] It is not difficult to see where these two themes meet in the middle—there seems to be a silent rehearsal of the cliché that becoming more reactionary with age is a natural and desirable side effect of maturity.

This is also evident in the musical form of 'Fiery Jack', with the song's rockabilly inflections immediately confirming its message regarding 'ageism'. The choice of musical elements is highly deliberate due to the genre being one which would likely have been to the taste of a middle-aged working class Mancunian in 1979, given the popularity of skiffle in the city's working men's clubs in the late 1950s. Smith coined the generic description 'Country "n" Northern' in the same year 'Fiery Jack' was released, claiming that 'we are a very retrogressive band in a lot of ways'.[54] He thus united formal traditionalism with political reaction, following the same logic but reacting in opposition to the equation made by post-punk groups like Scritti Politti between formal innovation and leftist politics.[55] Perhaps the most obvious indicator of the song's politics, however, is lyrical: Jack boasts of putting down left-wing 'tirades'.

It is significant that Jack is not a fan of the 'musical trades' either. This implies that those Smith had in mind when he discussed 'people [who] think they're smart when they're 21' may well have included contemporaries whose work interrogated the political implications of certain pleasures and freedoms. Here, the further significance of age becomes apparent along class and educational lines; the working class life experience of Fiery Jack is implicitly opposed to the presumed middle-class background of the young arts graduates who often featured in the line-ups of leftist post-punk bands. Smith would go on to characterise these bands' questioning stances as destructive of freedom and pleasure per se, something especially apparent during The Fall's period on Rough Trade.

'Just Sell the Record, You Hippy'

Between 1978 and early 1980, The Fall was signed to Step Forward, an independent set-up by Miles Copeland, the son of a co-founder of the CIA. Though Copeland employed punk ideologue Mark Perry, author of the influential fanzine *Sniffin' Glue*, the label's main aim was simply to capitalise on punk after Copeland's previous business involvements with progressive rock bands had faltered.[56] The Fall then moved to Rough Trade due to feeling sidelined on the former label by better-selling acts like The Police (featuring Copeland's brother, Stewart, on drums) and experiencing problems with royalties.[57] Dave McCullough's vision of a 'dream come true, like two sources of the same river joining' proved overly optimistic,[58] given that intervention of any kind on Rough Trade's part in The Fall's cultural production came to be viewed by Smith as unacceptably authoritarian and inappropriate in accord with his broader diagnosis of the libertarian left:

> They'd go, er, the tea boy doesn't like the fact that you've slagged off Wah! Heat on this number. And fuckin' ... the girl who cooks the fuckin' rice in the canteen doesn't like the fact that you've used the word 'slags' ... Y'know, 'it is not the policy of Rough Trade to be supporting...' and I'd go, what the fuck has it got to do with you? Just fuckin' sell the record you fuckin' hippy.[59]

The label's ethos of attempting to overcome the culturalist division between artistic freedom and the mechanical functionality of business, instead working co-operatively and democratically, was inexplicable anathema to Smith. In retrospect, it could be understood only as 'interfering' or in a manner which elided massively differing conceptions and practices of socialism with one another into one parody of authoritarianism: 'It was like living in Russia.'[60] Smith's conservative and individualist attitude towards the role of a record company could be seen in the fact that in order to play up his objections to critical feedback, he highlighted the supposed comments of employees whose roles would traditionally be seen as inferior and irrelevant to the music released. Furthermore, Smith joked significantly that only money could buy the right to an opinion: 'If they'd been a big label and gave me £50,000 then I might have let them have a say.'[61]

Smith's accusation that the label had failed to successfully promote and distribute The Fall's records,[62] his consistent view of The Fall as a job in contrast to this perceived laziness ('we wanted the money for a fair day's work. It's not an extension of your art-school course, it's work'),[63] and the description of Rough Trade as 'hippies' cemented what kind of a dynamic was operating here. Smith's memoir compares Rough Trade's staff to children 'who'd returned home from school, yapping about this new thing – indie music – and their mam had given them a few quid to go and immerse themselves in it – to shut them up'.[64] What is being articulated is a pastiche of a tabloid newspaper depiction of the countercultural left: overprivileged both in terms of class and education, naive, and workshy, which Smith opposes once more to his vision of authentic working class culture.

It is also notable that The Fall's 1982 album *Hex Enduction Hour*, released on the small independent Kamera during a hiatus from Rough Trade, opens with Smith's notorious reference to 'obligatory niggers' in 'The Classical'. Many of the post-punk bands on Rough Trade's roster, or who were associated with the label via its distribution network, drew on influences from the contemporary black music of the era in more or less conscious opposition to the spike in racism and neofascist activity of the period and Thatcherism's 'rooting of itself inside a particularly narrow, ethnocentric and exclusivist conception of "national identity"'.[65] In this context, it is possible to interpret the line as expressing a sense that influence by black music is somehow an authoritarian imposition, employed not out of authentic personal motivation but external political obligation. Such lyrical provocation is consistent throughout the album, as though Smith is revelling in a newfound absence of perceived constraint now that he is free of Rough Trade.

'Deer Park' deals more specifically with Rough Trade and its milieu, its musical accompaniment more than adequately expressing Smith's feelings towards the label. A furious backdrop of pummelling bassline, double drumkit beat and whining three-note synth pattern re-signifies the repetitive motifs of 1970s German progressive bands favoured by Smith, such as Neu! and Faust, conveying endless frustration in place of cosmic flow. Smith refers to the postcode of Notting Hill where Rough Trade's shop and offices were located, describing a 'sleeping' promotional department in a way that brings to mind his claims that the label had failed to promote The Fall. The comparison of the area to a deer park, meanwhile, encapsulates Smith's rooting of the opposition between his own cultural politics and those he associated with Rough Trade in class terms, presenting the latter not just as those of a minority middle-class fraction but comically exaggerating them as aristocratic. Relatedly, the song's title derives from Norman Mailer's *The Deer Park* (a favourite book of Smith's),[66] evoking parallels between Rough Trade and the corrupt elitism of Hollywood satirised in Mailer's novel.

This class division was parodic and could not account for the numerous working class employees of Rough Trade who shared the company's outlook. However, a further concern of Smith's regarding class and countercultural music formations did address a significant problem, which was not often dealt with by post-punk's libertarian left. This was an issue not just of production but also of consumption. It was a difficulty that provided momentum for the rhetoric of Oi! and new pop: the fact that despite Rough Trade's initial aim of directly challenging major labels through sales, much of its output until the arrival of The Smiths did not sell in comparable quantities to that released by major labels.

As discussed in Chap. 3, those associated with the 'real punk' of Oi! considered post-punk too obscure in its forms and concerns to have populist, including working class, appeal. This stance did not take account of the possibility that working class people were capable of enjoying more nuanced cultural production. Smith had reassuringly little time for this tendency, expressing ironic concern for its demagogue: 'Gary Bushell must have a really hard time interviewing all these bands who have nothing to say.'[67] He also attempted to circumvent Oi!'s questionable claims to be broadly representative of working class taste and concerns whilst simultaneously distancing The Fall from those he considered would only appeal to an apparently middle-class fraction of art school attendees, taking a position reflective of his autodidactic background. In a fanzine interview, Smith claimed: 'it was about time a fairly intelligent roots working class band did something as opposed to art school types'. Years later, he would reflect: 'there were no groups around that I thought represented people like me or my mates. If I wanted to be anything, it was a voice for those people ... The Fall had to appeal to someone who was into cheap soul as much as someone who liked [the] avant-garde. I even wanted the Gary Glitter fans.'[68]

Those drawn to new pop were usually far more successful than the Oi! bands in their attempts to reach a broad audience. But as in the case of Scritti Politti, their logic often involved a capitulation to existing conventions of popular musical production and consumption with reformist political parallels that were more than merely metaphorical. Smith declared: 'when I started out I wanted to wipe out pop music and start again and I thought there were some writers who felt the same way. Now ... being a pop musician is supposed to be something terribly clever and smart. Grown men and women write this crap. Well I'm still on the other side of the fence.'[69] This did not mean a desire to remain marginal—since the early days of The Fall, Smith has consistently stated his aim of reaching a wide audience without compromising on form and content. The *Sounds* journalist Ian Wood wrote: 'the first time I met [The Fall] they were working on a plot to play undercover at their local pub ... with plastic decor, piped muzak and a lousy jukebox. They reckoned they might cause a riot. "Music for the people that don't want it", grinned Mark.'[70]

Smith's wry aphorism highlights the key distinction between his own populism and that of new pop: a willingness to challenge market constructions of popular taste rather than adapt to them. This could also be seen in the decision to do a tour of working men's clubs in unglamorous locations such as Doncaster and Preston in 1980, captured on the live album *Totale's Turns*. The recording is not without audience friction. Furthermore, Smith's concern over the amount of promotion done by Rough Trade also begins to look different considered from the angle of new pop. Instead of a dismissal of 'hippies', it expresses the hope that significant sales can be achieved without the new pop strategy of signing to a major label, thus fitting in with Rough Trade's initial ambitions to be an oppositional challenge to major labels rather than falling into the role of minority alternative.

Ironically, Smith's populism was justified by the following distinction: 'There's entertainment and there's culture, and we're on the cultural side of the line.'[71] It is possible that the statement was a conservative and elitist formulation of high culture versus mass culture. Indeed, Jonathan Rose has argued that cultural conservatism is a persistent tradition amongst certain working class fractions due to a long history of belated exposure to canonical cultural production as a result of educational inequality.[72] There was, however, another possibility, with its roots in an aspect of Smith's background that preceded his autodidactic phase but nevertheless interacted with it. This was his attendance at grammar school in the late 1960s and early 1970s, which had a somewhat different influence on Smith to the comparable experience of Andy Gill and Jon King of Gang of Four.

Alan Sinfield has argued that left culturism permeated the education system in the postwar period.[73] Despite Smith's rejection of '*Jane Eyre* and irrelevant shit like that',[74] it may be that the attitudes of left culturism had an influence, even if its canonical texts were dismissed. For Sinfield, one of left culturism's flaws was its concentration on the traditional arts and its fetishism of state subsidy, leading to the 'historic missed opportunity' for the left of 'working with—politicising—actual popular cultures, "commercial" though they are'.[75] No doubt Sinfield is right to point out that there was not enough in the way of conscious attempts at alliance. Smith's curious take on populism, though, may be an example of the fact that a left culturist structure of feeling was bound at some point to appear in modified form in commercial popular cultural production, given its influence on the formative educational experience of a generation.

Smith's approach was not hugely successful to begin with. A contributor to *City Fun* noted 'the same old crowd' at a Fall gig in 1983, arguing that 'Smith didn't [sell out]. So what? [The Fall's] faith in their ability to educate their audience was misplaced.'[76] This was a problem that The Fall partially resolved only after the tension between post-punk and new pop had dissipated and reconfigured later in the 1980s, when the band experienced a period of increased coverage and higher sales despite remaining signed to an independent label and holding fast to the refusal of artistic compromise. Their 1988 album *The Frenz Experiment* went to number 19 in the mainstream charts.[77] It was soon followed up by *I Am Kurious Oranj*, a soundtrack to Michael Clark's avant-garde ballet themed around the 300th anniversary of William of Orange's accession to the British throne.

MOUNTAINS AND MYSTICISM

As with The Fall, there are hints in the work of the Blue Orchids of a new sensibility regarding pleasure and fulfilment, which nevertheless recognises that it alone cannot be socially transformative. This sensibility is also one that can be understood in terms of work, although from a different angle than The Fall. Rather than the projection of the supernatural onto an urban working class environment, the Blue Orchids stood apart from many of their urban-focused post-punk peers in their positive use of nature imagery.[78]

What does this have to do with work? As hinted at earlier, Marcuse argues that any socialism concerned with the qualitative transformation of human needs as well as the quantitative issue of egalitarianism would need to adapt the technological advances produced and shaped by capitalism to new functions and purposes.[79] This adaptation would build on the classical Marxist division between socialist production for need and capitalist production for profit. Once the imperative of the latter was abandoned, time spent on unpleasurable but socially necessary labour could be reduced by the development of technology to carry out functions that would normally require human input.

Thus there would be increased time for pleasurable forms of work and leisure which derived fulfilment from conscious connection with the surrounding environment, free of the ugliness and pollution generated by the irresponsibility of capitalism's profit-driven production. These kinds of work and leisure would be subject not to what Marcuse refers to as the performance principle (including the capitalist emphasis on productivity at all costs) but to the 'rhythm of those who wander ... who have the time and the pleasure to think, contemplate, feel and narrate'. There is thus, for Marcuse, a 'kernel of truth' in otherwise regressively conservative romantic idealisations of nature and the pre-industrial past; their 'most advanced positions' continue 'to haunt the consciousness with the possibility of their rebirth in the consummation of technical progress'.[80]

This is a pleasure that views fulfilment as contingent on our environment being shaped by socially just relations. In this sense, it is at odds with both Thatcherism's denial of social mutuality—'there is no such thing as society'—and with the individualistic, amoral pleasure discussed in relation to The Fall. Significantly, Marcuse argues that because of the historical malleability of human needs, the desire for such pleasures is diminished by those on offer from developed capitalism, which attempts to harmonise pleasure with its requirements of work and consumption.[81]

In its explorations of nature mysticism, however, there is the potential that the Blue Orchids' cultural production may act as a potent reminder of the pleasures so often denied by the combination of overwork and overconsumption which was promoted with aggressively renewed vigour by Thatcherism. Bramah has said of 'Sun Connection', the song which opens the band's debut album, that '[it] was [about] a particular trip where I saw the sun as a sentient being aware of me on a profound level, and that all these words for gods and deities were just ways of describing what was under our noses'.[82] Whilst the hallucinogenic experience described involved a fantasy of the sun as alive (perhaps inspired by Gurdjieff—his mentee P.D. Ouspensky recalled that 'what interested me was that G. spoke of the planets as living beings'),[83] the conclusion drawn from it was not religious mystification but the potential rooting of spiritual fulfilment in material reality.

The song begins with a guitar introduction whose major key and ascending melody evokes the jubilant mood that prevails throughout, excepting certain key moments. Baines' jaunty organ melody both complements the celebratory tone and the provocative lyrical statement that the narrator's mystical fulfilment goes hand in hand with the rejection of work, and presumably non-essential consumption, in favour of meagre unemployment benefits. The song was released in the year that the government's policy of dismantling British industry in favour of a finance and retail-based economy resulted in three million people unemployed for the first time since the 1930s.[84] It thus finds a positive angle to what was viewed as a disastrous situation by the left, without idealising unemployment: the lyrics note the precariousness of the rejection of work. By doing so, the song is similar to The Fall's use of the uncanny in that it allows for the possibility of a transformation of sensibility without giving the impression that it is easily attainable.

The next verse illustrates how the narrator uses the time granted by unemployment; the closest, but far from ideal, situation for many in a capitalist economy to Marcuse's hope of a society based on minimal unpleasurable labour: climbing and dancing on a 'green mountain'. Here, pleasure is obtained from movement and from an appreciation of the beauty of the earth, sky and sun. The use of the pronoun 'we' also makes fulfilment into a collective experience rather than a self-centred and alienated affair. Furthermore, this is a resolutely non-commodified enjoyment—the lyrics go on to speculate with heavy irony about climbing another kind of mountain, one made of money, in an attempt to purchase a soul.

There is, however, a repeated verse in the song where the musical accompaniment sounds more doubtful and hesitant, accompanying the evocation of an old anxiety that 'keeps you up all night'. The song concludes with this verse, Bramah's voice cracking slightly on the final note as if to reinforce the sentiment. To understand the nature of this doubt, it is worth considering another song that celebrates the pleasures of the natural environment, 'Hanging Man'. Its title, taken from tarot, is the first hint— the Hanging Man card often carries connotations of passivity. Amongst the lyrical imagery of mystic transcendence and nature, there is also a fatalistic pessimism regarding the conversion of this sensibility into a collective, politicised project. The sense of inevitability is compounded by the insistent drumbeat and repetitious rhythm of the bass and organ. This was a mood with residual roots in the band's countercultural influences: Paul Willis notes the way that hippies' rejection of the material world in pursuit of spiritual transcendence could result in a 'fatalist, quietist' culture.[85]

Bramah and especially Baines, however, were aware of this issue. In a *Melody Maker* interview at the time of the album's release, Baines admitted that the 'spiritual connotations of the band's work 'conjure up an image of something that's very up in the air', and then distanced herself from this interpretation: 'I mean, like the Krishna consciousness where you don't actually try and change anything in society because it's all your karma and you just *accept*. I'm totally *anti* that!'[86] This contradictory knot of left libertarian politics and esoteric bodies of knowledge with passive and fatalistic elements was one that would go on to mark every valence of the Blue Orchids' political concerns.

FREE TO ACT, FORCED TO PAY

In the politicised songs of the Blue Orchids, there is a continuation of the contradictions of those that communicate a new sensibility. In songs like 'Sun Connection' and 'Hanging Man', the language of mysticism can be read as pointing tantalisingly towards types of pleasure and fulfilment preferable to those which are currently dominant; pleasures which would only be possible for all in a politically transformed world. The commitment to such a political project, though, tends to waver under the influence of a mystic fatalism. In songs like 'Dumb Magician', meanwhile, the focus is more directly politically committed. The song is an astute and prescient critique of Thatcherite neoliberalism expressed in mystical terms that excoriate both the means and ends of aspiration that Thatcherism promoted—'a dreamer's critique of schemers', in the words of Simon Reynolds.[87] The contradiction, however, comes from what is offered as an alternative. Like 'Sun Connection', this is the pursuit of mystical enlightenment, though of a different variety to that discussed earlier. Instead of a metaphorical glimpse of a qualitative shift in pleasure, mysticism functions here as direct justification for the political pessimism that is occasionally apparent in the Blue Orchids' cultural production.

'Dumb Magician' starts with an organ intro by Baines modelled on fairground or circus music, thus evoking the magician of the title and his dumbness in its lurching discordance. Even before the lyrics begin, then, the song sets up the metaphorical terrain of spurious conjuring tricks, chiming with Bramah's view that 'the way society is structured at the moment, it's founded on illusion, not reality. There are no real values there.'[88] It soon becomes clear what the aims of such illusions and tricks are in the first two lines of the song, which describe being 'free to act' but 'forced to pay'. Bramah summarises the deregulatory economic zeal of the Thatcher government and the unspoken condition of this illusory version of freedom: its reliance on the possession of material wealth, which is unequally distributed, a situation exacerbated by Thatcherite policy. Here, a significant observation is succinctly made that consistently eluded Smith—the fact that freedom can be a political tool of conservatism.

The next two lines suggest the power that can be gained over others through being alert to their unconscious behaviour, connecting with the chorus's description of the dumb magician's instrumental acquisitiveness: 'this gets me that'. In these lines, the critique shifts from the theme of freedom to that of pleasure. They highlight the manipulative behaviour in pursuit of material gain and authority made possible by an awareness of the presence of power relations at the level of everyday life. Whether intentionally or not, this forms a bridge between the broader political conjuncture and post-punk, illustrating how a knowledge of the politics of the personal could be put to more cynical ends in the context of Thatcherism, as in the case of Scritti Politti. Simon Reynolds has speculated accurately that the song might 'be read as a dig at New Pop careerism';[89] when I interviewed Bramah, he said of this shift: 'You can over-intellectualise your grand ideas when at the end of the day you're just trying to make more money than you were making doing what you were doing previously.'[90]

When faced with the question by Reynolds, however, Bramah was more quietist, claiming that the song's theme was 'hubris' and the recommendation to 'keep your head above the temptations to manipulate the material'.[91] This description points towards the more passive elements of 'Dumb Magician', brought into focus by Bramah's explanation of the title of the band's album *The Greatest Hit (Money Mountain)*: 'I thought money was the great Satan, and international bankers have probably proved me correct. So I was just juxtaposing opposites: the spiritual quest (the holy mountain) versus the material game.'[92] It seems that Bramah was also interested in that variant of mysticism which views all materiality as sinful, unlike the nature mysticism of songs such as 'The Flood' and 'Sun Connection', where spirituality is located in the physical environment.

Seen from this perspective, the political critique of 'Dumb Magician' ebbs in two ways. Firstly, lyrics that may seem like an exposure of greed, ruthlessness, and a neoliberal definition of freedom as the free market instead imply not a specific critique but the imperative to reject conscious engagement with the material world. This is further given credence by Bramah's opinion of overt political themes in popular music: 'I'm wary of political bands, they tend not to last very long because their politics will become irrelevant [as] things move on and change.'[93] Secondly, the song's recommendation to 'turn the other cheek' and its suggestion that the 'only way out is up' acquire heightened significance in this context. They constitute the suggested alternative to social power struggles: passive contemplation and spiritual transcendence.

The political submission and deferred gratification potentially implied by the song suggest another, much earlier instance of the interaction of religion and working class culture noted by E.P. Thompson which may have been a very loosely residual influence: the disciplining function of Methodism on the new industrial working class from the early nineteenth century onwards, especially prevalent in Northern England, with its emphasis on poverty as a virtue and reward in the afterlife.[94]

The music of 'Dumb Magician' is profoundly symbolic of its thematic conflict. Possibly the most ecstatic song the band ever released, the ver-tiginously echoing vocal, lead guitar and organ melodies, and unstinting, martial drumbeat are capable of lending weight to both of the tendencies which are present within the lyrics. Evoking Bramah's love of The Doors, 'Dumb Magician' also echoes that band's pursuit of transcendence, cap-tured in their Blakean name. On the one hand, the rush of excitement that the song generates could be viewed as a passionate call to action and an infusion of political critique with pleasurable sensations, contradicting the dominant position, which often informed new pop, that such critique is puritanical and self-defeating. On the other hand, such sensations can be interpreted either as the giddy ecstasy of the dumb magician, subject to misguided 'hubris', or as the compensatory mystical frisson which can be obtained from the rejection of worldliness. Notably, Dave McCullough described the band's sound as a kind of 'sad euphoria'.[95]

The Weediest Gang in Salford

The Blue Orchids' approach to gender is best dealt with by considering the issue from the perspective of each of the two principal band mem-bers. Interestingly, both Bramah and Baines attributed the roots of their feminism directly to childhood. Bramah claims that Baines' discussions of the topic made sense to him due to the fact that he had already rejected the conservative gender expectations of a particular kind of working class upbringing, thus framing the question of gender as one of freedom:

> I've always been a very sensitive person, but as a working class kid in Manchester, as a man you're brutalised. Your education is to like [adopts

sarcastic tone] football and to hit anyone who disagrees with you. You don't sell your arguments intellectually, you just hit people and you get yourself a job and a wife. I refused to bow to that, I wanted to retain my sensitivity—I didn't want to leap classes—I am what I am, a working class kid but sensitive. So when I met Una I very much related to the things she had to say.[96]

There are numerous interesting things about the associations made between gender and other personal features in this statement. There is an implicit recognition of the complexity and variance of gender conventions between classes; for example, the rational intellect, though usually gendered as masculine, is not typically associated with working class masculinity. There is also an understanding of how certain expected kinds of behaviour tend to synchronise with expected roles and life decisions—'you get yourself a job and a wife'—and that by defying them, other routes of fulfilment may be opened up.

Bramah also recognises that for a working class man, an interest in intellectual development and fluency of emotional expression are often linked with class mobility in hegemonic terms. Bramah, though, does not see a continued loyalty to his class as incompatible with his desire for 'sensitivity', nor this desire as an aspirational one at odds with feminism's egalitarian aims. Furthermore, he has stated: 'I realised that being sensitive is strong',[97] contradicting the usual connection of sensitivity with passivity and thus femininity.

This class-based feminist stance overlapped with the band's interest in pagan traditions and embrace of nature with mixed results. Bramah remembers that he 'stole a copy of *The White Goddess* by Robert Graves as a teenager ... a treatise on the lost lore of the Druidic poets'.[98] Colin Wilson, another influence on both The Fall and the Blue Orchids, summarises Graves' theory of the white goddess as 'the goddess of magic, of the subconscious, of poetic inspiration'.[99] For Graves, the truth of poetry was the expression of a feminine freedom associated with the natural world, at odds with a controlling masculine reason.[100]

In the song 'Release' from the band's final EP *Agents of Change*, Bramah begins by evoking Wodin, the senior god in Northern European paganism and the representative of war, as tired and old, suggesting that a prime symbol of patriarchy and masculine aggression has become outmoded and is in need of nurturing. Wodin soon comes to stand for men in general, whilst the word 'paradise' becomes an extended metaphor binding femininity to nature and the maternal, but also to freedom or 'release'. The solution to patriarchal convention is an embrace of the feminised natural world, promising transcendence.

The lyrics invert gendered hierarchy by instructing 'brothers' to sink to their knees in respect of their 'mothers', though the inversion is reliant on an elision of the maternal with the feminine. Appropriately, the accompanying music is mostly composed of warm guitar chords, a gentle piano part and a steady tempo, sounding closer to countercultural singer songwriters influenced by folk and pagan traditions than to the Blue Orchids' punk roots. Hints of melancholy in the melody of the verses are replaced with the reassurance of the simple, reassuring three-note melody of the chorus, in which the song's message is condensed and affirmed. 'Release' therefore communicates Bramah's hopeful vision of the freedom of men to connect with emotive, nurturing values. It also obliquely implies the political advisability of doing so given its release immediately after the Falklands conflict.

For Baines, the relationship of feminism to cultural production also concerns both freedom and pleasure. Whilst she was in the Blue Orchids, Baines experienced a period of mental illness that required her to take time off. One of the most important goals of recovery for Baines was to return to the band, 'because my biggest fear was that I was gonna become a housewife and lose everything—nothing but dusting shelves for the rest of my life'.[101] Here, involvement in the Blue Orchids is viewed very directly as a liberating alternative to the dominant expectation of women to take full responsibility for time-consuming domestic labour.

It is the question of pleasure, however, which rewards closest consideration. Baines has long had a keen awareness of the sometimes politically fraught features of gendered desire. Disappointed that the concern with addressing this issue in punk and post-punk was uneven, she claimed about a band tour that 'it was like a nightmare being in a van … with a load of people talking about women like they're nothing more than something to screw'.[102] More recently, she has linked misogynistic pleasures on the part of male rock musicians with forms of amoral, excessive desire common to the field: 'It's almost as if you've got to have a serious drug and alcohol problem to be a cool male icon … [and] you've got to treat women with disrespect, that's a part of it.'[103]

This becomes apparent in the single 'Disney Boys', the lyrics of which were written by Baines, and which she described as being about 'men as illusions, full of shit'.[104] Bramah's summary of the song—'it's like the love affair with drug culture'[105]—hints at Baines' metaphorical connection between drug use and relationships. She recognised that mystical experiences occasioned by hallucinogens were a contradictory phenomenon, and in 'Disney Boys', this acknowledgement of troubled pleasure is applied to relations between men and women. This is not the only metaphor employed by the song—the lyrics also play on the fusion of pleasure with political reaction in the fairytale romances of Disney films, merging references to visual animation and childhood with allusions to the addictive but destructive effects of drugs.

The name 'Disney Boys' may also be indebted to the Beach Boys' 1957 song 'Disney Girls', in which the narrator yearns for the conservative idyll of a 'turned back world' that incorporates a happy-ever-after relationship whilst hinting at its fictional perfection and unattainability. Baines' lyrics go much further in their critique, repeatedly associating the seduction of the Disney boys with violence, lack of emotional warmth and unequal power relations. The masochism is reinforced by the song's dissonant development of its 1960s garage rock template: the sharp, discordant guitar strums with which it opens, its ominous yet captivating organ melody, Bramah's strained vocals and the brief, wistfully melancholy guitar figure which precedes the song's final verse in which the narrator resentfully concedes to the logic of the Disney boys.

The absence of an alternative to this portrayal of gender relations may have some connection with Baines' claim that 'I was always a bit of a clown [when I was young], but feminism was ever so serious ... I was one of those—what would have been described as "humourless feminists"'.[106] Here, she acknowledges a past susceptibility to one of the wider problems of the feminist movement in the early 1980s. This was the fact that it struggled to articulate an attractive alternative to its critique of the unequal power relations of gendered behaviour and desire, and was often parodied as falsely and joylessly identifying the presence of sexism in jokes and figures of speech which were considered 'just a bit of fun', beyond the reach of ideology. I return to this issue in more detail in the following chapter.

Baines, however, has for some time possessed a feminist vision of human flourishing influenced by paganism and tarot symbols, with an equal focus on personal fulfilment and collectivist nurture.[107] Aside from Bramah's call for men to adopt nurturing values in 'Release', however, there is little indication of such an alternative in the songs of the Blue Orchids in terms that relate specifically to gender. This is in line with Baines' feeling that there was an awkward disjunction between her sensibilities regarding other subjects and the puritanical seriousness that had become associated with feminism. It would take until Baines' all-female band The Fates' 1985 lost classic *Furia* for her alternative model of feminist fulfilment to be publicly expressed.

'POLITICS IS LIFE'

Aged only 20, in an early Fall interview, Baines argued that 'if you sing about life, you're singing politically. Politics is life, and society in its perversity has made it into something else', an attitude she took with her into the Blue Orchids.[108] Bramah describes Baines as 'a very powerful woman, in spirit', stating that 'she was a big influence on me'. This belief seems validated by the fact that nearly 34 years after Baines' comment, Bramah unconsciously echoed it in his claim that he sees himself as 'sharing things that might or might not be useful to other like-minded people [through music] and if that has political repercussions then that's fine because politics is life, isn't it?'[109]

Bramah has described the Blue Orchids' working relationship as a direct response to Smith's dictatorial assumption of control in The Fall, claiming that:

> It was the spirit of not having one genius leader, and everyone else has to do what they're told. Blue Orchids was kind of a reaction against that. We were crediting everyone with writing everything, so that the money was shared equally. I'm still paying people royalties now for playing the drums with us for six months, out of a sense of fairness.[110]

Unlike Gang of Four's attempts to translate their equal working relationships into the formal features of their music, there is little obvious sense in which the similar arrangements of the Blue Orchids can be detected musically. As the above comments by Bramah and Baines suggest, however, this does not mean that the pair's keen awareness of the politics of the personal did not make itself felt in their cultural production. Instead of a concern with personal politics at the level of intra-band relationships, what is most clear in songs such as 'Bad Education' and 'Work' is an oppositional ethos of personal fulfilment and development that is simultaneously libertarian and collectivist. This is an ethos already touched on in discussion of the band's nature mysticism, but it was also composed of a further feature. Influenced by an awareness of the alienation produced by capitalism, Bramah and Baines shared a focus on the notion of self-determination at odds with the possessive individualism that characterised Thatcherism.

Once more, mysticism was a touchstone, with Bramah reflecting on Gurdjieff: 'I dwell on his ideas quite a lot, but they're not seen as revolutionary ideas. They are to me, but the revolution is "examine yourself".'[111] Gurdjieff described most people as 'machines' and promoted greater self-awareness.[112] Self-awareness 'brings man to the realisation of the necessity for self-change'.[113] Gurdjieff, however, was no egalitarian on this issue, claiming: 'knowledge cannot belong to all, cannot even belong to many'.[114] Nor was he prescriptive on what the aim of fulfilment should be, claiming that 'when a man has an aim he "ought" to do only what leads him towards his aim and he "ought not" to do anything that hinders him from [it]'.[115] This was at odds with the Blue Orchids' view of the matter, which hoped for the self-realisation of the many and united ethics with pleasure and politics. Baines once claimed that 'the biggest tragedy that exists is that people don't develop their potential',[116] and Bramah has said, 'if you have a revolution on the streets it means nothing if you're not able to be a better person yourself'.[117]

What, then, was being 'a better person' for the Blue Orchids? A substantial residual contribution to Bramah and Baines' attitude was the long British working class tradition of educational 'mutual improvement' documented by Jonathan Rose and convincingly viewed as 'but one branch of a vast popular movement of voluntary collectivism' including economic initiatives such as friendly societies.[118] Embodied in these networks was a powerful faith in the value of education rooted in its lack of official provision for the majority of people. For many on the left, this extended not just to recognition of the benefits of education in the present but also to a belief in it as the principle of personal fulfilment in a future socialist society, beyond the equal distribution of wealth.[119] Combining grassroots co-operation and an autodidactic stress on individual interpretation, mutual improvement allowed for the potential of a left libertarian 'ethics of flourishing' as specified by Terry Eagleton, 'in which each attains his or her freedom and autonomy in and through the self-realisation of others'.[120] Accordingly, those who belonged to this tradition were often suspicious of the gradual state expansion of education in spite of its partially democratising effect due to its simultaneous tendencies towards paternalism and the inculcation of a passive mode of learning.[121]

Many decades later, there are close parallels with the band's outlook. Baines spoke of 'the debasement of education' and the way that 'it's the middle classes who communicate ... working class experience these days', believing instead in a system of collective responsibility.[122] Bramah has expressed his distrust of official institutions, including his school education:

> Being a kid I didn't fit into the education system so I was kind of against it on principle—I never took things as given or just because I was told it was so. I always gravitated towards things that interested me and pursued them. Very often it didn't fit in with what I was taught. I was trying to avoid school as much as I could, but I always thought about stuff, even from a young age.[123]

In line with the collectivism of mutual improvement, this was not a solitary pursuit—Bramah also notes: 'I was attracted to people [such as Baines and Smith] who did the same thing.' Nor was it self-aggrandising—Baines describes the song 'Low Profile' as 'about working without display ... while you're doing positive things to make changes. When it's about the ego, flaunting what you're doing and showing off ... then you're highlighting yourself and saying "look at me".'[124]

In 'Bad Education', Bramah uses the institution of education as a metaphor for the negative, pacifying effects of hegemonic values on individual perception, describing the 'sticky situation' of having read 'too many books' and watched 'too much TV' in a world-weary spoken-word refrain. The song avoids a collapse into individualism by directly addressing the listener from the beginning in a meekly charming idiom and by generalising its observations. 'Bad Education's conveyance of the passivity inculcated by social institutions and the failure to 'wake up' through its lulling melody does, however, tend towards the mystic fatalism evident elsewhere in the band's cultural production.

The Blue Orchids' second single 'Work' offers a more overt and positive solution. The resonances of its title fuse the dual influences on the band's personal politics of working class autodidact culture and mysticism; Gurdjieff referred to the process of developing self-awareness as 'the work'. Bramah stated of the song: 'it's about working on yourself before you can do anything else, attaining values and a conscience. Stripping down the illusions of life without being negative or flowery.'[125] The barked chorus of the song, consisting of the repetition of the word 'work', avoids the 'floweriness' suggested by the passivity of 'Bad Education', as does the disorienting organ melody. The brittle timbre of the drum machine accompaniment, meanwhile, is evocative of the 'crisis music' of the Blue

Orchids' post-punk peers. A purely negative effect, however, is avoided in the nature imagery of lines such as 'we'll be the gold salmon swimming against the tide'—there is a sense of pleasure as well as difficulty in the imagery and the tone in which the line is sung. The use of 'we' is consistent throughout in a song that concerns personal development, complementing the direct address of the listener in 'Bad Education' and further underlining the band's understanding of freedom and pleasure as collective, co-operative affairs.

'Working Without Display'

When asked if the Blue Orchids' ethos was more in tune with Rough Trade than Smith's, Baines agreed. She also compared the economic models used to run initiatives by the women's movement in Manchester to the co-operative manner in which Rough Trade operated, making a clear link between her cultural production and political activism.[126] Bramah, too, said, 'we thought things like Rough Trade would be collectives, would be communal ... getting things done without the businessmen ... not looking to make profit but just looking to make music and happenings and events'. As with the Blue Orchids' democratic working arrangements, though, this affinity is difficult to assess from close analysis of the band's cultural production due to Bramah's aforementioned culturalist suspicion of singing about their 'business affairs'.[127]

A more productive way of analysing the Blue Orchids' relationship with Rough Trade is to consider an ambiguity in the band's outlook rather than a harmony, one with parallels to the difficulties faced by Rough Trade. On the one hand, their stance was positive from the angle of pleasure. In line with Bramah and Baines' belief that personal fulfilment should not be a question of material acquisition, they valued cultural production for its own sake rather than in profit-driven, instrumentalist terms. Baines told me that 'we were just doing it for the sake of it', while Bramah said that he values his current arrangement of day job combined with his new band Factory Star: 'I can make money and make music but I don't have to stop making music if it's not making me any money. Some bands, it's all about a career, and if the career stops, the music stops, which is sad.'[128] In interview with Simon Reynolds, Baines claimed: 'we were pretty skint in those days, but we had a very interesting life. It's like, what do you call "rich"?'[129] Expanding on this theme when I interviewed her, she asked, 'don't you think people [who are concerned with status-driven consumption]—it's a bit sad? You know, "look at me with this big medallion" and you think "what a plonker"! Go and educate yourself, you know? Go and read some Oscar Wilde or something!'[130] Here, Baines unites the band's desire to make music for its own sake with the ethic of education discussed earlier.

On the other hand, there are two difficulties with framing the issue in this manner. The first concerns Baines' definition of pleasure. As noted in the previous chapter, both musicians and music press writers who had been involved with leftist post-punk were now beginning to characterise the Rough Trade milieu as joyless in contrast to the emergent formation of new pop. In this context, the Blue Orchids' aversion to a career and their willingness to live on very little in exchange for a life devoted to their art risked reinforcing this caricature of a puritanical scene; Baines claimed that they subsisted largely on porridge and lentils.[131] The recollection highlights a problem noted by David Hesmondhalgh in his sympathetic analysis of Rough Trade's long-term political effect on the British music industry. Hesmondhalgh argues that because the company only had limited resources in its early years, 'musicians were effectively trading in short-term financial security for a sense of collaboration and co-operation, and the feeling of a shared musical culture'. There was thus a tension between Rough Trade's attempt to foster creative freedom (which, as Hesmondhalgh argues, went beyond romantic culturalism by 'consciously forefronting the interdependence of creative and "commercial" work')[132] and their commitment to an egalitarian distribution of financial resources.

The other problem is directly related and is one of freedom; it is the question of who benefits from the allowance of institutional autonomy, free of record company assumptions of what will sell. The difficulty can be situated in the context of another of the new pop ideologues' characterisations of post-punk. This was the accusation that it had become a self-indulgent ghetto, which had lost touch with the fact that it was part of a popular music market whose aim was to cater for a broad audience. Paul Morley asserted: 'no longer is there an acceptance of the cobwebbed corner ... [new pop groups] want a big display in the supermarkets, not to be stuck on a high shelf in the corner shop'.[133] In this context, the Blue Orchids' aforementioned aim of 'working without display' may well have translated not as an admirable rejection of egotism but as a desire to remain marginal, making them prime targets of new pop critique. 'People will ... say you're opting out', worried McCullough in interview with them. 'But what are you competing with', Baines countered, 'except a lot of hip cynical people?'[134]

It should be acknowledged, however, that, like Smith, the Blue Orchids attempted to formulate an alternative populism, which they justified in terms of spreading their ideas rather than material ambition. In an interview at the time of their debut album's release, Bramah said: 'before you can tell anybody anything, they've got to be enjoying what you're saying or doing'. They implicitly distanced this stance from new pop, with Baines adding: 'we're not for people to escape to'.[135] Bramah, meanwhile, remarked of his musical contemporaries: 'some of them look very pretty, but they'd never change my life'.[136] Baines' anger about the contemporary music industry also shows an alertness to a problem often sidelined by new pop: an awareness that the market creates and meets pleasures moulded by dominant values rather than abstractly catering to free individuals. 'Now look at it, Simon Cowell and all that nonsense, where they just take the soul out of everything and regurgitate this shit at people, and people want it. Their lives are being narrowed down.'[137]

The logic of new pop, however, was not successfully circumvented in the long term. The *Melody Maker* music journalist Steve Sutherland, who had once championed the Blue Orchids, penned a deeply ambiguous review of the band's final EP littered with backhanded compliments: 'the Blue Orchids' appeal is viral, a sort of sapping sympathy for a sound so fragile it could just as easily expire as pull through'.[138] Simon Reynolds has noted the prevalence of metaphors of health and sickness in the language of new pop, employed in order to give the impression of post-punk as stagnant and decaying in contrast to an emerging aspirational stance.[139] What goes unmentioned by Reynolds, however, is an undeniable parallel between this rhetoric and Thatcher's positing of her government's policies as 'medicine' in response to the media portrayal of Britain as 'the sick man of Europe'.[140] It is perhaps unsurprising, then, that fellow *Melody Maker* journalist Paolo Hewitt once described Sutherland as 'a right wing shit' who 'toadied up to management'.[141] With regard to this portrayal of post-punk as entropic, the Blue Orchids were once again vulnerable. In 1981, they had acted as tour band for Nico, formerly of The Velvet Underground, who had a chronic heroin addiction and was surrounded by others in a similar position. Bramah briefly experimented, whilst the band's long-term bassist and live guitarist became hooked and left to join Nico's backing band full-time.[142]

This shift is reflected in some of the songs from the band's final EP, which was released in late 1982. One such example is 'The Long Night Out'. The song uncharacteristically employs a synthesiser with a tone and melody faintly suggestive of fellow Mancunian post-punks Joy Division, whose singer Ian Curtis had committed suicide two years before. Its slow, listless pulse and mournful piano is comparable to the trudge of 'The Eternal' from Joy Division's final album *Closer*, which dealt morbidly with funereal imagery. The lyrics of 'The Long Night Out', meanwhile, evoked the addictive yet destructive properties of heroin, observing its stultifying effect. These lines seemed a world away from the band's promotion of positivity and action in interviews and the counterparts of this attitude in other examples of their cultural production. The song, which is the last on the EP, features a bleak spoken finale, asking where it is possible to go in a world that 'stinks'. The question remains unanswered, a fact reflected in the musical conclusion of an unresolved chord progression that slowly fades out.

Vibrations That Live On

Reflecting on The Fall years which this chapter has dealt with, Smith has claimed that 'I always used those right-wing comments to wind [*NME*] up because I knew how narrow-minded they were'.[143] This defence—'it was a joke all along'—is a cunning move, rendering any objection to the views Smith has expressed on the left as confirmation of their apparent veracity. It is a move that has bothered me numerous times when reading back the more critical analyses of Fall songs I nevertheless enjoy for all sorts of reasons. Have I simply taken Smith too seriously? Is my analysis, despite my own working class background, an example of 'middle class revolt', as a Fall album title would have it? To accept this, though, would be to accept Smith's portrayal of the left as uniformly puritanical, lacking even the ability to appreciate ironic humour.

It would also leave the views expressed in The Fall's cultural production unexamined on the assumption that they will always be taken with a pinch of salt rather than crystallising or reinforcing such views in listeners. This is a difficult assumption to make, since at the time Smith was clearly mobilising a particular structure of feeling shared by certain other participants in post-punk, such as *Sounds* journalist and Fall champion Dave McCullough. McCullough's hostility to the leftist and feminist art school bands The Raincoats and The Mekons was motivated by the same attribution of such views to naive middle-class students—'self-righteous do-gooding … [a] conceited student mentality … irretrievably jinxed by [its] own middle-class, haplessly patronising attitudes'—and the same accusation of joylessness: '*The Raincoats* is … an album void of love.'[144]

More recently, it is also worth speculating whether potential contemporary listeners influenced by the pernicious ideological rhetoric of 'political correctness gone mad', in other words the neoliberal re-casting of progressive and leftist freedoms as authoritarian impositions, may well interpret aspects of Smith's outlook as complementary with their views. In the late 1970s and early 1980s, the phrase had yet to gain the purchase it now holds, but it is telling that Smith claims some of the band's output 'was totally un-PC for Rough Trade' in his recent memoir, going on to assert that 'a lot of so called hipsters are very conservative like that. There are more taboos in their world than there are in that of the fucking Tories they purport to despise.'[145] Here, Smith's individualism is united with the logic of those who object to 'political correctness' on the basis that true freedom is the freedom to express reactionary views without being questioned or challenged.

For all these gestures, however, The Fall's post-punk period shows a complex, contradictory and sharply witty mind at work. Smith created a grotesquely entertaining alternative reality of Manchester that is still unsurpassed. He broached certain crucial issues which many on the post-punk left never quite managed to address convincingly or at all, such as the relationship between class, populism, the market, and countercultural music formations and institutions.

Smith commented in a 1987 interview that 'when I was moving house I found a *New Musical Express* from 1981 ... those times were like the intellectual times of music, weren't they? Philosophical bullshit. Now it's like a complete reaction against that ... in a way, I like it better like this.'[146] The relief from leftist post-punk's culture of scrutiny may have been seductive, but an awkward and conflict-ridden belonging to this formation of 'philosophical bullshit' often brought out the best in Smith and his band. It would be a shame for this to be buried under the vacuous and insulting stereotype of truculent, incomprehensible middle-aged Northern alcoholic that now tends to frame Smith in the media, as 'the demonisation of the working class' proceeds apace.[147] Recently, too, Smith has mocked the Tories and described left-wing Labour leader Jeremy Corbyn as 'eminently sensible'.[148]

Meanwhile, Simon Reynolds has argued that the legacy of the Blue Orchids was to have 'anticipated the "zen apathy", indolence-as-route-to-enlightenment, anti-stance of Happy Mondays' "Lazy-Itis"', and more broadly, the 'defeatism as dissidence' attitude of early 1990s 'slacker' alternative rock.[149] This view is clearly informed by an awareness of the political implications of the Blue Orchids' tendencies to fatalism and their rejection of material acquisition in the context of new pop. However, Reynolds presents the outlook of the band as far more pessimistic than it ever was in reality. The summary neglects to consider that the Blue Orchids built and committed to a consistent, convincing oppositional ethos of pleasure and freedom, in addition to critiquing the dominant articulations of these themes.

Nor have the band relinquished this ethos over the past three decades. Bramah is still devoted to making music without the motive being profit or ego. Baines, meanwhile, has remained involved in political activism and community work with an emphasis on collective, non-acquisitive personal fulfilment, such as running a women's group at her local Sure Start centre and volunteering to make music with people suffering from mental health problems. In an echo of the Blue Orchids' nature mysticism, Baines was also recently part of a group that opposed the felling of established trees in her local area. She believes that 'we'll look back on the 60s, 70s, 80s [countercultural and leftist movements] as golden years' but expresses a guarded hope that the global communication enabled by the internet has some transformative potential despite problems of censorship and private ownership. Baines also notes the existence of new co-operative, counter-cultural initiatives in Manchester.[150] We can only hope that such developments, informed by an oppositional tradition to which the Blue Orchids made an important if overlooked contribution, continue to flourish in our currently interesting times.

NOTES

1. See for example, Simon Ford, *Hip Priest: The Story of Mark E. Smith and The Fall* (London: Quartet, 2003), p. xi; Mick Middles and Mark E. Smith, *The Fall* (London: Omnibus, 2003), p. 278; Taylor Parkes, 'The Fall and Mark E. Smith as a Narrative Lyric Writer', *The Quietus*, 19 March 2010, available online at http://thequietus.com/articles/03925-the-fall-and-mark-e-smith-as-a-narrative-lyric-writer, accessed 8 October 2015; Michael Goddard and Benjamin Halligan (eds.), 'Introduction', in *Mark E. Smith and The Fall: Art, Music and Politics* (Farnham: Ashgate, 2010), p. 5.

2. Wilson Neate, interview with Simon Reynolds for *Perfect Sound Forever*, February 2006, available online at http://www.furious.com/perfect/simonreynolds31.html, accessed 8 October 2015.

3. Middles and Smith, *The Fall*, p. 79.

4. *The Fall: The Wonderful and Frightening World of Mark E. Smith*, BBC4, 2005.
5. Richard Witts, 'Building Up a Band: Music for a Second City', in *Mark E. Smith and The Fall: Art, Music and Politics*, ed. Goddard and Halligan, pp. 19–31 (p. 30).
6. Ford, *Hip Priest*, pp. 14–15.
7. Sinfield, *Literature, Politics and Culture in Postwar Britain*, 3rd ed. (London: Continuum, 2004), p. 178.
8. Keith Gildart, 'From "Dead End Streets" to "Shangri Las": Negotiating Social Class and Post-War Politics with Ray Davies and the Kinks', in *Youth Culture, Popular Music and the End of 'Consensus'*, ed. The Subcultures Network (London: Routledge, 2015), pp. 9–34 (p. 14).
9. Ian Penman, 'The Fall', *NME*, 19 August 1978.
10. Ford, *Hip Priest*, p. 77.
11. Simon Reynolds, *Totally Wired: Post-Punk Interviews and Overviews* (London: Faber and Faber, 2009), p. 210.
12. James Nice, 'The Blue Orchids Biography', available online at http://www.ltmrecordings.com/bobio.html, accessed 8 October 2015.
13. Reynolds, *Totally Wired*, p. 209.
14. Gary Lachman, *Turn Off Your Mind: The Mystic Sixties and the Dark Side of the Age of Aquarius* (London: Sidgwick and Jackson, 2001), p. 69.
15. Paul Morley, 'They Mean It, Ma-a-a-nchester', *NME*, 30 July 1977.
16. Dick Witts quoted in Clinton Heylin, *Babylon's Burning: From Punk to Grunge* (London: Penguin, 2008), p. 313.
17. Ford, *Hip Priest*, pp. 24–25.
18. Dave Simpson, *The Fallen: Life in and out of Britain's Most Insane Group* (Edinburgh: Canongate, 2008), p. 93.
19. Oliver Lowenstein, 'A New Career in a New Town', *Melody Maker*, 18 January 1978.
20. Middles and Smith, *The Fall*, p. 84.
21. Ford, *Hip Priest*, p. 8.
22. George Kay, 'The Fall of Slick, Mark E. Smith's Hex Enduction Hour', *Rip It Up*, September 1982.
23. Jon Lawrence and Fiona Sutcliffe-Braithwaite, 'Thatcher and the Decline of Class Politics', in *Making Thatcher's Britain*, ed. Jackson and Saunders (Cambridge: Cambridge University Press, 2012), pp. 132–147 (p. 139).
24. Gildart, 'From 'Dead End Streets' to 'Shangri Las', p. 10.
25. Middles and Smith, *The Fall*, p. 28.
26. Mat Snow, 'Before and After The Fall', *NME*, 3 November 1984.
27. Smith on KPFA Radio, San Francisco, broadcast 10 July 1981.
28. Gavin Martin, 'Revolting Soul', *NME*, 30 August 1986.
29. Reynolds, *Totally Wired*, p. 207.

30. Author interview with Martin Bramah, 2011.
31. Bramah quoted in Ford, *Hip Priest*, pp. 25–26.
32. Author interview with Una Baines, 2012.
33. Author interview with Una Baines.
34. Lynn Hanna, 'When Reality Rears Its Orchidacious Head', *NME*, 20 June 1981.
35. Author interview with Una Baines.
36. Reynolds, *Totally Wired*, pp. 210–214 and author interviews with Martin Bramah and Una Baines.
37. Author interview with Martin Bramah.
38. Jonathan Rose, *The Intellectual Life of the British Working Classes* (New Haven and London: Yale University Press, 2001), pp. 12–18.
39. Sandy Robertson, 'Hex Education', *Sounds*, 8 May 1982.
40. Barney Hoskyns, 'Hip Priest: The Mark E. Smith Interview', *NME*, 14 November 1981.
41. Mark E. Smith and Austin Collings, *Renegade: The Lives and Tales of Mark E. Smith* (London: Penguin, 2009), pp. 77–78.
42. Mark Fisher, 'Memorex for the Krakens: The Fall's Pulp Modernism', in *Mark E. Smith and The Fall*, ed. Goddard and Halligan, pp. 95–110 (p. 104).
43. Ian Pye, 'The Fall Go to the Wall', *Melody Maker*, 6 June 1981.
44. Colin Irwin, review of The Fall—*Hex Enduction Hour*, *Melody Maker*, 6 March 1982.
45. Margaret Thatcher in Richard Benson, *The Wit and Wisdom of Margaret Thatcher and Other Tory Legends* (Chichester: Summersdale, 2010), p. 48.
46. Herbert Marcuse, 'The End of Utopia', in *Five Lectures: Psychoanalysis, Politics, and Utopia*, trans. Jeremy J. Shapiro and Shierry M. Weber (London: Allen Lane, 1970), pp. 64–67.
47. Tony Herrington, 'Mancunian Candidate', *The Wire*, September 1996.
48. Ford, *Hip Priest*, p. 72.
49. Reynolds, *Totally Wired*, p. 415.
50. Dave McCullough, 'Totale Turnaround', *Sounds*, 21 June 1980.
51. Smith and Collings, *Renegade*, p. 89.
52. Simon Reynolds and Joy Press, *The Sex Revolts* (Cambridge: Harvard University Press, 1996), pp. 141–147.
53. McCullough, 'Totale Turnaround'.
54. Simon Reynolds, *Rip It Up and Start Again: Postpunk 1978–1984* (London: Faber and Faber, 2005), p. 195.
55. Smith's views on this matter remained contradictory, however, due to the simultaneous pursuit of formal idiosyncrasy which contributes towards the band's post-punk status, and his consistent hostility towards punk bands who continued to follow the generic template established in the move-

ment's first two years. Even The Fall's rockabilly and 'Country "n" Northern' songs like 'Fiery Jack', 'The Container Drivers' and 'Fit and Working Again' avoided pastiche, a fact implicit in the neologism Smith used to describe them.

56. Alex Ogg, *Independence Days: The Story of UK Independent Record Labels* (London: Cherry Red, 2009), pp. 142–150.

57. Ford, *Hip Priest*, p. 80.

58. Dave McCullough, 'Society's Scourge', *Sounds*, 17 May 1980.

59. David Cavanagh, 'The Fall', *Volume* 4, September 1992.

60. Smith and Collings, *Renegade*, p. 91.

61. George Kay, 'The Fall of Slick…'.

62. Edwin Pouncey, 'Rough Justice', *Sounds*, 9 June 1984.

63. Smith and Collings, *Renegade*, p. 65.

64. Smith and Collings, *Renegade*, pp. 65, 90.

65. Stuart Hall, *The Hard Road to Renewal: Thatcherism and the Crisis of the Left* (London: Verso, 1988), p. 8.

66. Mark E. Smith, 'Portrait of the Artist as a Consumer', *NME*, 15 August 1981.

67. Ian Penman, 'All Fall Down', *NME*, 5 January 1980.

68. Lisa Verrico, 'Are You Talking to Me?', *Dazed and Confused*, December 1998.

69. Steve Lake, 'After The Fall', *Melody Maker*, 21 April 1984.

70. Ian Wood, 'The Fall Stumble into the Void', *Sounds*, 8 April 1978.

71. Smith on Dave Fanning's radio show, RTE (Ireland), broadcast 18 October 1980.

72. Rose, *The Intellectual Life of the British Working Classes*, p. 116.

73. Sinfield, *Literature, Politics and Culture in Postwar Britain*, p. 282.

74. Ford, *Hip Priest*, p. 12.

75. Sinfield, *Literature, Politics and Culture in Postwar Britain*, p. 283.

76. *City Fun* 3, no. 6, 25 June 1983.

77. Available online at http://www.officialcharts.com/artist/21777/fall/, accessed 8 October 2015.

78. The only other prominent post-punk band to do so was The Slits, a theme examined in the following chapter.

79. Herbert Marcuse, 'The End of Utopia', pp. 64–68.

80. Herbert Marcuse, *One Dimensional Man* [1964] (London: Routledge, 1991), pp. 62–63.

81. Marcuse, *One Dimensional Man*, p. 77.

82. Reynolds, *Totally Wired*, p. 211.

83. P.D. Ouspensky, *In Search of the Miraculous* (New York: Harcourt, Brace and Company 1949), p. 25.

84. *BBC News*, 'On this Day 1950–2005—26 January 1982', available online at http://news.bbc.co.uk/onthisday/hi/dates/stories/january/26/newsid_2506000/2506335.stm, accessed 8 October 2015.
85. Paul Willis, *Profane Culture* (London: Routledge, 1978), p. 133.
86. Steve Sutherland, 'The Sane Old Blues', *Melody Maker*, 1 May 1982.
87. Reynolds, *Rip It Up*, p. 449.
88. Lynn Hanna, 'When Reality…'.
89. Reynolds, *Rip It Up*, p. 449.
90. Author interview with Martin Bramah.
91. Simon Reynolds, *Totally Wired*, p. 213.
92. Reynolds, *Totally Wired*, p. 213.
93. Author interview with Martin Bramah.
94. E.P. Thompson, *The Making of the English Working Class* (London: Victor Gollancz, 1963), pp. 358–363. The simultaneous stresses of Methodism on the work ethic and abstinence were clearly less influential, however, given Bramah's rejection of a 'factory fodder' destiny and his self-confessedly prodigious consumption of psychedelics.
95. Dave McCullough, 'Flower Power Revisited', *Sounds*, 12 June 1982.
96. Author interview with Martin Bramah.
97. Author interview with Martin Bramah.
98. Reynolds, *Totally Wired*, p. 210.
99. Colin Wilson, *The Occult* (St. Albans: Mayflower, 1973), p. 82.
100. Robert Graves, *The White Goddess: A Historical Grammar of Poetic Myth* (London: Faber and Faber, 1961).
101. Sutherland, 'The Sane Old Blues'.
102. Sutherland, 'The Sane Old Blues'.
103. Author interview with Una Baines.
104. Simon Reynolds, 'Rip It Up—The Footnotes', available online at http://ripitupfootnotes.blogspot.co.uk/2008/11/footnotes-24-chapter-23-glory-boys.html, accessed 8 October 2015.
105. Reynolds, *Totally Wired*, p. 211.
106. Author interview with Una Baines.
107. Author interview with Una Baines.
108. Chris Brazier, 'United They Fall', *Melody Maker*, 31 December 1977.
109. Author interview with Martin Bramah.
110. Author interview with Martin Bramah.
111. Author interview with Martin Bramah.
112. Ouspensky, *In Search of the Miraculous*, p. 21.
113. Ouspensky, *In Search of the Miraculous*, p. 145.
114. Ouspensky, *In Search of the Miraculous*, p. 37.
115. Ouspensky, *In Search of the Miraculous*, p. 152.
116. Sutherland, 'The Sane Old Blues'.

117. Author interview with Martin Bramah.
118. Rose, *The Intellectual Life of the British Working Classes*, p. 59.
119. Rose, *The Intellectual Life of the British Working Classes*, p. 53.
120. Terry Eagleton, *After Theory* (London: Penguin, 2003), p. 170.
121. Rose, *The Intellectual Life of the British Working Classes*, p. 57.
122. McCullough, 'Flower Power Revisited'.
123. Author interview with Martin Bramah.
124. Author interview with Una Baines.
125. Hanna, 'When Reality...'.
126. Author interview with Una Baines.
127. Author interview with Martin Bramah.
128. Author interview with Martin Bramah.
129. Reynolds, 'Rip It Up—The Footnotes', available online at http://ripi-tupfootnotes.blogspot.co.uk/2008/11/footnotes-24-chapter-23-glory-boys.html
130. Author interview with Una Baines.
131. Author interview with Una Baines.
132. David Hesmondhalgh, 'Post-Punk's Attempt to Democratise the Music Industry: The Success and Failure of Rough Trade', *Popular Music* 16, no. 3 (Oct 1997), 255–274 (p. 262).
133. Quoted in Reynolds, *Rip It Up*, p. 364.
134. McCullough, 'Flower Power Revisited'.
135. Sutherland, 'The Sane Old Blues'.
136. Hanna, 'When Reality...'.
137. Author interview with Una Baines.
138. Steve Sutherland, 'On the Sick List', *Melody Maker*, 27 November 1982.
139. Reynolds, *Rip It Up*, p. 364.
140. Available online at http://www.britishpoliticalspeech.org/speech-archive.htm?speech=131, accessed 8 October 2015.
141. Paul Gorman, *In Their Own Write: Adventures in the Music Press* (London: Sanctuary, 2001), p. 275.
142. Reynolds, *Totally Wired*, p. 214.
143. Middles and Smith, *The Fall*, p. 229.
144. Dave McCullough, 'Shrieks from the Grove', *Sounds*, 8 December 1979.
145. Smith and Collings, *Renegade*, p. 90.
146. Charles Neal, *Tape Delay* (Harrow: SAF, 1987), p. 95.
147. Owen Jones, *Chavs: The Demonisation of the Working Class* (London: Verso, 2011).
148. Tony Dewhurst, 'The Fall's Mark E. Smith Talks Television, Politics and New Technology', *The Bolton News*, 7 October 2015, available online at http://www.theboltonnews.co.uk/news/13809653.The_Fall_s_Mark_E_Smith_talks_television__politics_and_n/, accessed 8 October 2015.

149. Simon Reynolds, *Melody Maker* review of the Blue Orchids compilation 'A View from the City', available online at http://ripitupfootnotes.blogspot. co.uk/2008/11/footnotes-24-chapter-23-glory-boys.html
150. Author interview with Una Baines.

CHAPTER 6

Desires Bound with Briars: Freedom, Pleasure and Feminism

The Slits and The Raincoats were perhaps the two most emblematic female post-punk bands in Britain. Their diverse backgrounds and styles resist equivalence on the basis of sex and gender alone. In the late 1970s, The Slits' Ari Up was a dreadlocked Bavarian teenager and the extroverted daughter of a wealthy media heiress, for instance, whilst The Raincoats' Ana da Silva was a contemplative Portuguese émigré in her late 20s. Yet productive comparisons can be made, and as women situated within British post-punk, all shared a formation.[1] In this instance, though, habitus does not play the same unifying role as in previous chapters. Instead the argument is situated in relation to the difficult and fragmentary situation of the women's movement in the late 1970s and early 1980s, and its partial incorporation by the dominant culture. In doing so, I aim to historically contextualise the two bands in a way that has only been gestured towards so far, exploring interwoven questions of agency, pleasure, gendered consumerism, and women's engagement with cultural production during Britain's shift to neoliberalism.

Lynne Segal has observed that in an era of neoliberal hegemony, feminism is being incorporated as individual success within the terms of the dominant culture. It is a process of 'expedient accommodation', which selectively appropriates particular feminist ideas 'even as it rejects or ridicules' others. A significant element of this rejection is the notion of feminism as a collective, consciously politicised movement.[2] Angela

© The Editor(s) (if applicable) and The Author(s) 2016
D. Wilkinson, *Post-Punk, Politics and Pleasure in Britain*,
DOI 10.1057/978-1-137-49780-2_6

McRobbie, too, has argued that 'post-feminism positively draws on and invokes feminism as that which can be taken into account, to suggest that equality is achieved, in order to ... emphasise that it is no longer needed'.[3] Zoe Williams, noting that the head of the International Monetary Fund, Christine Lagarde, has attributed her success to her 'feminine softness', summarises just such a structure of feeling as 'capitalism with tits'.[4]

It is in this context that a biography of The Slits was published in 2009, built on new interviews with band members. Throughout, its author Zoe Street Howe frames interview questions and deploys the band's responses to support her claim that the key value of The Slits' work is the individual freedom it celebrates and the pleasure to be gained from this. This is an angle that is often framed in post-feminist terms.[5] Thus, Street Howe declared in a promotional interview for *The Quietus* that 'I ... was inspired by ... [the band's] refusal to label themselves "feminist"',[6] characterising The Slits as 'liberated ... feminist-without-using-the-feminist-label'.[7]

There are elements of The Slits' cultural production that could, in certain lights, be interpreted as part of an inchoate 'post-feminist' sensibility. At the time their work was released, however, many had little difficulty in presenting it as a development of the gains of women's liberation and more broadly oppositional in a libertarian left sense. Such figures included Lucy Toothpaste (real name Lucy Whitman), author of the fanzine *Jolt* and contributor to women's movement magazine *Spare Rib*;[8] as well as Lucy O'Brien, an author, *NME* journalist and member of punk band The Catholic Girls.[9] Retrospectively, too, guitarist Viv Albertine recalls the direct influence of the women's movement on her work,[10] somewhat complicating Street Howe's biography of the band.

In an article for *The Quietus*, meanwhile, Charles Ubaghs suggests that The Raincoats 'embodied the spirit' of post-punk, a 'spirit' defined purely in formalistic terms. Unsurprisingly, such an interpretation plays down the band's feminism and libertarian left politics.[11] Reviews of Raincoats reissues tend to pay lip service to the band's politics too.[12] As will become clear, such portrayals are even more debatable than Street Howe's portrayal of The Slits.

Not all retrospective writing slots the two bands into a post-feminist narrative. There has been much attention devoted to the potentially feminist qualities of The Slits' and The Raincoats' formal innovations.[13] Feminist sociological studies of women in the popular music industry, too, have focused on The Slits and The Raincoats.[14] As yet, though, there has been no account that explicitly aims to bridge this disciplinary division.

Along with historical contextualisation, this is a key aim of cultural materialism. It is this relationship between cultural production, post-punk as formation and the broader conjuncture that can help us understand why the two bands might be represented as they are today, and how we might question such portrayals.

Sheila Rowbotham has pointed out that Margaret Thatcher's strategic deployments of traditional images of femininity were a central aspect in securing electoral consent for her government's reforms, thus tying them to a New Right vision of freedom and pleasure: 'Utopia had lurched dramatically to the right and Hayek's neo-liberal economics had transmogrified into British housewifery and a new common sense.'[15] How did the women's movement respond to this situation?

In *Is The Future Female?* Lynne Segal noted the dominance by the early 1980s of an essentialist, often puritanical and separatist tendency within the movement. In its retreat to the personal elements of feminist politics, this tendency could also tend to neglect consideration of the interrelation of patriarchal and capitalist inequality, or reduce the latter to the former. Segal recognised that broader determinations had contributed to this shift, noting that the fall-back on personal politics was reflective of leftist pessimism in the face of the New Right[16] and that fear and suspicion regarding the implication of pleasure in inequality and violence echoed New Right sexual moralism.[17] Nevertheless, she has remained ruefully critical of this tendency's limitations, observing the problems created from the prescriptive inversion of '"the personal is political" into "the political is personal" and "the personal is sexual"'. Where once the women's movement had freed women from self-loathing by showing them that problems they may have considered the result of their own failings were social in origin, 'it now served more to induce personal guilt and self-blame, where some feminists felt accused of involvement in "incorrect" sexual and personal relationships'.[18]

As I argued in Chap. 3, this turn was a significant factor in the wariness of many women, otherwise on the left of post-punk, over associating themselves with feminism. This wariness could result, as in the case of The Slits, in a residual countercultural individualism in tension with the dominant direction of the women's movement, with ambiguous political consequences. The Raincoats' greater willingness to declare their feminist allegiances, by contrast, has meant that the band has been tarnished by suggestions of puritanism. Each band's exploration of libertarian left freedoms and pleasures, though, suggests a structure of feeling that built on early women's liberation, offering alternatives to the prevailing feminist divisions of the early 1980s that also possess an urgent contemporary significance.

'It Seemed So Doable'

One of the shared aspects of each band's situation was their involvement in the London punk and post-punk scenes. Both The Slits and The Raincoats were consciously aware of the significance of their sex within this context. Early in their existence, Lucy Toothpaste asked The Slits 'if you couldn't find a girl bassist, would you accept a bloke?' to which they replied, 'No, we're The Slits! It wouldn't matter so much if we'd already been going some time but we want to start off as an all-woman band.'[19] Gina Birch of The Raincoats, meanwhile, recalls that although seeing the Sex Pistols was one of her initial inspirations, it was going to a gig by the all-female Slits which finally swayed her into buying a bass guitar and forming a band: 'When I saw [The Slits] play … it seemed so extraordinary and so … *doable* somehow. Suddenly the possibility was there … and I so wanted to be part of it.'[20]

There were further similarities of habitus, including residual connections with the counterculture. The Slits' singer, Ari Up (real name Ariane Forster), was the daughter of middle-class dissident Nora Forster. Forster was an actor, model and heiress of the German newspaper *Der Spiegel*, who moved to London in the late 1960s and became a promoter of the city's music scene. Her house became a meeting point for psychedelic, progressive and punk rock figureheads, such as Jimi Hendrix, Jon Anderson of Yes and Joe Strummer of The Clash.[21] The influence of Nora's 'free parenting style' meant that the teenage Ari was often more comfortable in such circles than with her own peer group.[22]

The band's guitarist Viv Albertine, by contrast, was working class. She and her sister lived in a council flat in Muswell Hill and were brought up by her mother, who worked as a library assistant and a cleaner, after Albertine's abusive father left the family early in her childhood.[23] A full eight years older than Ari Up, who was only fourteen when The Slits formed in 1976, Albertine bonded with the singer through a comparable immersion in the counterculture. London's patchwork geography of class fractions played a strong part in this; in one of the many present-tense vignettes of Albertine's brilliant recent memoir *Clothes Music Boys*, she claims her North London school friends 'come from shabby, bohemian stripped-pine furniture houses with Che Guevara posters on the walls; their parents are communists, artists and intellectuals'.[24] Attending the progressive scout organisation the Woodcraft Folk in the late 1960s, Albertine evokes an 'arty, bohemian vibe ... living ... close to nature', which was also 'educational about global poverty, conflict and the peace movement'.[25] The teenage Albertine was devoted to countercultural rock, ranging from cult figures like Captain Beefheart to the chart topping glam of T Rex.[26]

Albertine's attraction was based not only on the culturalist dissidence of the counterculture, but on what she perceived as its humanistic egalitarianism, which she considers to have been continuous with punk.[27] Evoking The Fall and the Blue Orchids, Albertine also notes the way it acted as a conduit to cultural and political knowledge:

> The music I was exposed to was revolutionary and because I grew up with music that was trying to change the world, that's what I still expect from it.... Songs ... made us interested in politics; they were history lessons in a palatable, exciting form. We demonstrated against the Vietnam and Korean wars, discussed sexual liberation ... and read books by Timothy Leary, Hubert Selby Jr and Marshall McLuhan because we'd heard all these people referred to in songs and interviews.[28]

In part, Albertine owed her anti-culturalist critique to the counterculture too. She traces the punk shock tactics of her art school work, aimed at sweeping away 'preconceptions' and cutting through 'habits and learnt behaviour', to 'the sixties: hippies and yippies used it a lot'. Art school provided her with further historical precedent, with lessons on surrealism and Dada.[29] Counteracting the prevalent elision of higher education with being middle class in post-punk discourse, Albertine notes the mixed-class background of Hornsey: 'It's OK to be poor here.'[30] The guitar style that Albertine developed reflected this fusion of culturalism and anti-culturalism. Recalling being sat in her squat, learning to play, she claims both that 'I want to develop a distinct personality' and that 'I need to be sure that I am conveying the right message with my instrument'.[31]

Bassist Tessa Pollitt, too, was drawn to the tradition of artistic dissidence from childhood, revealing that her grandfather had worked as a restorer for the Pre-Raphaelite painter Holman Hunt.[32] The band's first drummer, Paloma Romero (known as Palmolive), had experience of the counterculture in simultaneously culturalist and politically oppositional terms. Described as 'a restless soul, bright and independent', she fled Francoist Spain at 17 to live in a succession of 'mouldy hippy squats' in London.[33]

Palmolive also contributed this sensibility to The Raincoats, on whose first album she played drums, and the rest of the band had similar experience; guitarist Ana da Silva was a poet with 'a thesis on Dylan under her belt'[34] and a faith in the transformative power of music,[35] whilst Gina Birch recalls that while living in a squat in Ladbroke Grove, 'we all used the Tea Room, which was a kind of local cafe and food co-op ... The punks and the hippies really joined at this point and in some ways the DIY ethic chimed with many of the hippie ideals.'[36] Like Albertine, Birch had studied at Hornsey College of Art, aforementioned site of student revolt in 1968. Whereas Albertine's anti-culturalism was rooted in countercultural rebellion and the European avant-garde, Birch had been involved with Art and Language since her foundation degree in her home city of Nottingham.[37] This meant that, like Gang of Four, Birch was also possessed of an explicitly politicised impulse to demystification. It was, however, tempered by da Silva's more 'elliptical and poetic' leanings.[38]

Birch's stance was also complemented by the approach of another key figure within the band, Vicki Aspinall. Aspinall was directly involved in the women's movement and had previously played in the feminist avant-garde band Jam Today, which shared the libertarian left politics of early women's liberation.[39] She brought not only a consciousness of socialist feminism to The Raincoats, but also, as Mavis Bayton has argued, the focus on direct democracy of the women's movement and a 'questioning of established norms and conventions'. This extended as far as the band's approach to musical production,[40] thus linking politics and form as with many leftist post-punks.

It was this balance of experience within The Raincoats that shaped the band's distinctive politics. It was also what distinguished them from The Slits. Though The Slits shared the anti-culturalist tendencies common to post-punk—'we spend hours talking about our look, our stance on all sorts of subjects, from feminism to what is good and bad in music', Albertine recalls of the early days of the band[41]—these tendencies had been encountered in a manner less explicitly connected to leftist involvement. In the context of the rise of neoliberalism and the puritanical turn of the women's movement, this could have consequences that are difficult to finally interpret, providing inadvertent material for Street Howe's post-feminist agenda. The band's simultaneously oppositional sensibilities, informed by countercultural anti-consumerism, mysticism and respect for the natural world, tend to undermine such interpretations, however.

'WE ARE FEMINISTS IN A WAY'

The Slits' culturalist investment in post-punk had a profound influence on their attitude towards women and freedom. Their cultural production counteracted not only stereotypes of passive femininity with the imperative to rebellious creative activity, but also hinted at the possibility of a world beyond the limitations of gender in its promotion of transformative self-fulfilment. Palmolive's claim in an interview with *Jolt* summarises such implications: 'we are feminists in a way—we don't want to tell anyone how to act, we just want to show them what we're doing, what girls can do'.[42]

Their avoidance of didacticism, however, foregrounds the band's individualist leanings and highlights some of the ambiguities of their outlook. To begin with, there was a reluctance to commit to any collective movement out of the perceived threat to individual freedom that this posed. Ari Up has claimed that 'I'm not into anything that has an "-ism", because right away that gets into rules ... you lose yourself in a movement'.[43] Albertine doubted being in an all-girl band at first as 'gimmicky and tokenistic' because 'I read a lot about feminism and I'm a feminist, apply it to everything I do, but I don't want to be labelled in any way'.[44] It should be noted, though, that both statements are retrospective.

With the weakening of feminism as a collective movement in the three decades since The Slits were first active, the band's contemporary disassociation from women's liberation has been presented by Street Howe as an astutely liberating move. For Street Howe, freedom is defined as the freedom to succeed in the popular music marketplace: 'If only they had a pound for every assumption they must have been militant, bra-burning feminists ... this form of "acceptance" was often a barrier of its own kind ... and left The Slits ... struggling to shake off any association with feminism in its more political, militant sense.' For Street Howe, this was an association that 'wasn't going to do them any favours'.[45] At this point, it is worth turning to an analysis of one of the band's best-known songs, their debut single 'Typical Girls', to assess whether such judgements stand up.

'Typical Girls' begins quietly at a slow tempo, with an aimless-sounding guitar melody and a rhythm section accompaniment suggestive of plodding, tedious movement which was likely to have been initially bewildering for those used to The Slits' noise and speed-driven live performances of their early punk era songs. The function of the introduction soon becomes clear, however: it reinforces the first two lines' ironic instruction not to 'create' or 'rebel'. Ari Up delivers these lines wearily and languidly, thus associating 'typical girls' with passivity and conformity. The phrase 'can't decide' further helps explain the aforementioned aimlessness. The dub echo effect placed on it, however, draws attention to the concurrent and sudden change of tempo, rhythm and melody, immediately suggesting that the bands are atypical in their decisiveness. The up-tempo nature of the shift also conveys activity rather than passivity. Furthermore, in contrast to Ari Up's claim that typical girls are predictable, the structure of the song is unpredictable, alternating in a jittery manner between three different motifs rather than a standard verse/chorus structure.

The song's framing of gender and freedom indicates that there is a value to non-conformity in the face of dominant gendered expectations and behaviour; stresses activity in contrast to passive constructions of femininity; and consciously incorporates unpredictability into musical form, reclaiming it as disruptive agency rather than an inescapable biological limitation. The opposition to 'typical girls' does tend to affirm the role of outsider individual for women, rather than a more collectivist libertarianism. There is the potential here for an interpretation that sees any individualist activity on the part of women as positive, as in the case of Street Howe's advocacy of the band for their lack of association with the women's movement.

However, the song's reference to young women's anxieties over body image and 'natural smells' suggests a simultaneous celebration of 'natural femininity', a theme I go on to explore in more detail when considering the band in relation to new sensibilities. Ari Up, looking back, reflects that: '"Typical Girls" was … a satire. We're so not typical … but in the end there's a twist. Yes, we *are* really typical girls, but not by the standards of society, the magazines, the fashion industry … the music industry.'[46] Interestingly, this belief in natural femininity was fairly close to the growing essentialism of the women's movement at the time the song was released.

Furthermore, the line 'just another marketing ploy' displays the influence of a more socialist strand of the women's movement in its recognition that limiting social constructions of typical girls can often be traced to the profit motive. The tone is also playful, counteracting the possibility of its themes being rejected on the basis of being too serious, as the women's movement risked at this time. The mood is created not only in Ari Up's yodelling, ironic delivery but also through a bouncing bass part and capering piano triplets strongly influenced by reggae rhythms. Given the sexism prevalent amongst certain reggae artists, including high profile and otherwise progressive figures such as Bob Marley (who allegedly removed a reference to The Slits in his song 'Punky Reggae Party' upon discovering they were women)[47] and the 'apocalyptic', 'evangelical' sensibility of the Rastafarianism which sometimes informed the genre,[48] The Slits' irreverent use of its formal features to affirm the song's themes is an entertaining, appropriative move.

'A Feminist? Why the Hell Would I Not Be?'

The Raincoats had a similarly conflicted, but overall far more committed, stance regarding feminism and the women's movement. Unlike The Slits, they gave their official support to the grassroots Rock Against Sexism (RAS) organisation. RAS was set up in response to the success of Rock Against Racism and supported by a coalition of leftist post-punk bands like Gang of Four and This Heat, anarcho-punks such as Crass and Poison Girls and the protest rock of Tom Robinson. The Raincoats' support was not without reservations, however: in an interview with feminist post-punk fanzine *Brass Lip*, Palmolive was clear that 'we didn't agree with the bureaucracy of the organisation'. This was not an opposition to collective political action per se, as with The Slits, but a libertarian left concern regarding democracy. Aspinall claimed: 'the way you organise is very important … they're not very open to suggestions. It's very difficult to work with them if you disagree.'[49]

As the only member of The Raincoats directly involved with the women's movement, Aspinall was less concerned about anxieties regarding a potential conflict of personal freedom and feminist politics. In an *NME* feature on 'Women in Rock', which interviewed numerous female post-punk bands, Barbara Gogan of The Passions expressed her anger that many women musicians were afraid of being labelled a feminist. Aspinall responded: 'which is why I think it's very important that we should come out and talk more strongly about it'.[50] There was, however, an internal tension on this matter. Gina Birch remembers that:

> Vicky … had been involved in feminist politics, which was a whole different world to us. We were more grounded in art, language and philosophy … this whole other agenda was forced upon us, the idea that politics couldn't be ignored. Once the feminist word got out of the bag we were asked about it all the time … I'm quite proud of what we did. But at that time there was such a dreary aspect to feminism … what exactly were you *allowed* to do?[51]

Due to The Raincoats' respect for internal democracy, though, these differences of emphasis often had a highly productive effect on the band's output rather than remaining an unresolved source of conflict. One such instance was 'Baby Song' from *Odyshape*, the topic of which is worth contextualising. Caroline Coon perceptively notes that it was not just tabloid demonisation of the women's movement that contributed to a suspicion on the part of women involved in punk's fallout, but also 'broadsheet feminism … ghettoised on *The Guardian*'s women's pages'. Coon characterised the position of such writing as 'generally an essentialist, mother … female goddess "respectable" feminism … it was not … attractive to young women who were yet to have children'.[52]

Yet what the band managed with 'Baby Song' was to incorporate the topic of motherhood for consideration within a post-punk framework. Positing it as a role that could be reclaimed as a tool of freedom, the song shares The Slits' concern with the limiting expectations of conventional femininity. The understanding of freedom displayed in the song's lyrics, however, differs from the individualism of 'Typical Girls'. The evocation of limits being broken not only subtly evokes childbirth through the word 'stretch', but also suggests a conception of agency strongly redolent of humanistic socialism: a belief in individual intention within given circumstances.

Indeed, the power of hegemonic constructions of motherhood as biological destiny and duty is not underestimated; the singer expresses uncertainty about the risks of attempting to reclaim the role, wondering about this in a subdued, muttering style. The unease is supplemented by the choppy, nagging tone and rhythm of Aspinall's guitar line. The sense of exploring a possibility whilst being subject to limitations is also represented at a musical level, given that Aspinall was not a trained guitarist and played the instrument on 'Baby Song' as part of the band's policy of swapping musical roles for democratic reasons[53] and to stimulate innovation.[54]

It is not only the song's presentation of agency which differs from The Slits, but also its understanding of the concept in directly political terms. Where 'Typical Girls' can be read as suggesting individual freedom for women, 'Baby Song' conveys a more collectivist libertarianism. The singer experiences pregnancy as personal liberation, her body beating to 'new rhythms', while the autonomy of women is stressed by the fact that in a song concerning pregnancy, childbirth and motherhood, there is no mention of men. However, she also acknowledges motherhood in terms of nurturing and the way this difficult but valuable work is often taken for granted. In this, the song also goes beyond the essentialist feminism concurrent with it by emphasising motherhood as potentially progressive not because it is feminine, but because it offers the possibility of fulfilment through the nurture of others, a value neglected by the Thatcherite rhetoric of self-advancement. Such fulfilment is also expressed in 'Baby Song's' music; while not as overtly playful as 'Typical Girls', the fraught guitar and hesitant vocals of the verses, which carry the ideological possibility of being interpreted as joyless in line with their feminist preoccupations, are counteracted by the pleasurable melody of the chorus, the lyrics of which emphasise the theme of mutual warmth in their entreaty for intimacy.

Satisfying Empty Feelings

As we saw earlier, The Slits' rejection of conventional femininity went beyond the individualism projected onto them by Street Howe. Though the band avoided specific allegiance, the fact that they played a benefit for Communist newspaper the *Morning Star*[55] and developed friendships and relationships with The Pop Group would seem to confirm a general leftist slant. The band's lyrics, for instance, showed a clear recognition of the vested economic interests behind the attempts of the marketing industry to reproduce women's desire for the attainment of conventional femininity through consumption. Furthermore, songs like 'Spend, Spend, Spend' demonstrated a critical awareness of the dominant association between consumerism and femininity on the basis of the supposed superficiality of both, in its narrator's admission of their desire for something 'new' and 'trivial'.

Instead of reinforcing portrayals of women as shallow, however, 'Spend, Spend, Spend' repeatedly suggests that its narrator is compulsively searching for pleasure and a deep sense of fulfilment through shopping due to an absence of such fulfilment in other areas of her life. The title references the much-publicised pools-winner Viv Nicholson, whose rapid exhaustion of her fortune and subsequent downward spiral became the subject of a BBC play in 1977. Each verse of the song focuses on aspects of the problem at hand. In the first verse, the narrator reflects on her dysfunctional relationship, while in the second, she yearns for a sense of domestic community. In the third verse, the theme is the exhaustion and lack of joy of the narrator's job and its dehumanising effect on her behaviour. This is complemented musically; the lyrics of the verse melody consistently follow awkward patterns of phrasing in relation to the rhythms of the guitar, bass and drum parts, suggesting the sensation of disjunction, alienation and inability to connect with others that characterises the lyrical themes of the verses. The sensation is reinforced still further by the spaced-out production and a scratchy, brittle guitar timbre strongly connotative of a scarcity of the warmth usually associated with mutually nurturing human connection.

Reynolds and Press note that 'even the language of [the narrator's] inner life has been colonised by advertising: shopping, she says, offers "a new improved remedy" for her angst'.[56] Furthermore, the melody of this line is the only one of the song that sounds positive rather than melancholy or desperate. Its positivity, however, sounds deliberately unconvincing and faintly absurd in a manner that is suggestive of advertising jingles. On its first appearance, this parody is deliberately exaggerated by Ari Up's warbling delivery, whilst on the second, a heavy dub-style echo is placed on the vocal, further compounding the effect with a sense of distance and space evocative of the narrator's alienation and the disconnect between her desire and the means through which she attempts to satisfy it.

'Spend, Spend, Spend' thus differs from 'Typical Girls' in its suggestion that personal fulfilment should be more than a matter of individual freedom, also requiring a mutuality which is choked by alienated labour and insufficiently compensated for with a consumer culture that reproduces limiting and insulting definitions of femininity. Additionally, the implication of the narrator in consumerist desire is signalled through a dialogue with the backing vocals, which sound a cautioning note. The song thus recalls Gang of Four's exploration of 'false consciousness in rebellion against itself', though it adds a more fully social, and optimistic, dimension of critique by featuring different and dissident voices.

'ODYSHAPE'

Curiously for a band considered so close to the Rough Trade ethos, The Raincoats rarely connected their feminist politics with broader leftist themes overtly in their cultural production beyond their democratic intra-band collectivism. Nor did they foreground such beliefs frequently in the media at the time, with Birch's description of Thatcher as a 'battleaxe'[57] and da Silva's view that 'it's necessary to boycott those powers that have money as the main reason for their actions'[58] dating from more recent interviews. Members of the band have often recalled that a shared shyness and cautiousness marked their public engagement. This also had consequences for the band's negotiation of the music industry, and on the terrain of politics, it led Dave McCullough to fulminate when reviewing their debut album:

> Why the half-hearted promotion of the politics? Bands like the Raincoats, whether they're Marxist-motivated, feminist-motivated or Sooty-motivated always seem to HIDE the exact nature of their attitudes ... What's wrong, for God's sake? Are you FRIGHTENED of saying what you are and who you are? Or is it confidence you lack?[59]

In the same review, McCullough contradictorily accuses the band of overplaying political themes, which according to him deprives their music of 'love'. Such an irrationally aggressive reaction to The Raincoats' cultural production from journalists like McCullough may well have been a key explanation for their hesitant approach. As women who explicitly raised political themes, they were damned by McCullough from two angles. Firstly, engaging in 'politics' dominantly understood as disinterested and rational meant that they could be presented as unnaturally rejecting a realm of emotions (or 'love') which is typically gendered feminine, and were thus incapable of making pleasurable music. Secondly, their engagement could be presented as a failure in other ways related to their sex, with the suggestion that their output was unclear and timid evoking sexist understandings of women as prevaricating and passive. These objections came from the same journalist who celebrated the work of the all-male Scritti Politti and seemed overawed in interviews with them by the band's ability to ruthlessly interrogate the practices of rock.

The Raincoats, however, were not entirely dissuaded by such reception, with the song 'Odyshape' from their second album of the same name covering similar ground to The Slits in its concern with women and consumerism. The song begins with lines that associate a woman's embarrassed reaction to her reflection with reading a magazine. Thus, it establishes its focus on the negative body image and low self-esteem inculcated in women in order to motivate continual consumer spending on products and services that promise to rectify these anxieties.

As with 'Baby Song', these lines demonstrate a humanistic understanding of how our actions are determined, expressed through their play on the word 'looks' regarding agency and perspective: the subject of the song 'looks' in magazines, suggesting that active input and consent is necessary in order for constructions of femininity to be taken on board. This allows for the possibility that such constructions may be rejected. It's a possibility that is given voice when the song's protagonist interrogates the expectations of others and asks whether she is owed an explanation for her predicament. The song avoids underestimating the power of the media, however, by flipping the usage of the word 'looks' between an active, subjective sense—'she looks in mirrors'—and a sense of objective scrutiny—'she looks embarrassed'. These shifts in perspective continue throughout, initially through the adoption of a bitter spoken-word section in the first-person perspective in which the protagonist expresses her insecurities, which is overlaid with sung phrases of third-person observation. The effect of these differing lyrical perspectives is to undermine the false universalism of hegemonic standards of beauty.

Entirely at odds with McCullough's assessment of the band's work, 'Odyshape' is an especially successful fusion of what each of the main members contributed to The Raincoats' collective ethos. Aspinall's political activism is represented in the feminist awareness of the naturalisation of false beauty standards and objectification; the protagonist sees herself as a 'blot' marring the landscape and reflects that she is 'no ornament'. da Silva's culturalism, meanwhile, shows through in the emphasis on emotions and psychological suffering, whilst the conceptualism which Birch inherited from her association with Art and Language is evident in the shifts in perspective and the fact that there is a clear relationship between musical form and lyrical content.

The issue of pleasure unites these emphases on form, politics and emotion. The song points out that images of beauty which are supposed to be fulfilling actually induce misery and, in its description of painfully tight-fitting clothes, that this is a material process. The alternative to such misery, though, lies in the song's music. Its lolloping, expansive bass and shifting tempo and rhythms may evoke the awkward, amorphous and conventionally unattractive 'odyshape'[60] of the woman described in the lyrics, with the twanging guitar and minor key melody conveying her anxiety and sadness. However, they are also possessed of a fragile beauty augmented by the plaintive, empathetic concern with which Birch sings the lines that adopt a second- and third-person perspective on the song's protagonist, laced with the conviction of folk-style ornamentation. The song's influence by emerging 'world music', too, could be read as a celebration of a more diverse and inclusive understanding of physical attractiveness threatened by the narrow, frequently sexist and often unattainable images promoted by the fashion and beauty industries. Doing so alleviates Birch's worry that the 'dreary feminist books' she had read contributed to writing 'some depressing songs'.[61]

'GOD IS RIDDIM AND SO IS THE EARTH GOING ROUND'

Numerous Slits songs from *Cut* investigate the troubled pleasures of gendered identity and male–female relationships, warding off the association with puritanical sobriety that this topic threatened to provoke through the playful humour that they shared with 'Typical Girls'. 'So Tough' mocks the machismo of certain manifestations of the punk fallout and interrogates the desires for money and girls of the male figure that is its target. It also contains joyful, wordless rhythmic yells, the repeated imperative to avoid seriousness and comical rhymes like 'star/wunderbar' set to a skipping beat and careening bassline. 'Love Und Romance', meanwhile, opens with Ari Up's potentially sanctimonious declaration that 'Babylon lovers are Babylon-lovers', fusing a critique of conventional femininity to a broader politics of culturalist anti-capitalism with hints of Rastafarianism. Any risk of overzealousness, however, is defused by the wry intonation of the final 'lovers'; the breathless, ironic embrace of overly possessive relationships ('who wants to be free?'); along with the adoption of a giggling, infantilised style when Ari Up adopts the perspective of the woman trapped in such a relationship and the gleeful backing shouts of the rest of the band on the final lines of the chorus.

Unlike Gang of Four, though, the band could not sustain a sense of pleasure that derived only from critique. Interestingly, The Slits' disavowal of conscious association with the women's movement did not extend to a related rejection of considering a politics of the senses. The way the band eventually negotiated this issue was comparable to the Blue Orchids, perhaps because of their similarly autodidactic approach to social critique. As Reynolds and Press have succinctly observed, 'The Slits were ... strung out on the tensions between revolt ... and the longing for a holistic, grounded way of life. Their aesthetic veered from demystification to mysticism.'[62] They go on to summarise the sensibility that began to take shape in the ranks of the band:

> The Slits' ... trajectory took them through demystification of the feminine towards a more affirmative politics of the body and a return to a less alienated ... way of life. And this shift to an investment in nature was matched by an almost mystical belief in 'natural rhythm': the undulating grooves of reggae, funk and African music were seen as less forced, less masculine than rock ... They took from Rastafarianism not just bass-heavy rhythms but the idea of a spiritual migration back to the Motherland, an escape from the alienation of 'Babylon' (Western consumer capitalism).[63]

Interviewing Albertine during the period in which this trajectory was developing, *NME* journalist Deanne Pearson reported: 'Viv believes that women are naturally attracted to a more rhythmic, lighter music because they're naturally more balanced and rhythmic than men. Their whole body, in fact, is geared to a monthly cycle.'[64] Meanwhile, on the terrain of rhythm, race and gender, Ari Up described the cover of *Cut* to Reynolds in the following manner: 'We just decided "let's cover ourselves in the mud, be naked but *natural*. Ruin that image that females need to be sexy by dressing sexy" … naked, without being pornographic.' This attitude was linked to 'that reggae tribal aspect'.[65] Furthermore, the band's image shifted emphasis from a punk bricolage style to elements taken from Rastafarian and traditional African dress.

When it came to the desire for human connection as against alienation, Ari Up referred to the black wife of her stepfather: 'The white women hanging around my mum were posh and very uptight around kids. My mum wasn't very warm either … When Jenny came, it was the first time I had warmth of feeling. She gave me a big impression, subconsciously, of the African side of things.'[66] Thus was a counterpoint to individualism instilled in the band's outlook. The lyrics of 'Difficult Fun', from second album *Return of the Giant Slits*, reflected searchingly that oppositional pleasures were 'hard to find'.

An unsympathetic reading of such an outlook might go as follows. It was not only that The Slits seemed to have been loosely influenced by the growing turn towards essentialism and irrationalist mysticism among one faction of the women's movement at this time, a tendency that coalesced around the anti-nuclear peace camp at Greenham Common which has been persuasively and sensitively critiqued by Kate Soper.[67] It was also that the desire for a simple life unmarked by alienation was linked with both black people and black music, risking the reproduction of understandings of blackness as primitive and presenting musical styles developed historically by predominantly black cultural formations as essentially bound to race. These takes on femininity and race were often articulated together, giving the impression of some natural connection between black people and women based on a shared closeness to nature and tendency to nurture. Reynolds notes this dual articulation in his observation that '*Cut*'s cover [on which the band posed as naked, mud-covered Amazons] echoes the photo of the Mud People of Papua New Guinea on the front of *Y*, the debut album by The Pop Group, who also flirted with the 'idealisation of noble savagery'.[68]

Little of this went unnoted amongst well-read music press writers keen to make their names with provocative critique. Ian Penman, for example, wrote a profoundly spiteful review of the 1980 single 'In The Beginning There Was Rhythm', the first instance of The Slits' cultural production which conveyed this new oppositional formulation of fulfilment: 'Naiveté ... lofty effusions ... Oh, they *mean it*, mon [sic].' Penman went on to accuse the band of 'bullshitting, imitating West Indian religions and patois ... and generally being a precious, artsy fartsy pain in the pants'.[69] A post-structuralist-indebted anti-essentialism framed his insults. The exaggerated hostility, though, and Penman's introduction of competition with the suggestion that the band had no right to even exist when others like Scritti Politti had done their 'political homework', were suggestive of the move away from solidarity towards the aspirational stance of new pop that such theoretical loyalties would later facilitate for Penman and others. More recently, Reynolds' description of The Slits 'drift[ing] along' and 'submitting to a ... mystic pantheism'[70] suggests a lack of empathy with their apparent naiveté that is a slightly more tolerant version of Penman's scorn.

The scrutiny of these writers, though, is somewhat lofty and patronising itself, and is counteracted by analysis of the song at hand. What is interesting about 'In The Beginning There Was Rhythm' in this context is that its lyrics never refer to women or feminine attributes being more in tune with the mystical notion of rhythm it proposes. Indeed, its mystic monism would seem to transcend gender dualism. There is a potential ambiguity in terms of race, given that musically the song is made up of elements of funk, dub, hip-hop and Jamaican Rasta patois, perhaps implying that these styles are naturally appropriate means of conveying its lyrical themes. However, the song's fusion of diverse genres and the fact that the music is played by an all-white, mixed sex band[71] tend to work against an essentialist interpretation.

The Slits' new sensibility, however, was not notable simply because it was not essentialist. The ecological implications of a respect for nature ('Earthbeat' anxiously imagined the clouds 'coughing' over thunderous, elemental percussion); the dissident culturalism of a mystical elevation of musical rhythm; the search for gender equality; and the highlighting of ways of life elsewhere in the world which were not focused on overproduction and overconsumption ('Walkabout' humorously but earnestly celebrated tribal cultures whose diet did not include 'frozen peas') connected quite directly with a broader structure of feeling on the libertarian left at this time.

There was a Marcusean precedent here: discussing the women's movement, Marcuse pointed out that the sexist attribution of 'tenderness' and 'sensuousness' to femininity possessed a dialectical possibility of radicalism in its preservation of such human qualities in the face of the utilitarian brutality of capitalism.[72] Such links to libertarian left thought are also made by the indie singer songwriter Momus in the following recollection, indicating that the band were quite rightly not simply interpreted as credulous primitivists:

> The exotic warmth of [the band's second album *Return of the Giant Slits*] was important to me in the Aberdeen winter of 1981. I remember listening to it on Baker Street, sharing a flat with my communist friends Babis and Catherine. I made a Matisse-like mural of a reclining, Gaian woman out of cut coloured paper. The room was furnished with books—Ivan Illich on radical education, Erich Fromm's *To Have or To Be*, *How the Other Half Dies* by Susan George, Mary Daly's *Gyn/Ecology*, poetry by Brecht.

Momus also directly relates this to the key institution of the post-punk left, noting that The Slits' 'scatty, quirky, baba-boho radicalism led you … to a core of hip, post-materialist districts … places where people were united in a common left-wing bohemianism … exactly the atmosphere I was to encounter the following year … [in] Rough Trade's Blenheim Place warehouse'.[73]

Furthermore, the band's stance was consciously oppositional, defining itself against the incorporative shift of new pop and its complicity with the dominant structure of feeling of the new decade. 'The eighties went so yuppie', Ari Up remembers. 'It was the cocaine age. But I just literally continued with the earthbeat thing and went into the jungle … trying to find … if there were any spots left on earth that weren't in that Babylon situation.' Though she discovered that such purity did not exist, recalling, for example, 'the Indonesian government coming in to blackmail the tribes or push stuff on them', she was also inspired by aspects of tribal life which emphasised fulfilment through nurture, in ways which could be interpreted as breaking down gendered divisions of labour: 'Tribal men were … carrying the babies … they were very soft and tolerant … when it came to equal emotional support, they [men and women] would both share in child upbringing.'[74]

JOYS AND DESIRES

The Raincoats, too, explored a variety of techniques to convey potential new sensibilities. Ana da Silva, like Una Baines, has referred to the pervasive power of the Catholicism she grew up with, emphasising her rejection of its guilt-inducing attitude: 'Catholicism is so much part of you. It gives you a strong sense about right, wrong, guilt and repression. And trying to come out of that in the strongest possible way you use punk.'[75] Birch, meanwhile, has long recognised the danger of neglecting alternative models of fulfilment from a feminist perspective: 'It wasn't particularly joyful, reading a book on women's position in the world. Sometimes you need to look at all the bad stuff … but then you need to move on from it.'[76]

Yet The Raincoats' avoidance of an overtly sexualised image, the feminist critique of their lyrics and their aforementioned shyness have led to persistent suggestions of puritanism often framed in sexual terms. The band's look, however, was not always 'a strident abstention from glamour', as Reynolds has described it.[77] Birch astutely recognises in such statements the implicit association of the band with the direction of the women's movement at this time. She notes: 'it's been put across as a dowdy feminist thing', recalling some of her more outré outfits in opposition to this portrayal.[78]

The association began in an *NME* piece, which critiqued Rock Against Sexism on the basis of both freedom and pleasure. Presumably referring to the aim of the organisation 'to fight sexism in music and to use music to fight sexism at large',[79] the article characterised rock music as amorally individualistic and sex-focused, framed RAS as censorious, unsexy and overcerebral ('Do You Think I'm Brainy?'), and implied that the organisation wished to place certain elements of rock history off-limits: 'Bo Diddley might preen and roar out for his women to git on with the grits, but I for one ain't giving up that man's music for anybody's cause.'[80] Simon Reynolds and Joy Press take up a similar critique with a specific focus on The Raincoats in *The Sex Revolts*, arguing that 'demystification is The Raincoats' thing' and claiming notably that 'where combat rock like The Clash turns oppression into a self-glamourising drama of Us against Them, The Raincoats focus on more routine forms of immiseration'.[81]

The everyday sexual oppression of women is indeed documented in various Raincoats songs, including two notable examples from their first, self-titled album. 'Off Duty Trip' was based on a court case in which a soldier convicted of raping a woman received a lenient sentence so as to avoid a negative effect on his military career.[82] 'Life On The Line', meanwhile, concerns a woman being stalked. Each emphasises that the incidents they depict are not aberrations, but are bound up with hegemonic attitudes towards women: 'Off Duty Trip' ironically claims that the woman's ignored screams are interpreted by passers-by as 'love's young dream', and that the soldier's overpowering of her is an indication of his desirability. Furthermore, it makes the link between media objectification and sexual violence, describing the woman as 'pinned up on the wall'. 'Life On The Line', meanwhile, suggests that there is no hiding place from its protagonist's sensation of being observed. Musically, too, both songs convey tension, panic and anger at this state of affairs, expressed in the former through the appropriately machine-gun-like rhythm of the drums and an itching guitar riff and in the latter through disorienting shifts of tempo and Aspinall's scraping, Velvet Underground-style violin which accompanies da Silva's repeated exclamation regarding the stalked woman's attempt to escape: 'But she could not!'

While both songs might seem to confirm critiques of the band's supposed suspicion of sex and pleasure more generally, it is worth bearing in mind Lucy Toothpaste's claim that:

> The Raincoats' music is often discordant and rough-edged and this can be off-putting ... I like harmonious, melodious music too, but I get more of a thrill, more of a shock of recognition, when I hear certain quite difficult bands such as The Raincoats ... They give me more of a sense that my own experience is being expressed—my feeling that life is painful, dangerous, exciting and full of contradictions.[83]

In a similar manner to Gang of Four, then, the band's critiques of the sexual oppression of women can be considered a form of sensuous reason. Rational critique of unequal power relations is delivered in a manner inseparable from the visceral emotions produced by the situation it describes; emotions capable of eliciting the pleasure of solidarity that can come from hearing your life experience confirmed and expressed in cultural production.

Just as The Slits' new sensibilities cannot only be defended in negative terms, though, so the same is true of The Raincoats. By the time of their third and last album *Moving*, Birch's anxiety regarding the neglect of pleasure in the feminist work she had been reading was at the forefront of her lyrical concerns. There is a clear effort to break through this deadlock, often specifically in terms of sensual pleasure, which is hinted at in the album's title.

'Ooh Ooh La La' draws directly on early English romanticism, specifically the progressive elements of its sexual politics, encompassing both critique and alternative whilst maintaining a culturalist focus on the emotions and the senses. Its lyrics quote William Blake's 'The Sick Rose' to describe the situation of the 'bitter' and 'denying' girl to whom the song is addressed.[84] Within the context of the song's theme, the connotations of the destructive 'worm' invading the protagonist's 'bed of crimson joy' may seem to suggest a continuation of the band's earlier focus on the sexual violence experienced by women at the hands of men. However, the lyrics also counsel their addressee that 'joy' is also possible. In contrast to the harshness of songs such as 'Off Duty Trip', the music is driven by languid, interlocking rhythms of bass guitar and bongos and overlaid with luxuriant saxophone riffs whose melodies are often anticipated and echoed by both the lyrics and the wordless backing vocals, evoking harmonious, mutual sensual relations.

This turn to pleasure has not gone unnoticed, but has been critically regarded as unsuccessful. Accepting that critique was not the band's sole focus, Reynolds and Press remained dubious in *The Sex Revolts*, referring to the closing song of *Moving*, 'Animal Rhapsody':

> Over a loose and limber shuffling groove, the Raincoats chant phrases like 'get to know your body/get to know your mind'—giving off a pungent whiff of holistic therapy. The joy of unfettered sexuality and natural harmony has seldom seemed less enticing. As with a lot of the demystification bands ... the Raincoats' discovery of desire and the pleasures of the body couldn't escape being rendered dull and worthy by the programmatic nature of their politics.[85]

Reference to the band's 'programmatic' stance frames the issue as one of freedom, implying a connection with the censoriousness of the women's movement at this time. This questionable attribution of an overly didactic stance to The Raincoats is reflected in the misquotation of the song's lyrics: Birch does not instruct listeners to get to know their bodies and minds, but, in the role of the song's narrator, claims that she is attempting such understanding herself. Thus, 'Animal Rhapsody' conveys experience rather than the potential authoritarianism of the imperative mode. Reynolds and Press admittedly draw attention to the notion that sensual pleasure is sometimes bound up with a surrender of ego in the claim that 'attempts to avoid being controlled ... spilled over into an oppressive self-control'.[86] They nevertheless appeal to a supposed realm of unconscious freedom outside of social relations, one in line with the pair's broader interpretation and celebration of rock history as a kind of libertine individualism.

By contrast, 'Animal Rhapsody' can be more productively analysed in the following terms. Discussing the relationship between countercultural non-conformity and libertarian left politics, Marcuse notes: 'Do one's thing, yes, but the time has come to realise that not *any* thing will do ... Individual liberation ... must incorporate the images and values of a future free society ... within the unfree society. For instance, the sexual revolution is no revolution if it does not ... converge with political morality.' He goes on to distinguish between individualist 'self-indulgence' and personal liberation that is simultaneously collectivist and egalitarian in its implications.[87] This distinction is expressed in specifically sexual terms in *One-Dimensional Man*, which argues that sexual freedom has become alienated and 'marketable', obscuring the possibility of an inwardly fulfilling yet outwardly facing eroticism unbound by capitalist functionalism.[88]

This seems a reasonable position, though it risks the excessive pre-scriptivism regarding 'correct' sexual relations that was later to develop in the women's movement. The lyrics to 'Animal Rhapsody', though, never identify specific practices as either acceptable or taboo. The song's occasionally critical, as opposed to affirmative, lines, directed at a presumably male partner, are better interpreted in the context of its empowering feminist stance with regard to sensual pleasure; the singer implicitly refers to a history of female objectification, rejecting it and asserting her right to erotic satisfaction. The perspective, however, is not purely self-centred. In the refrain, a shared sense of sensual pleasure is evoked through the word 'mingling', one which entails direct, as opposed to alienated, connection—a kind that reaches the 'root'—and is conveyed by the song's absorbing, collectively produced rhythmic groove.

The use of 'mingling' also has a further connotation; although 'Animal Rhapsody' stresses the necessity of a sensuous reason through its focus on knowledge and control, it also allows for the temporary abdication of selfhood in sensual pleasure which Reynolds and Press claim the song denies. In addition to the suggestion of two personalities becoming one, the singer also acknowledges that something happens in her brain that

cannot be explained. She teasingly warns her partner that the same surrender is necessary on his part to avoid the premature end of their fun, with a
playful innuendo-laden reference to rockets launching into orbit that miti-
gates any risk of pleasure-killing prohibition. Rather than a sanctimonious
sex manual, then, the song is a joyful, liberating conclusion to the band's
final album. The lukewarm reception of *Moving* in the music press of the
era had far more to do with its timing than its content, as we will see.

'WHEN YOU'RE INTO A THING FOR MONEY…'

The Slits were possessed of a feminist-influenced, anti-culturalist consciousness of the potential of record company exploitation that was continuous
with their punk formation. It meant that the band refrained from signing
a record deal for the first two years of their existence. Albertine recalls that
'the blokes in the record companies are not the sort you would associate
with, totally naff human beings, and there you are trying to deal with
them … we got offered contracts quite early, and we didn't want them'.[89]
Like the Blue Orchids, The Slits also had a culturalist, anti-instrumentalist
understanding of the motivations for their cultural production; reflecting
on the various factors which contributed to the band's break-up in 1982,
Albertine evokes the movement towards new pop and its complicity with
broader political change: 'Things just shifted … Thatcher got in, people
were making music to make money and … The Slits didn't fit in [with]
that.'[90]

The more wayward elements of this culturalism, however, meant that
the band's path through the music industry throughout their six years
of existence was somewhat fraught. The Slits' leanings towards countercultural individualism resulted in them signing to the independent label
Island, based on its association with countercultural rock and reggae.[91]
Island's culture of production, though, was far from the leftist and feminist leanings of Rough Trade. Street Howe's celebration of the label's
'honourable history'[92] sits uncomfortably with her simultaneous docu-
mentation of Island's mistreatment of The Slits in a manner which united
sexist and economic exploitation. Ari Up recalls that the art department
tried to force a record cover on them that would have conventionalised
their image and was 'trashy, fluorescent … with zippers all over it. Like
insinuating that when you open the zipper, there's The Slits.'[93] Albertine,
meanwhile, remembers that 'one of Island's A&R men was trying to get
me chucked out of The Slits … it was back-stabby … [because] … you

didn't kowtow or flutter your eyelids'.[94] After releasing *Cut*, the band left the label following a financially based legal dispute.[95]

As The Slits moved towards a more oppositional ethos of fulfilment, so they signed to Y, a small label set up by Pop Group manager Dick O'Dell after discovering that their previous employers Radar had links to the global arms trade.[96] Y was supported by Rough Trade, and, as hinted at in the earlier quotation from Momus, the structure of feeling embodied in The Slits' post-*Cut* cultural production seemed to complement the world of Rough Trade. For their final album, however, The Slits' negotiation of the music industry changed once more. Sensing the shift to new pop, they signed with US major label CBS, the same company which had famously exploited The Clash. Yet unlike other new pop groups, the band's strategy did not combine attempts at greater musical 'accessibility' with major label backing. In fact, the reverse was true: much of *Return of the Giant Slits* was far more experimental and less melodically oriented than their previous work, coinciding with band members' discovery of avant-garde jazz and African music. As Simon Reynolds has noted, the album 'fell into a hostile marketplace',[97] and Ari Up's claim that 'it was underpromoted … CBS were using us as a tax write-off and they stuck us on the shelf'[98] sadly comes as little surprise.

'COSY CAMDEN LOCK SWEATERS'

The Raincoats shared the same anti-instrumentalist attitude of The Slits regarding the music industry, with da Silva recalling that 'there was no thought of career … it was purely for the sake of just doing it'.[99] By contrast though, the band remained signed to Rough Trade throughout the post-punk era. In many ways, they came to epitomise its ideals, engaging in co-operative collaboration with other bands signed to the label in Rough Trade 'super-group' The Red Crayola. Band members also contributed to Geoff Travis' anti-culturalist aim of breaking down barriers between 'artists' and staff by working shifts in the label's record shop and warehouse. This association became even more prominent once Green Gartside adopted a new pop strategy, leaving The Raincoats as Rough Trade's standard-bearers; Birch remembers 'we were absolutely shocked when one day it was announced that Green was going to be the leader of Scritti Politti, that it was no longer a democracy'.[100]

The affinity between band and label, though, meant that The Raincoats' fate was bound up with that of the first phase of Rough Trade. As new pop eclipsed the label's oppositional leftism, so the music press began to present The Raincoats as marginal. In a comment that was as revealing of changes in the broader political landscape as it was about those in British popular music, *Melody Maker* journalist Ian Pye claimed in 1982 that 'they find themselves the reluctant ... mouthpiece for "women in rock music" ... there appears to be a notable lack of volunteers willing to run the media's gauntlet of potentially damning brands that threaten to stamp the protagonist with ... passé IDs like "feminist" [and] "liberationist".'[101]

Such media manoeuvres were consciously gendered. They elided the band's avoidance of conventionally feminine pop style with the supposed joylessness of the Rough Trade milieu: Pye asserted that 'the grass roots worthiness of their image probably hasn't been helped by their long running association with Rough Trade'.[102] Steve Sutherland, who had subtly taken the knife to the Blue Orchids, was more openly scathing in his review of *Moving*. Sutherland drew on a similar rhetoric to Mark E. Smith in his implication that The Raincoats were representative not only of the supposedly outmoded stance of Rough Trade, but also of a complacent, insular and worthy leftist middle-class fraction. His comments, too, featured a gendered focus on dress and style in order to convey the point:

> All was splendidly healthy and right-thinking [then] ... Duran Duran shifted the centre of the universe ... but the Raincoats stayed put and came to be seen as the archetypal *Observer* colour supplement band in their cosy Camden Lock sweaters ... what once seemed ripe to change the world never even grasped the importance of changing a hairstyle.[103]

There is one further gendered link between The Raincoats and the new pop's critique of Rough Trade. This was the band's lack of assertion in response to media scrutiny of their status as politicised female musicians. In Pye's interview, for example, the band's awkwardness—'Gina shifts and squirms'—is noted alongside the more overtly political reasons for them being unfashionable in a new pop climate. Such hesitance became bound up with Rough Trade's gradual shift from oppositional populism—its attempt to directly challenge the operations of major labels—to its passive acceptance of marginal culturalist dissidence, as noted in Chap. 3.

The Raincoats, too, began to internalise this self-consciously marginal position, as Gartside had feared would be the fate of Scritti Politti if they did not change tack.[104] Birch recalls that '[we were] pretty cut off from the mainstream. I think I despised anything that wasn't what I was doing, because what I was doing was a revolution ... we were on a mission and what was going on outside was really just irrelevant.'[105] When the band covered the Sly Stone song 'Running Away', Birch made clear that it was not 'a desperate bid to break into the charts'. In the same interview, da Silva guardedly claimed that they would consider playing Top of the Pops 'not because we like the show, but to reach more people'. This, though, was a rare display of interest in populism. The Raincoats' attitude set them apart from bands like The Fall and the Blue Orchids, who remained on Rough Trade whilst espousing a different approach to populism to that of new pop. Although Pye tried half-heartedly to promote the band ('why not try them out?'), the title of his interview—'An Old Raincoat'—could not have done them any favours.[106] By the time of Graham Lock's lone celebration of the 'delights' of *Moving* as 'a splendid swansong ... sensuous music ... spiced with a feminist perspective',[107] it was already too late.

Although media reception ranging from the uncertain to the downright hostile was not the most immediate cause of The Raincoats' break-up (which occurred before *Moving* was released), it probably contributed to the sense of doubt that led Birch and Aspinall into pursuing a late new pop direction from 1985. The pair formed a new band, Dorothy, and signed to Geoff Travis' major label-supported subsidiary Blue Guitar.[108] Despite The Raincoats' successful attempt to explore oppositional pleasures on their final album, Birch continued to be unsure about the 'dowdy' portrayal of the band. As with Green Gartside, it was an interest in post-structuralism that contributed to the seductiveness of the new pop strategy, this time with direct reference to gender. In interview with Simon Reynolds, Birch recalled:

> I just thought [Cindy Sherman's] photographs were fantastic ... Judith Williamson had written a fantastic article on Sherman's work in *Screen* ... I really liked the fact that you could put on this item of clothing and throw off your personal shackles—all the kind of introspection that went into lyrics like 'she looks embarrassed' on *Odyshape* ... it was very liberating to be, you know, a sex kitten if you felt like it.[109]

Williamson had argued of Sherman's images that: '"Essentially feminine" as they all are, they are all different. This not only rules out the idea that any one of them *is* the "essentially feminine", but also shows, since each *seems* to be it, that there can be no such thing.'[110] In this perspective, there was no possibility of a liberating move beyond gender distinctions as hoped for in the early stages of the women's movement, only an endless 'playful' postmodern questioning of the authenticity of femininity. In terms of pleasure, Williamson implicitly suggested that those who objected to Sherman's work on the basis of its perceived sexism were puritanical, using the pejoratively loaded phrase 'Right On' to describe a man at a gallery discussion who made such a critique. She went on to claim that the man's discomfort arose from the realisation that his own desires were implicated in conventional constructions of femininity. What she did not openly acknowledge was that her celebration of Sherman's photography might have had something to do with her own pleasurable investment in such constructions.[111]

This structure of feeling was present in Dorothy's first single 'Loving Feeling', which drew on a camp sensibility implicit in the band's *Wizard of Oz*-referencing name to convey its ironic pastiche of feminine glamour. The song featured lyrics such as 'I'll wear my best new dress' delivered in a coy, girlish manner, accompanied by music reminiscent of concurrent singles by Madonna, who was also toying ambiguously with stereotypes. Madonna declared of the cover to *Like A Virgin* that 'people were thinking who was I pretending to be—the Virgin Mary or the whore? ... I wanted to play with them. I wanted to see if I can merge them together ... the photo was a statement of independence, if you wanna be a virgin, you are welcome. But if you wanna be a whore, it's your fucking right to be so.'[112]

The video for 'Loving Feeling', directed by Birch, featured herself and Aspinall in evening gowns, sequinned gloves and elegant tailoring, driving an open-topped car in front of obviously superimposed backdrops, with vogueing, eyebrow-raising and knowing winks galore. 'Loving Feeling' is undeniably sophisticated fun. Yet its simultaneous gentle mockery of and desire for all the off-the-shelf clichés of femininity and heteronormative romance, like Madonna's pseudo-empowering assertion of women's right to take apparent control of the limiting roles forced upon them, is far from the oppositional pleasures of *Moving*.

It was also a sensibility that went hand-in-hand with the undermining of The Raincoats' commitment to making music for its own sake, rather than being subordinated to success defined in commercial terms. With hindsight, Birch claims of Dorothy that 'I turned the screw in my own destruction'. She refers to the 'nightmare' of becoming 'consumed' by the idea of selling records[113] and recognises that a prior ethos of co-operation was replaced by one of marketplace jostling: 'There was this group, a model and a make-up artist or something, and I remember feeling very competitive with them. There wasn't room for both of us.'[114]

DIFFICULT FUN

After the break-up of The Slits in 1982 and Ari Up's temporary relocations to the jungles of Borneo and Belize, the singer settled in Jamaica and became involved in the dancehall music scene, an emergent development of reggae. Its individualism and frequent promotion of conspicuous consumerism, homophobic machismo and the objectification of women were bound up with the island's political shift from the government of the left social democratic People's National Party to that of the Jamaica Labour Party, which initiated the movement towards neoliberalism that has continued to the present.[115] Simon Reynolds has attempted to establish a progressive continuity between the outlook of The Slits and Ari Up's reinvention of herself as the dancehall artist Madussa, noting in interview that 'it brought you back to the original Slits spirit. Rasta's idea of proper womanhood is submissive' to which Ari Up responded, 'and the dancehall idea of a woman is she don't take no shit!'[116]

Reynolds' and Ari Up's connection between dancehall and 'the original Slits spirit' is partly accurate. A YouTube search for 'Madussa' brings up a video from 1996, posted after the singer's untimely death from cancer in 2010: it features Ari Up at a dancehall festival 'shocking out' by allowing various men to simulate violent sex with her in front of a large audience.[117] There is a kind of continuity here between the early individualism promoted by The Slits and the strategies of post-feminism, whereby gender roles remain unchallenged, but power relations are apparently shifted by women's supposed 'ownership' of such roles, a logic whose alienating implications reveal the determining pressures of neoliberalism upon it. Yet when Ari Up and Tessa Pollitt reformed a version of The Slits in the mid-2000s, new songs like 'Babylon' reaffirmed the band's mystical, ecological critique.

Furthermore, the mystical turn of The Slits cannot be dismissed as easily as it has been both then and since. While not explicitly articulated in politicised terms, it can, however, be viewed as a utopian sensibility which evolved in part from the band's critique of gendered consumerism and unequal relations between men and women. It was a sensibility at odds with the individualist tendencies also evident in the band's cultural production, one which continued to emphasise freedom and pleasure whilst suggesting in terms very similar to the libertarian left that a genuinely liberated, fulfilling life for all required a radical undermining of the assumption that endless capitalist growth was both beneficial and sustainable.

The Raincoats, meanwhile, have thankfully not only been misrepresented by recent journalistic retrospectives and portrayed as puritanical by Reynolds and Press. They became a key reference point for the neo-punk 'riot grrrl' movement of the early 1990s and beyond. Their democratising legacy in terms of inspiring successive generations of young women to get involved in making rock music has often been stressed.[118]

What has not been celebrated are the libertarian left understandings of pleasure and fulfilment developed by The Raincoats. The way they affirmed the possibility of enjoyable, mutual sensual relations without exploitation begins to address some of the difficulties faced by the women's movement in the late 1970s and early 1980s. It is also powerfully relevant in a contemporary era in which media objectification of women has spiralled in line with intensified commodification. This is clearly evident within popular music, not least in much of the supposedly 'indie' descendants of post-punk. Catfish and the Bottlemen, signed to The Slits' former home, Island Records, are the latest in a long line of marketable 'lad rock' bands. Their merchandise stands at gigs offer a tongue-in-cheek price list for various groupie-style activities. 'Signed titties', anyone?

NOTES

1. In response to post-structuralist critiques of biological essentialism, Toril Moi has drawn on Simone de Beauvoir and Maurice Merleau-Ponty to argue that: 'Considered as a situation, the body encompasses both the objective and the subjective aspects of experience ... the body is our perspective on the world, and at the same time that body is engaged in a dialectical interaction with its surroundings ... The way we ... live ... is shaped by this interaction. The body is a historical sedimentation of our way of living in the world, and of the world's way of living with us.' Toril Moi, 'What is a Woman?', in *What is a Woman? And Other Essays* (Oxford: Oxford University Press, 1999), pp. 3–120 (p. 68).

2. Lynne Segal, *Why Feminism? Gender, Psychology, Politics* (Cambridge: Polity, 1999), p. 226.

3. Angela McRobbie, 'Post-feminism and Popular Culture: Bridget Jones and the New Gender Regime', in *Media and Cultural Theory*, ed. James Curran and David Morley (London: Routledge, 2006), pp. 59–69 (p. 59).

4. Zoe Williams, 'Nine Lessons We can Learn from Thatcher', *Compass*, 23 April 2013, available online at http://compassonline.org.uk/news/item. asp?n=17179

5. Zoe Street Howe, *Typical Girls? The Story of The Slits* (London: Omnibus, 2009).

6. Huw Nesbitt, 'The Author Speaks: Zoe Street Howe on Writing the Slits' Story', *The Quietus*, 1 July 2009, available online at http://thequietus. com/articles/02022-the-author-speaks-zo-street-on-writing-the-slits-story, accessed 8 October 2015.

7. Street Howe, *Typical Girls*, p. 86.

8. Lucy Toothpaste, interview with The Slits, *Jolt*, 2 summer 1977 and 'Women and Popular Music', *Spare Rib* 107 (June 1981), 6–8.

9. Cazz Blase, 'Women of the Punk Era—Part Three', *The F Word*, 24 April 2010, available online at http://www.thefword.org.uk/features/2010/04/ women_of_the_pu, accessed 8 October 2015.

10. Viv Albertine, *Clothes Music Boys* (London: Faber, 2014), p. 201.

11. Charles Ubaghs, 'Post-Punk Distilled: The Raincoats' Debut Album 30 Years On', *The Quietus*, 26 October 2009, available online at http:// thequietus.com/articles/03050-post-punk-distilled-the-raincoats-debut-album-30-years-on-the-raincoats, accessed 8 October 2015.

12. Chris Power, review of *The Raincoats* re-release, *Drowned in Sound*, November 2009, available online at http://drownedinsound.com/ releases/14871/reviews/4138182; Noel Gardner, review of The Raincoats—*Odyshape* re-release, *Drowned in Sound*, September 2011, available online at http://drownedinsound.com/releases/16469/reviews/ 4143468?relevant-artist, accessed 8 October 2015.

13. See, for example, Caroline O'Meara, 'The Raincoats: Breaking Down Punk Rock's Masculinities', *Popular Music* 22, no. 3 (2003), 299–313; Lucy O'Brien, *She Bop II: The Definitive History of Women in Rock, Pop and Soul* (London: Continuum, 2002), p. 147; Brian Cogan, 'Typical Girls? Fuck Off, You Wanker! Re-Evaluating The Slits and Gender Relations in Early British Punk and Post-Punk', *Women's Studies: An Interdisciplinary Journal* 41, no. 2 (2012), 121–135.

14. Helen Reddington, *The Lost Women of Rock Music: Female Musicians of the Punk Era* (Bristol: Equinox, 2012); Mavis Bayton, *Frock Rock: Women Performing Popular Music* (Oxford: Oxford University Press, 1998).

15. Sheila Rowbotham, *A Century of Women: The History of Women in Britain and the United States* (London: Penguin, 1999), p. 426.

16. Lynne Segal, *Is The Future Female? Troubled Thoughts on Contemporary Feminism* (London: Virago, 1994), p. 43.

17. Segal, *Why Feminism?*, p. 28.

18. Segal, *Is the Future Female?*, p. 96.

19. *Jolt* issue 2, Summer 1977.
20. Blase, 'Women of the Punk Era'.
21. Simon Reynolds, *Totally Wired* (London: Faber and Faber, 2009), pp. 3–4.
22. Albertine, *Clothes Music Boys*, p. 162.
23. Albertine, *Clothes Music Boys*, pp. 23–25, p. 105.
24. Albertine, *Clothes Music Boys*, p. 30.
25. Albertine, *Clothes Music Boys*, pp. 35–36.
26. Thomas Hasson, 'Like Choosing a Lover: Viv Albertine's Favourite Albums', *The Quietus*, 18 April 2013, available online at http://thequietus.com/articles/12018-viv-albertine-the-slits-interview-favourite-albums, accessed 8 October 2015.
27. Jon Savage, *The England's Dreaming Tapes* (London: Faber, 2009), p. 286.
28. Albertine, *Clothes Music Boys*, p. 39.
29. Albertine, *Clothes Music Boys*, p. 11.
30. Albertine, *Clothes Music Boys*, p. 62.
31. Albertine, *Clothes Music Boys*, p. 102.
32. Gregory Mario Whitfield, interview with Tessa Pollitt, available online at http://www.3ammagazine.com/musicarchives/2003/nov/interview_tessa_pollitt.html, accessed 26 August 2015.
33. Street Howe, *Typical Girls?*, p. 6.
34. Reynolds, *Rip It Up*, p. 213.
35. Ozgur Cokyuce, interview with Ana da Silva for *Punk Globe*, available online at http://www.punkglobe.com/anadasilvainterview0710.html, accessed 8 October 2015.
36. Neil Taylor, *Document and Eyewitness: An Intimate History of Rough Trade* (London: Orion, 2010), p. 118.
37. Taylor, *Document and Eyewitness*, p. 118.
38. Richie Unterberger, interview with Gina Birch, available online at http://www.richieunterberger.com/birch.html, accessed 8 October 2015.
39. Bayton, *Frock Rock*, p. 202.
40. Bayton, *Frock Rock*, p. 67.
41. Albertine, *Clothes Music Boys*, p. 159.
42. *Jolt* 2.
43. Reynolds, *Totally Wired*, p. 10.
44. Albertine, *Clothes Music Boys*, p. 153.
45. Street Howe, *Typical Girls?*, pp. 53–54.
46. Street Howe, *Typical Girls?*, p. 86.
47. Street Howe, *Typical Girls?*, p. 42.
48. Reynolds, *Rip It Up*, p. 88.
49. *Brass Lip*, fanzine issue 1 1979, interview with The Raincoats, available online at http://www.tumblr.com/tagged/brass-lip, accessed 8 October 2015.

50. Deanne Pearson, 'Women in Rock', *NME*, 20 March 1980.
51. Taylor, p. 120. Birch has since become less conflicted about her alignment, claiming, 'now I would say "well yes of course I'm a feminist" ... and I have written a song about it'.—see Cazz Blase, 'Women of the Punk Era—Part Three'. The song in question contains the refrain 'When you ask me if I'm a feminist, I say "why the hell would I not be?"' A live version can be found on YouTube: http://www.youtube.com/watch?v=Lg3UN7nYpJM
52. Blase, 'Women of the Punk Era'.
53. Vicki Aspinall interview in *The Angry Violist*, zine no. 4, copies available online at http://angryviolist.wordpress.com/tag/vicki-aspinall/
54. Reynolds, *Rip It Up*, p. 216.
55. Taylor, *Document and Eyewitness*, p. 152.
56. Simon Reynolds and Joy Press, *The Sex Revolts: Gender, Rebellion and Rock 'n' Roll* (Cambridge: Harvard University Press, 1996), p. 353.
57. Blase, 'Women of the Punk Era'.
58. Ozgur Cokyuce, interview with Ana da Silva, *Punkglobe*.
59. Dave McCullough, 'Shrieks from the Grove', *Sounds*, 8 December 1979.
60. The phrase is also suggestive of *The Odyssey*, inviting metaphorical parallels between the body of its protagonist and the non-linear structure of Homer's epic.
61. Reynolds, *Totally Wired*, pp. 200–202.
62. Reynolds and Press, *The Sex Revolts*, p. 307.
63. Reynolds and Press, *The Sex Revolts*, p. 307.
64. Pearson, 'Women in Rock'.
65. Reynolds, *Totally Wired*, p. 7.
66. Reynolds, *Totally Wired*, p. 4.
67. Kate Soper, 'Patchwork Dragon Power?', in *Troubled Pleasures: Writings on Politics, Gender and Hedonism* (London: Verso, 1990), pp. 165–174.
68. Reynolds, *Rip It Up*, p. 84.
69. Ian Penman, review of The Slits—'In the Beginning There was Rhythm', *NME*, 15 March 1980.
70. Reynolds, *Rip It Up*, p. 89.
71. The band's drummer at this time was Bruce Smith of The Pop Group.
72. Herbert Marcuse, *Counterrevolution and Revolt* (Boston: Beacon Press, 1972), p. 77.
73. Momus, 'Return to the Giant Slits', 29 September 2008, available online at http://imomus.livejournal.com/403645.html, accessed 8 October 2015.
74. Reynolds, *Totally Wired*, pp. 13–14.
75. O'Brien, *She Bop*, p. 408.
76. Reynolds, *Totally Wired*, p. 200.
77. Reynolds, *Rip It Up*, p. 214.
78. Blase, 'Women of the Punk Era'.

79. *Drastic Measures*—Rock Against Sexism, fanzine issue 1, 1979.
80. Martha Zenfell, 'Love Sex, Hate Sexism?', review of Rock Against Sexism gig, *NME*, 7 April 1979.
81. Reynolds and Press, *The Sex Revolts*, p. 311.
82. Reynolds, *Rip It Up*, p. 214.
83. Lucy Toothpaste, 'Women in Popular Music'.
84. Blake's 'The Garden of Love' is also paraphrased in the lyrics to the song which follows 'Ooh Ooh La La' on *Moving*, 'Dance of Hopping Mad'.
85. Reynolds and Press, *The Sex Revolts*, p. 311.
86. Reynolds and Press, *The Sex Revolts*, p. 314.
87. Marcuse, *Counterrevolution and Revolt*, pp. 49–50.
88. Herbert Marcuse, *One-Dimensional Man* [1964] (London: Routledge, 1991), pp. 77–78.
89. Savage, *England's Dreaming*, p. 486.
90. Will Parkhouse, 'I Do not Believe in Love: Viv Albertine on Life Post The Slits', *The Quietus*, 25 February 2010, available online at http://thequietus.com/articles/03789-viv-albertine-of-the-slits-interview-on-new-ep-never-come, accessed 8 October 2015.
91. Street Howe, *Typical Girls?*, p. 99.
92. Street Howe, *Typical Girls?*, p. 99. Jason Toynbee has also noted that Island's founder Chris Blackwell shared the 'ambitious', 'petit bourgeois' background of other key figures centrally involved in Jamaica's nascent music industry—see Jason Toynbee, *Bob Marley: Herald of a Postcolonial World?* (Cambridge: Polity, 2007), p. 86.
93. Street Howe, *Typical Girls?*, p. 101.
94. Street Howe, *Typical Girls?*, p. 152.
95. Street Howe, *Typical Girls?*, p. 177.
96. Street Howe, *Typical Girls?*, p. 193.
97. Reynolds, *Rip It Up*, p. 90.
98. Reynolds, *Totally Wired*, p. 12.
99. Ozgur Cokyuce, interview with Ana da Silva, *Punkglobe*.
100. Reynolds, *Rip It Up*, p. 199. Tom Morley, whom Gartside had spurned for a drum machine, later found work playing guest drums on 'No One's Little Girl' from *Moving*.
101. Ian Pye, 'An Old Raincoat...', *Melody Maker*, 21 August 1982.
102. Pye, 'An Old Raincoat...'.
103. Steve Sutherland, review of The Raincoats—*Moving*, *Melody Maker*, 28 January 1984.
104. Taylor, *Document and Eyewitness*, p. 134.
105. Reddington, *The Lost Women of Rock Music*, p. 119.
106. Pye, 'An Old Raincoat...'.
107. Graham Lock, 'Big Macs Go for It!', *NME*, 4 February 1984.

108. 'Your Heart Out' music blog, available online at http://yrheartout. blogspot.co.uk/2011/05/hiss-shake-leggs-eleven-pt-8.html, accessed 8 October 2015.
109. Reynolds, *Totally Wired*, p. 202.
110. Judith Williamson, 'Images of 'Woman'—Judith Williamson Introduces the Photography of Cindy Sherman', in *Screen* 24, no. 6 (Nov/Dec 1983), 102–116 (p. 105).
111. Williamson, 'Images of 'Woman', p. 103.
112. Debbi Voller, *Madonna: The Style Book* (London: Omnibus, 1999), p. 18.
113. Reddington, *The Lost Women of Rock Music*, p. 152.
114. Reddington, *The Lost Women of Rock Music*, p. 188.
115. Donna P. Hope, *Inna Di Dancehall: Popular Culture and the Politics of Identity in Jamaica* (Kingston: University of the West Indies Press, 2001).
116. Reynolds, *Totally Wired*, p. 15.
117. Available online at https://www.youtube.com/watch?v=kvHPGwH1kQc, accessed 27 August 2015.
118. See, for example, Nadine Monem (ed.), *Riot Grrrl: Revolution Girl Style Now!* (London: Black Dog, 2007).

CHAPTER 7

Agents of Change: Post-Punk and the Present

I started this book with the claim that it was worth questioning some of the more pessimistic assessments of post-punk's political trajectory. Looking back over the central chapters, it might seem as though the stances of writers like Simon Reynolds are more accurate than it is comfortable to admit. It has to be asked how much impact left post-punk bands and institutions could have had, given the historical circumstances they were part of. One small countercultural formation, after all, could not have mitigated the British ruling class's adoption of neoliberalism and its all-out assault on the broad left upon which post-punk in part relied for its existence.

In a broadly hegemonic sense, elements of left post-punk chimed with the neoliberal turn in terms of freedom and pleasure. The experiences of bands such as Gang of Four and Scritti Politti indicated the immense difficulties entailed in a project of prefigurative politics, whilst the legacies of Mark E. Smith and The Slits echo the ambiguities of countercultural individualism. And although labels like Rough Trade helped see through a democratised access to popular musical production, an oppositional populism was not achieved from the perspective of consumption. Often it was the most visionary, uncompromising bands like the Blue Orchids and The Raincoats that had the least market reach. 'Indie', Reynolds notes, gradually became a signifier for a 'sort of resentfully impotent opposition to mainstream pop'.[1]

© The Editor(s) (if applicable) and The Author(s) 2016   189
D. Wilkinson, *Post-Punk, Politics and Pleasure in Britain*,
DOI 10.1057/978-1-137-49780-2_7

It should be noted, too, how often structuralism, post-structuralism and postmodernism provided the intellectual rationale for political accommodation. This was by no means uniformly the case—the idiosyncrasies of The Fall and The Slits stand out, for example. These theories, though, mediated the directions not only of bands like Gang of Four, Scritti Politti and The Raincoats, but also of the new pop music press ideologues who helped set the agenda of the post-punk moment. It may well be that Simon Reynolds' doubts about the political achievements of post-punk are also connected with the post-structuralist theories which have influenced his earlier work. Comparable tendencies can be detected at the level of British Cultural Studies' influential interaction with political thought in the 1980s on the pages of *Marxism Today*. Jeremy Gilbert has recently argued that the 'soft left', influenced by such intellectual work, made an uneasy alliance with the New Labour project that has not ended well.[2]

There is surely a lesson to be learned from post-punk on this score for anyone attempting to produce oppositional intellectual work via institutions in which post-structuralist and postmodernist assumptions are often so hegemonic that their philosophical basis and their historical origin as pessimistic responses to a specific moment of defeat for the left go unacknowledged. This might seem like a tangential niche concern, until we consider that the expansion of higher education has meant hundreds of thousands of students in Britain graduate every year with some experience of such an intellectual culture.

Despite all this, left post-punk was remarkably successful in two respects given the historical circumstances it was part of. Firstly, there was the establishment of an independent and frequently oppositional institutional infrastructure within the British music industry that outlasted post-punk itself by a decade, despite the emergence of new pop's 'subvert from within' rhetoric and the rapid boom and bust cycles of the British economy in the 1980s and early 1990s. Secondly, post-punk bands often worked up countercultural utopianism into a genuinely qualitative opposition to capitalism at a time when the rest of the left were either neglecting or struggling with this issue. Both of these achievements offer pertinent resources of hope in our current moment. In order to understand how, it is necessary to ask: what happened in-between?

LOSING ITS EDGE

From 2001 onwards, a large-scale and lasting revival of interest in post-punk began to occur, somewhat taking the music press by surprise; *NME*'s predictions for that year were a motley collection of stale post-Britpop bands, US nu-metal imports and the dying embers of 1990s dance.[3] A drip-feed of seductively packaged post-punk compilations, CD reissues of long-lost classics, media features anticipating Reynolds' book-length history[4] and themed clubnights[5] combined with a slew of new bands displaying appropriate musical and visual citations. Though many echoed post-punk by virtue of being signed to independents or major label subsidiaries, this was more or less where the similarities ended. The revival's frequently explicit pastiche was somewhat at odds with post-punk's emphasis on innovation. Very few bands, too, displayed an interest in the oppositional politics that often animated the original wave of post-punk, with the exception of the odd cult act like the strikingly named Selfish Cunt. Their single, 'Britain Is Shit', remains an under the radar classic, a caustic and surreal response to New Labour's wars in Afghanistan and Iraq.

Coverage of the post-punk revival in *NME* actually coincided with the gradual muting of the magazine's residually left-leaning tone, in line with a sense of fatalistic resignation marked by the government of New Labour. Instead, a selection of bands such as The Rapture were celebrated as a much-needed revolution of the wheel of popular musical fashion—'the sound of now'[6]—rather than a new wave of countercultural opposition. The same issue that announced Scottish art school band Franz Ferdinand's debut 'Darts of Pleasure' as single of the week featured a reader's letter that lamented the decline of radicalism in popular music. Its writer declared 'commercialism' to be 'the enemy of progress', advocating the politicised use of then-new digital and online technologies against a music industry motivated solely by profit. The letter was followed by a mocking response by Sarah Dempster (now a journalist for *The Guardian*), which dismissed its sentiment as 'hippy-fied poppycock'.[7]

In an article for *The Quietus*, Joe Kennedy has argued that:

> The revival came across ultimately as a rather crass attempt to refit the sonics of an alienation arising from the collapse of post-war social democracy for the carefree spirit of an economic ... boom ... The tendency of first-wave post-punks such as Gang of Four and Scritti Politti to keep up to date with radical developments in aesthetic and sociological theory was replaced by an off-the-shelf performance of bookishness.[8]

Kennedy has a point. Bands like Franz Ferdinand were celebrated for appearing 'clever', without much indication of what this cleverness consisted of.[9] In Britain especially, post-punk's incorporation was bound even more directly to the New Labour boom years. When I reflect with

hindsight on being swept up in the revival as a teenager, there was a defi-
nite structure of feeling that fused the predominantly urban, 'arty' and
intellectual aura of post-punk to the mania of speculative apartment building which reached its peak on the brink of 2008's global economic crash.
In Manchester, the sensibility of local post-punk independent Factory was
drawn on in a move that exhumed the city's musical past to advertise the
supposedly sophisticated glamour of city-centre living, surrounded by the
trappings of a 'post-industrial' creative economy. It was a myth mostly
exploited by out-of-town investors and buy-to-let landlords. The most
visible and talked-about symbol of this was the building of the luxury
'Hacienda' apartment block on the site of Factory's legendary nightclub,
its base adorned with an industrial-chic, die-cut mural depicting key events
in the club's story. Lately, a featureless plaza between a new multi-storey
car park and an office block has been named 'Tony Wilson Place'.

Meanwhile, post-punk became, and to some extent remains, a form
of what Sarah Thornton has theorised as 'subcultural capital',[10] an elitist marker of distinction amongst music fans within a shifting and indi-
rectly acknowledged hierarchy of taste. A tongue-in-cheek article for *The
Guardian* in 2003 advised on 'What To Say About the Real 80s Revival',
its standard-issue postmodern irony detracting from the real work of cultural distinction that it was effectively carrying out.[11] Post-punk's complex
tensions of class and education have been eerily re-animated in a social
context where there's an ever-growing disconnect between the precarious
lower rungs of the working class and those whose cultural and educational
capital has placed them at the centre of the 'flat white economy'.[12] This is
often culturally expressed as a division between despised 'chavs' and savvy
'hipsters'. Recently I spotted a fanzine for sale in an independent record
shop in Brighton, its cover adorned with the phrase 'Die Inbred Chav
Scum Die! Die!' and an illustration of its author's fantasies rendered in
twee cartoon graphics.

For Kennedy, the harsh and insecure climate of global recession and a
shift to the right in the governance of Britain has provided much-needed
perspective on all this. It's also appropriately closer to the historical conditions in which post-punk first coalesced. Highlighting examples of
recent comeback albums by first-wave post-punk bands like Public Image
Limited, he argues that such music 'matche[s] the requirements of new
political anxieties' by reflecting them at a formal level, differing from the
triviality of the earlier revival.[13]

Flickers of opposition can be detected in newer post-punk inspired artists, too, such as Lonelady (aka Julie Campbell). Though it avoids political commentary, *Hinterland*, Campbell's second album, invests Manchester's inner-city ruins with an imaginative utopianism that recalls the new sensibilities of first-wave post-punk. In interview, Campbell has celebrated networks of affordable, independent rehearsal and recording space, asserting, 'you can't just have middle-class people making music'.[14] Such urban-focused music also offers a stark alternative to the way that, as Alex Niven observes, the right has incorporated the bucolic elements of the counter-culture over the last decade or so. 'Nu-folk' acts like the privately educated Mumford and Sons resonate with the latest articulation of the age-old 'neo-feudal ... pastoral myth' of the British establishment, recurrently drawn on to mask inequality.[15]

Make a Connection

The work of Lonelady is just one example of how both the 'systematic' and the 'heuristic' utopianism of post-punk, its prefigurative institutional practices and oppositional sensibilities, continue to resonate. With regard to the former, the case of Rough Trade is especially compelling. After collapsing during the recession of the early 1990s, the label made an appropriately timed return during the post-punk revival, mostly stripped of its old values and working methods. Geoff Travis now speaks loosely of 'doing business in a fair-minded way',[16] whilst Patsy Winkelman, an employee of the company, justifies the label's new aim of serving a niche market by reference to neoliberal hegemony and, in the light of the political and economic upheaval of recent years, a now fairly dated-sounding postmodern defeatism:

> You can't tag politics onto music and make a big movement in a way that you could even as late as the 1980s ... it seems to me that everything has become so postmodern and broken down and no-one bothers to revolt anymore ... we play our part now by recognising the genius and releasing records that nobody else can quite see.[17]

Yet the very aspect of Rough Trade that seems most pressing in current circumstances is its early commitment to prefigurative strategies with the aim of a leftist, grassroots transformation of popular musical production. Despite large-scale structural and technological developments within the cultural industries since the 1980s that might seem to render the label's efforts irrelevant, equally significant continuities exist. David Hesmondhalgh has argued that the cultural industries as a whole are still dominated by what Raymond Williams called corporate professionalism (see Chap. 2).[18] In this context, the label's understanding of freedom, consisting of the democratisation and decentralisation of cultural production, is vital.

It's not only continuity but also change within the cultural industries that highlights these particular values of Rough Trade's post-punk phase. There has been a trend towards conglomeration, with the corollary of ever-greater concentrations of capital and power, and a tendency for small companies to operate more and more in a hierarchical relationship of interdependence with major corporations.[19] 'Record Store Day', a global marketing event for independent music shops sold as a celebration of alternative musical culture, has led to pressing plants shunning small orders by independent labels in favour of churning out vinyl reissues of classic rock guaranteed to sell in high numbers.[20]

The much-vaunted neo-DIY aspects of the internet are also dubious from a libertarian left perspective: rather than Rough Trade's support for autonomous musical production, musicians now often have to carry out time-consuming, uncompensated labour attempting to promote their work online.[21] They are also pressured into deals that newly exploit other profitable aspects of their output now that file-sharing and websites, such as YouTube, have devalued recorded music as a commodity.[22]

The increased prevalence of copyright has meant that creative labour is now more often thought of in terms of individual property rather than 'social or collective creativity'.[23] Meanwhile, intensified marketing has encroached on the institutional autonomy[24] that, as I argued in Chap. 2, is central to a sense of cultural production as consisting of more than capitalist imperatives, or of being in direct opposition to them. Chillingly, music industry employees are now more likely to listen for a 'synch' than for a single: an aspect of the music that would render it appropriate for licensing to advertisers. Many companies have whole departments devoted to advertising placement,[25] a world away from Rough Trade's commitment to popular musical production for its own sake as an enriching experience for both producers and listeners.

Hesmondhalgh's more recent work draws on his earlier research on UK independent labels, juxtaposing Rough Trade with contemporary trends. He points to the label's significance as an attempt to 'transform the apparatus of *commercial* cultural production' rather than more marginal interventions 'known only to small groups of activists and intellectuals'. Nevertheless, Hesmondhalgh contends that 'in the end, the … rebellion was unsuccessful',[26] recalling Simon Reynolds' pessimistic view of the politics of post-punk more generally.

Whilst it is true that little remains of this idealistic moment, the co-operative working practices of the original Rough Trade—such as collective ownership, democratic structures, positive discrimination and the privileging of music over profit—continue to be potential inspirations for contemporary oppositional musical production. It is these kinds of specifics that can further flesh out the growing number of populist critiques of the music industry, such as that of Robert Barry. Barry situates its current operations within the increased dominance of neoliberalism and argues hopefully:

> I'd like to propose an alternative, one of those alternatives that we keep being told don't exist. You are the music industry. We all are … So perhaps it is time we started, collectively and cooperatively, to take some responsibility for it, instead of waiting for this nebulous ghost called 'the music industry' to take responsibility for us.[27]

The resonance of the post-punk left's heuristic utopianism, meanwhile, has to do with the connection between the way in which culture gets made and its resultant characteristics. This is an issue that is particularly well suited to a cultural materialist approach, with its insistence on analysis that mediates between close reading, means and conditions of production and historical context. Hesmondhalgh warns against assumptions that the content of popular culture has become more conservative and neatly congruent with the interests of big business in line with developments in the cultural industries over the past 30 years.[28] The generalised assessments that Hesmondhalgh critiques are tempting, but would require a huge amount of evidence and analysis to back them up. They also have the ring of totalising pessimism that still lingers on the cultural left.

Nevertheless, assessments of particular instances of cultural change are more manageable, especially via a cultural materialist method that considers specific formations and institutions. In the case of Rough Trade, there is little doubt that with the odd exception, much of what the label has promoted over the past decade and a half falls far short of the aesthetic and political radicalism of its output in the late 1970s and early

1980s. Examples include the garage rock pastiche of The Strokes, the 1960s female pop-soul template through which Duffy was marketed and more recently, the diminishing returns of formulaic 'indie rock' bands such as Palma Violets, recalling Reynolds' critique of pop culture's spiralling 'retromania'.[29]

By contrast, those bands whose ethos was closest to that of Rough Trade in its post-punk phase, like the Blue Orchids and The Raincoats, were not only formally innovative in a manner which Williams identified as an essential feature of emergent cultural production.[30] They also had the most fully formed libertarian left notions of freedom and pleasure; of a life which rejects alienation and exploitation in favour of openness to learning, mutual nurture, respect for and appreciation of the natural world, and playful, egalitarian erotic relations. These notions were fragile, for sure—the Blue Orchids' 'sad euphoria' captures this well—but all the more affecting for that.

Such bands were an emergent, progressive development from the often abstracted idealism of an earlier counterculture because they were supported by a sympathetic institution at the point of production. Thus, their oppositional visions appeared not only necessary but also, one day, possible. For Simon Reynolds, 'post-punk's struggle to avoid escapism and superficiality had led either to hair-shirt propaganda ... or the existential abyss'.[31] In the light of analysis, however, this summation of unworkability seems more like a convenient narrative device to ease readers into the second, new pop-centred half of *Rip It Up and Start Again*. Its implications of post-punk's joylessness and ghettoised extremity also bear a strong resemblance to the rhetoric of new pop. The rise of that movement was not due to insurmountable puritanism on the part of the post-punk left, but rather new pop's loose affinity with the emerging dominance of the New Right and the transformation of the left that followed.

Given that this is the case, it might appear that pinning any hopes on the utopian projections of left post-punk in the present is a futile gesture. Indeed, Paul Morley, one of the key architects of new pop, has suggested that rock's history is now so incorporated that any new youth culture with radical intentions must reject its legacy entirely.[32] This, though, is a simplistic proposal, relying on a narrative which substitutes a sensationalist account referring only to the Rolling Stones and Glastonbury festival for a more nuanced historical reflection that acknowledges residual possibilities. Moreover, this sensationalism is itself reminiscent of the 'spinning', 'distracting' and passivity-inducing media tactics of corporate entertainment that Morley argues are responsible for repressing and sublimating contemporary rebellious urges. In its resemblance of the very forces it opposes, Morley's article, despite its no-doubt sincere desire for a new counterculture, is new pop all over again.

A New Kind of Politics

Post-punk's legacy has contemporary repercussions that go beyond popular musical production to encompass political theory and practice. Once again, this can be framed in 'systematic' and 'heuristic' terms. Let's take systematic utopianism first.

For Hilary Wainwright, the libertarian left's participatory, decentralising and creative characteristics broke the ideological deadlock of that especially effective neoliberal opposition between the paternalistic, unresponsive statism of the postwar consensus, and the dynamic 'freedom' of the capitalist market. What's more, such practices remain capable of doing so: Wainwright points to Greece's Syriza as an example, having used its newly won state influence to strengthen the hand of the diverse popular movements which helped propel it into power.[33] There are echoes here of Rough Trade's relationship with the libertarian left-controlled Greater London Council, an institution whose working methods Wainwright sees as historically reminiscent of those of Syriza. As the last remnants of postwar public services and welfare are either privatised or annihilated in Britain, it is also no surprise that a new edition of *Beyond The Fragments* has been republished, containing essays which consider the insights of the book's original pieces within present circumstances.

Until very recently, the majority of the British left remained mired in the deadlock identified by Wainwright. In the wake of its defeat in the general election of 2010, the parliamentary Labour Party floundered in a post-New Labour landscape: it was unable to renege on its acceptance of neoliberalism due to continuing alliances with business and the right-wing media, not to mention remaining significantly populated by figures at ease with the party's transformation under Tony Blair. Yet the party was also aware of the toxicity of New Labour in the hearts and minds of many potential supporters, given that Blair and Gordon Brown lost around five million votes between 1997 and 2010. Global recession, too, had shattered the 'end of history' narrative upon which that political project was in part based. Knowing that there was some political capital in re-energising a core vote by talking left in response to Tory assaults on the working poor and the disabled, the party lost the 2015 election partly due to a confused message. Lacking an overall vision, it offered a few token moderations of Tory policy alongside a commitment to further public service cuts and savage scapegoating of the unemployed that justified the ideological fiction of Labour's 'overspending' as the cause of economic crisis.

Beyond the parliamentary circus, the prevailing mood on the left has been defensive and nostalgic, captured by the longstanding and endlessly repeated use of the phrase 'resistance' to describe attempts to conserve what little remains of the welfare state in the face of the intensified neoliberalism of austerity. Ken Loach's documentary film *Spirit of '45* is evocative of this structure of feeling: intended as a rallying device, Loach used the film's release to publicly call for the formation of a new leftist political party. Its tone, however, suggests that hope lies in some rosy vision of the postwar consensus, conveyed by a final scene in which the black and white archive footage used throughout is replayed, but has now been vividly colourised.

As I write, however, Westminster has just witnessed the most seismic political shift in a generation. Against all odds, a campaign to elect left-wing backbench MP Jeremy Corbyn as Labour leader propelled him to victory with an astounding majority, outstripping even that of Tony Blair's historic 1994 mandate. Labour's decision to open up the process to a newly created category of 'supporters', who could pay £3 to get a vote, arose from machinations on the party's right to reduce the weight of affiliated trade union votes in leadership elections. In the event, though, it gave the election of a left candidate extra democratic legitimacy, with an electorate of over 550,000. The vast majority voted, nearly 60% of whom chose Corbyn over the other three candidates.

Corbyn's outlook was formed through involvement in the libertarian left in the exact historical circumstances dealt with by this book. Leo Panitch places him within the Bennite Labour tradition, formed by 'the effects of the 1960s New Left, anti-Vietnam activism, the beginning of the women's movement, the general thrust for participatory democracy'.[34] Corbyn's close political ally John McDonnell, once the Chair of Finance for the Greater London Council, spoke of community budgeting and workplace democracy in his first TV interview as shadow chancellor.[35] A photo of the new Labour frontbench circulating on social media, with Corbyn and McDonnell accompanied by fellow left-winger Diane Abbott and the first ever majority female cabinet, brings to mind Lenin's quote that 'there are decades where nothing happens, and there are weeks when decades happen'.

It's hard to say whether Corbyn's leadership will last long in the face of hysterical reaction from the media and the Labour right. Nevertheless, his election represents a profound shift: a populist and longstanding yearning for a 'new kind of politics' (Corbyn's campaign slogan) finally achieving coherence and a potential connection to the levers of state power through mass Labour Party membership. This movement is part of a broader resurgence of left-wing opposition across the West; it echoes the electoral successes of the Scottish National Party on a social democratic platform, Greece's Syriza and Spain's Podemos, alongside the groundswell behind Bernie Sanders' campaign for US presidential nomination. Its longevity, though, is by no means guaranteed. That will only come if Corbyn's vision of Labour as 'social movement' transpires.[36]

Part of establishing such a broad movement would undoubtedly involve backing contemporary oppositional and independent popular cultural production with its roots in postwar countercultures. This is a move likely to further cement support from younger people increasingly schooled in the 'creative industries' who face precarious employment and significantly lower life chances than the baby boomer generation of welfare-capitalism. In this context, labels like Rough Trade offer a practical historical example of how policy could be developed that would suture Corbynism's classically Labourist promise of publicly funded arts to its democratising policy aims elsewhere (e.g. in energy and transport) and its gestures to small businesses and co-operatives.[37]

As for heuristic utopianism, this new movement will face many challenges, but one in particular which stands out is the need for a qualitatively distinct vision of what a liberated and fulfilled life might look like as part of a socialism of the twenty-first century. Until Corbyn's election, Labour remained weak on this point in a manner that was entirely congruent with the era I discussed in Chap. 3. Even with a neoliberal Labour Party, the same dynamic between the right's seizure of individual aspiration and the left's cornered role of dutiful provision played out. Before the 2015 election, the Tories claimed they would not raise income tax rates or VAT; Labour responded by warning of Tory cuts to child benefit and tax credits.[38]

There is a risk that this dynamic may continue, despite initial successes. *Coronation Street* actress Julie Hesmondhalgh captured a renewed investment in social solidarity in her description of Corbyn's packed-out campaign rallies as 'the mass movement of giving a toss about stuff'.[39] The MP's 'parsimonious' expenses record[40] has likewise gone down well, with public trust in politicians at an all-time low. Both the right-wing and the liberal media, however, have wasted no time in wheeling out age-old portrayals of the left as puritanical and dogmatic. *The Telegraph*'s profile of the mild-mannered Corbyn calls him a 'firebrand', mocks his sartorial choices, and notes his avoidance of extravagant personal spending alongside his 'strict' vegetarianism.[41] Its hegemonic reach is apparent in the satirical Twitter account @corbynjokes. The account's tagline is 'Jeremy hasn't heard or told a joke since 1964'.[42] *The Guardian*, meanwhile, ran an article that claimed of Corbyn: 'He has engaged young voters for the first time … we should judge him for that, rather than for how he dresses', despite the fact that its entire focus was on the way he dressed.[43]

It is tempting to dismiss such coverage as predictable, superficial or even irrelevant in a social media era that has the potential to counteract dominant media narratives. However, whether Corbyn's leadership lasts or not, a reinvigorated labour movement must learn from a past that continues to haunt it, tapping in more successfully to personal hopes and desires as a practical means of neutralising perennial accusations of worthiness. The structures of feeling explored by left post-punks may be one promising resource of hope in this struggle. Feminism and pleasure; sensuous reason; anti-consumerism; aesthetic investment in the natural environment; these are after all hardly archaic concerns at a moment of 'lad culture', widespread frustration at cynical political spin, popular culture that is dominantly fixated on conspicuous consumption and growing awareness of climate change.

Thankfully, the decay of leftist post-punk's oppositional visions of freedom and pleasure is not only a matter of rueful reflection. At a point when Margaret Thatcher is dead but Thatcherism is rampant beyond the wildest dreams of the governments she led, post-punk offers us much more than just a formal means of capturing the dread of ordinary lives ruined by bearing the brunt of a crisis they did not cause. Far from being the story of bands that failed, it is proof that radical popular cultural production can come out of moments of political difficulty for the left and still maintain, like the work of Raymond Williams, a guarded hope for the future. Whatever the chances of a renewed left turn out to be, in an era of growing inequality, ecological devastation, and the conservative anxieties provoked by geopolitical power shifts, the utopian sensibilities of post-punk remain profoundly and urgently relevant.

Notes

1. Simon Reynolds, *Rip It Up and Start Again: Postpunk 1978–1984* (London: Faber, 2005), p. 519.
2. Jeremy Gilbert, 'What Hope for Labour and the Left? The Election, the 80s and "Aspiration"', *Open Democracy*, 28 July 2015, available online at https://www.opendemocracy.net/ourkingdom/jeremy-gilbert/what-hope-for-labour-and-left-election-80s-and-'aspiration', accessed 22 September 2015.
3. '2001: An Ace Odyssey', *NME*, 6 January 2001, p. 13.
4. See, for example, the 'Beyond Punk!' special issue of *Mojo*, January 2004.
5. Peter Robinson, 'Indie Sexy Cool: The Coolest UK Clubs', *NME*, 12 April 2003, pp. 26–29.
6. April Long, live review of The Rapture, *NME*, 11 May 2002.
7. Sarah Dempster, 'Angst', *NME*, 6 September 2003.
8. Joe Kennedy, 'Dance 'Til the Police Come: Post-Punk Politics in 2012', *The Quietus*, 14 December 2012, available online at http://thequietus.com/articles/10981-post-punk-politics-revival-now-not-shit-the-rakes, accessed 8 October 2015.
9. Alexis Petridis, review of Franz Ferdinand—*Franz Ferdinand*, *The Guardian*, 30 January 2004.
10. Sarah Thornton, 'Understanding Hipness: "Subcultural Capital" As Feminist Tool', in *The Popular Music Studies Reader*, ed. Andy Bennett, Barry Shank and Jason Toynbee (London: Routledge, 2006), pp. 99–105.
11. Michael Hann, 'What to Say About the Real 80s Revival', *The Guardian*, 1 July 2003.
12. Felix Martin, 'Love Them or Hate Them East London's Hipsters have Fuelled a Vast Economy', *New Statesman*, 19 May 2015, available online at http://www.newstatesman.com/politics/2015/05/love-or-hate-them-east-london-s-hipsters-have-fuelled-vast-economy, accessed online 18 September 2015.
13. Kennedy, 'Dance 'Til the Police Come'.
14. John Doran, 'Interiority Complex: Exploring Manchester's Hinterlands with Lonelady', *Quietus*, 5 February 2015, available online at http://the-quietus.com/articles/17173-lonelady-interview-hinterland, accessed online 18 September 2015.
15. Alex Niven, *Folk Opposition* (Winchester: Zero, 2012), p. 39.
16. Neil Taylor, *Document and Eyewitness: An Intimate History of Rough Trade* (London: Orion, 2010), p. 393.

17. Taylor, *Document and Eyewitness*, p. 400.
18. David Hesmondhalgh, *The Cultural Industries—2nd Edition* (London: Sage, 2007), p. 303.
19. Hesmondhalgh, *The Cultural Industries*, pp. 167, 176.
20. Mike Campbell, 'How Independent Artists and Labels are Getting Squeezed Out by the Vinyl Revival', available online at http://noisey.vice.com/blog/how-independent-artists-and-labels-are-getting-squeezed-out-by-the-vinyl-revival?utm_source=noiseyfbus, accessed 16 September 2015.
21. Wyndham Wallace, 'How the Music Industry is Killing Music and Blaming the Fans', *The Quietus*, 24 May 2011, available online at http://thequietus.com/articles/06318-how-the-music-industry-is-killing-music-and-blaming-the-fans, accessed 8 October 2015.
22. Matt Stahl and Leslie Meier, 'The Firm Foundation of Organisational Flexibility: The 360 Contract in the Digitalizing Music Industry', *Canadian Journal of Communication* 37, no. 3 (2012), 441–458.
23. Hesmondhalgh, *The Culture Industries*, p. 154.
24. Hesmondhalgh, *The Culture Industries*, p. 189.
25. Wallace, 'How the Music Industry is Killing Music and Blaming the Fans'.
26. Hesmondhalgh, *The Culture Industries*, p. 209.
27. Robert Barry, 'Who's Afraid of the Big Bad Music Industry? In Search of the Beast', *The Quietus*, 29 June 2011, available online at http://thequietus.com/articles/06502-music-industry-beast, accessed 8 October 2015.
28. Hesmondhalgh, *The Culture Industries*, pp. 282–283.
29. Simon Reynolds, *Retromania: Pop Culture's Addiction to Its Own Past* (London: Faber, 2011).
30. Raymond Williams, *Marxism and Literature* (Oxford: Oxford University Press, 1977), p. 126.
31. Reynolds, *Rip It Up*, p. 377.
32. Paul Morley, 'The Rolling Stones will Reign Supreme Until There is a New Counterculture', *The Observer*, 31 March 2013.
33. Hilary Wainwright, 'Political Organisation in Transition', *Red Pepper*, January 2013, available online at http://www.redpepper.org.uk/essay-political-organisation-in-transition/, accessed 8 October 2015.
34. Leo Panitch, 'Can Jeremy Corbyn Redeem the Labour Party?', *Jacobin*, 11 September 2015, available online at https://www.jacobinmag.com/2015/09/jeremy-corbyn-benn-miliband-leadership-election/, accessed 18 September 2015.
35. 'John McDonnell Talks to Jon Snow: In Full', *Channel 4 News*, 14 September 2015, available online at https://www.youtube.com/watch?v=cGDla6aSwng, accessed 18 September 2015.

36. Jeremy Corbyn interviewed on *The Andrew Marr Show*, BBC One, 26 July 2015, available online at http://www.bbc.co.uk/programmes/p02y2ffn, accessed 21 September 2015.

37. Jeremy Corbyn for Labour Leader, 'Policy Documents', available online at http://www.jeremyforlabour.com/policy, accessed 21 September 2015.

38. Rowena Mason, 'Tory Income Tax Lock a 'Gimmick', says Ed Balls', *The Guardian*, 21 September 2015, available online at http://www.theguardian.com/politics/2015/apr/29/tory-david-cameron-income-tax-lock-gimmicked-balls-general-election, accessed 21 September 2015.

39. Helen Pidd, 'Welcome to the Mass Movement of Giving a Toss About Stuff', *The Guardian*, 30 August 2015, available online at http://www.theguardian.com/uk-news/the-northerner/2015/aug/30/jeremy-corbyn-manchester-rally, accessed 21 September 2015.

40. In 2010, in the wake of the parliamentary expenses scandal, Corbyn's annual claim was the lowest of all 650 MPs. Meyrem Hussein, 'Islington North MP Jeremy Corbyn is the Country's Lowest Expense Claimer', *Islington Gazette*, 8 December 2010, available online at http://www.islingtongazette.co.uk/news/politics/islington_north_mp_jeremy_corbyn_is_the_country_s_lowest_expenses_claimer_1_748369, accessed 8 October 2015.

41. Rosa Prince, 'Jeremy Corbyn: Full Story of the Lefty Candidate the Tories Would Love to See Elected as Labour Leader', *The Daily Telegraph*, 22 July 2015, available online at http://www.telegraph.co.uk/news/politics/labour/11710685/jeremy-corbyn-profile.html, accessed 8 October 2015.

42. Available online at https://twitter.com/corbynjokes, accessed 8 October 2015.

43. Morwenna Ferrier, 'Jeremy Corbyn: From Home-Knitted Jumpers to Harrington Jackets, His Style Evolution', *The Guardian*, 19 August 2015, available online at http://www.theguardian.com/fashion/2015/aug/19/jeremy-corbyn-style-jumper-newsnight, accessed 22 September 2015.

BIBLIOGRAPHY

BOOKS AND CHAPTERS IN EDITED COLLECTIONS

Adorno, Theodor. 1991. *The Culture Industry: Selected Essays on Mass Culture.* Edited by J. M. Bernstein. London: Routledge.

Albertine, Viv. 2014. *Clothes Music Boys.* London: Faber.

Althusser, Louis. 2008. *On Ideology.* London: Verso.

Anderson, Perry. 1983. *In the Tracks of Historical Materialism.* London: Verso.

Bakhtin, Mikhael. 1981. *The Dialogic Imagination.* Edited by Michael Holquist. Austin: University of Texas Press.

Barthes, Roland. 1975. *The Pleasure of the Text.* Translated by Richard Miller. New York: Hill and Wang.

Bayton, Mavis. 1998. *Frock Rock: Women Performing Popular Music.* Oxford: Oxford University Press.

Bennett, Andy, Barry Shank, and Jason Toynbee, eds. 2006. *The Popular Music Studies Reader.* London: Routledge.

Benson, Richard. 2010. *The Wit and Wisdom of Margaret Thatcher and Other Tory Legends.* Chichester: Summersdale.

Bourdieu, Pierre. 1984. *Distinction: A Social Critique of the Judgement of Taste.* Translated by Richard Nice. London: Routledge and Kegan Paul.

CCCS. 1978. *On Ideology.* London: Hutchinson.

Clarke, John. 1977. "Skinheads and the Magical Recovery of Community." In *Resistance Through Rituals: Youth Subcultures in Postwar Britain*, edited by Stuart Hall and Tony Jefferson. London: Hutchinson.

© The Editor(s) (if applicable) and The Author(s) 2016   205
D. Wilkinson, *Post-Punk, Politics and Pleasure in Britain,*
DOI 10.1057/978-1-137-49780-2

Cobb, W. Mark. 2004. "Diatribes and Distortions: Marcuse's Academic Reception." In *Herbert Marcuse: A Critical Reader*, edited by John Abromeit and W. Mark Cobb. London: Routledge.

Cowling, Maurice. 1978. "The Present Position." In *Conservative Essays*, edited by Cowling. London: Cassell.

Derrida, Jacques. 1995. "A 'Madness' Must Watch Over Thinking." Interview with Francois Ewald, *Le Magazine Litteraire*, March 1991 in Elizabeth Weber (ed.), *Points...: Interviews 1974–1994*, translated by Peggy Kamuf. Stanford: Stanford University Press.

Doggett, Peter. 2008. *There's a Riot Going On: Revolutionaries, Rock Stars and the Rise and Fall of '60s Counter-Culture*. Edinburgh: Canongate.

Dworkin, Dennis. 1997. *Cultural Marxism in Postwar Britain*. Durham: Duke University Press.

Eagleton, Terry. 1976. *Criticism and Ideology*. London: New Left Books.

Eagleton, Terry. 1990. *The Ideology of the Aesthetic*. Oxford: Blackwell.

Eagleton, Terry. 2003. *After Theory*. London: Penguin.

Ford, Simon. 2003. *Hip Priest: The Story of Mark E. Smith and The Fall*. London: Quartet.

Foucault, Michel. 1998 [1976]. *The History of Sexuality: Volume One—The Will to Knowledge*. Translated by Robert Hurley. London: Penguin.

Frith, Simon, and Howard Horne. 1987. *Art into Pop*. London: Methuen.

Gildart, Keith. 2015. "From 'Dead End Streets' to 'Shangri Las': Negotiating Social Class and Post-War Politics with Ray Davies and the Kinks." In *Youth Culture, Popular Music and the End of 'Consensus'*, edited by The Subcultures Network, 9–34. London: Routledge.

Gitlin, Todd. 1997. "The Anti-Political Populism of Cultural Studies." In *Cultural Studies in Question*, edited by M. Ferguson and P. Golding, 25–38. London: Sage.

Goddard, Michael, and Benjamin Halligan, eds. 2010. *Mark E. Smith and The Fall: Art, Music and Politics*. Farnham: Ashgate.

Goodyer, Ian. 2009. *Crisis Music: The Cultural Politics of Rock Against Racism*. Manchester: Manchester University Press.

Gorman, Paul. 2001. *In Their Own Write: Adventures in the Music Press*. London: Sanctuary.

Gorz, André. 1989. *Critique of Economic Reason*. London: Verso.

Graves, Robert. 1961. *The White Goddess: A Historical Grammar of Poetic Myth*. London: Faber and Faber.

Hall, Stuart. 1988. *The Hard Road to Renewal: Thatcherism and the Crisis of the Left*. London: Verso.

Hall, Stuart, and Martin Jacques, eds. 1983. *The Politics of Thatcherism*. London: Lawrence and Wishart.

Hebdige, Dick. 1979. *Subculture: The Meaning of Style*. London: Methuen.

Hesmondhalgh, David. 2007. *The Cultural Industries*. 2nd ed. London: Sage.

Hesmondhalgh, David. 2013. *Why Music Matters*. Oxford: Wiley Blackwell.

Heylin, Clinton. 2007. *Babylon's Burning: From Punk to Grunge*. London: Penguin.

Hindess, Barry, and Paul Hirst. 1977. *Mode of Production and Social Formation*. London: Palgrave Macmillan.

Hope, Donna P. 2001. *Inna Di Dancehall: Popular Culture and the Politics of Identity in Jamaica*. Kingston: University of the West Indies Press.

Jackson, Ben, and Robert Saunders, eds. 2012. *Making Thatcher's Britain*. Cambridge: Cambridge University Press.

Jones, Owen. 2011. *Chavs: The Demonisation of the Working Class*. London: Verso.

Jones, Paul. 2004. *Raymond Williams' Sociology of Culture*. Basingstoke: Palgrave Macmillan.

Kellner, Douglas, ed. 2005. *Herbert Marcuse: The New Left and the 1960s*. London: Routledge.

Lachman, Gary. 2001. *Turn Off Your Mind: The Mystic Sixties and the Dark Side of the Age of Aquarius*. London: Sidgwick and Jackson.

Laclau, Ernesto, and Chantal Mouffe. 1985. *Hegemony and Socialist Strategy*. London: Verso.

Laing, Dave. 1985. *One Chord Wonders: Power and Meaning in Punk Rock*. Milton Keynes: Open University Press.

Lester, Paul. 2008. *Gang of Four: Damaged Gods*. London: Omnibus.

Marcus, Greil. 1994 [1980]. "It's Fab, It's Passionate, It's Intelligent! It's the Hot New Sound of England Today!." In *In the Fascist Bathroom: Writings on Punk 1977–1992*, 128–129. London: Penguin.

Marcuse, Herbert. 1970. "The End of Utopia." In *Five Lectures: Psychoanalysis, Politics, and Utopia*, translated by Jeremy J. Shapiro and Shierry M. Weber, 64–67. London: Allen Lane.

Marcuse, Herbert. 1972a. *An Essay on Liberation*. Harmondsworth: Pelican.

Marcuse, Herbert. 1972b. *Counterrevolution and Revolt*. Boston: Beacon Press.

Marcuse, Herbert. 1991 [1964]. *One Dimensional Man*. London: Routledge.

Marx, Karl. 1975. *Early Writings*. Harmondsworth: Penguin.

Marx, Karl. 1976 [1867]. *Capital Volume 1*. Translated by Ben Fowkes. Harmondsworth: Pelican.

McGuigan, Jim. 2009. *Cool Capitalism*. London: Pluto.

McRobbie, Angela. 2006. "Post-Feminism and Popular Culture: Bridget Jones and the New Gender Regime." In *Media and Cultural Theory*, edited by James Curran and David Morley, 59–69. London: Routledge.

Medhurst, John. 2014. *That Option No Longer Exists: Britain 1974–76*. Alresford: Zero.

Middles, Mick, and Mark E. Smith. 2003. *The Fall*. London: Omnibus.

Middleton, Richard. 1990. *Studying Popular Music*. Milton Keynes: Open University Press.

Miles, Barry. 2010. *London Calling: A Countercultural History of London since 1945.* London: Atlantic Books.

Milne, Seumas. 1994. *The Enemy Within: The Secret War Against the Miners.* London: Verso.

Milner, Andrew. 2002. *Re-Imagining Cultural Studies: The Promise of Cultural Materialism.* London: Sage.

Moi, Toril. 1999. "What is a Woman?" In *What is a Woman? And Other Essays*, 3–120. Oxford: Oxford University Press.

Monem, Nadine, ed. 2007. *Riot Grrrl: Revolution Girl Style Now!* London: Black Dog.

Mulhern, Francis. 2000. *Culture/Metaculture.* London: Routledge.

Naylor, Liz. 2007. "Must the Haçienda Be Built?" In *New Perspectives in British Cultural History*, edited by Rosalind Crone, David Gange, and Katy Jones, 255–265. Newcastle: Cambridge Scholars Publishing.

Naylor, Liz. 2010. "Various Times." Unpublished MA thesis quoted in Owen Hatherley, *A Guide to the New Ruins of Great Britain*, Verso, London.

Neal, Charles. 1987. *Tape Delay.* Harrow: SAF.

Negus, Keith. 1996. *Popular Music in Theory.* Cambridge: Polity.

Negus, Keith. 1999. *Music Genres and Corporate Cultures.* London: Routledge.

Neville, Richard. 1970. *Play Power.* London: Jonathan Cape.

Nice, James. 2010. *Shadowplayers: The Rise and Fall of Factory Records.* London: Aurum.

Niven, Alex. 2012. *Folk Opposition.* Winchester: Zero.

Nuttall, Jeff. 1970. *Bomb Culture.* London: Paladin.

O'Brien, Lucy. 2002. *She Bop II: The Definitive History of Women in Rock, Pop and Soul.* London: Continuum.

Ogg, Alex. 2009. *Independence Days: The Story of UK Independent Record Labels.* London: Cherry Red.

Ouspensky, P. D. 1949. *In Search of the Miraculous.* New York: Harcourt, Brace and Company.

Petley, Julian. 2005. "Hit and Myth." In *Culture Wars: The Media and the British Left*, edited by James Curran, Ivor Gabor, and Julian Petley, 85–107. Edinburgh: Edinburgh University Press.

Pimlott, Herbert. 2015. "Militant Entertainment? 'Crisis Music' and Political Ephemera in the Emergent 'Structure of Feeling', 1976–1983." In *Fight Back: Punk, Politics and Resistance*, edited by The Subcultures Network, 268–286. Manchester: MUP.

Pollock, Griselda. 1987 [1982]. "Theory and Pleasure." In *Framing Feminism*, edited by Rozsika Parker and Griselda Pollock. London: Pandora.

Quilley, Steve. 2002. "Entrepreneurial Turns: Municipal Socialism and After." In *City of Revolution: Restructuring Manchester*, edited by Jamie Peck and Kevin Ward, 76–94. Manchester: Manchester University Press.

Reddington, Helen. 2012. *The Lost Women of Rock Music: Female Musicians of the Punk Era*. Bristol: Equinox.

Renton, Dave. 2006. *When We Touched The Sky: The Anti-Nazi League 1977–1981*. Cheltenham: New Clarion Press.

Reynolds, Simon. 1990 [1985]. "New Pop and Its Aftermath." In *On Record: Rock, Pop and the Written Word*, edited by Simon Frith and Andrew Goodwin, 466–471. London: Routledge.

Reynolds, Simon. 2005. *Rip It Up and Start Again: Postpunk 1978–1984*. London: Faber.

Reynolds, Simon. 2009. *Totally Wired: Post-Punk Interviews and Overviews*. London: Faber.

Reynolds, Simon. 2011. *Retromania: Pop Culture's Addiction to Its Own Past*. London: Faber.

Reynolds, Simon, and Joy Press. 1996. *The Sex Revolts*. Cambridge: Harvard University Press.

Rose, Jonathan. 2001. *The Intellectual Life of the British Working Classes*. New Haven and London: Yale University Press.

Rowbotham, Sheila. 1999. *A Century of Women: The Story of Women in Britain and the United States*. London: Penguin.

Rowbotham, Sheila, Lynne Segal, and Hilary Wainwright. 1979. *Beyond the Fragments: Feminism and the Making of Socialism*. London: Merlin.

Samuel, Raphael. 1989. "Born-Again Socialism." In *Out of Apathy: Voices of the New Left 30 Years On*, edited by Oxford University Socialist Discussion Group, 39–59. London: Verso.

Sandbrook, Dominic. 2012. *Seasons in the Sun: The Battle for Britain, 1974–1979*. London: Allen Lane.

Savage, Jon. 2005. *England's Dreaming: Sex Pistols and Punk Rock*. 2nd ed. London: Faber.

Savage, Jon. 2009. *The England's Dreaming Tapes*. London: Faber.

Segal, Lynne. 1994a. *Is the Future Female? Troubled Thoughts on Contemporary Feminism*. London: Virago.

Segal, Lynne. 1994b. *Straight Sex: Rethinking the Politics of Pleasure*. Berkeley: University of California Press.

Segal, Lynne. 1999. *Why Feminism? Gender, Psychology, Politics*. Cambridge: Polity.

Simpson, Dave. 2008. *The Fallen: Life In and Out of Britain's Most Insane Group*. Edinburgh: Canongate.

Sinfield, Alan. 1992. *Faultlines: Cultural Materialism and the Politics of Dissident Reading*. Berkeley: University of California Press.

Sinfield, Alan. 2004. *Literature, Politics and Culture in Postwar Britain*. 3rd ed. London: Continuum.

Smith, Mark E., and Austin Collings. 2009. *Renegade: The Lives and Tales of Mark E Smith*. London: Penguin.

Soper, Kate. 1990. "Patchwork Dragon Power?" In *Troubled Pleasures: Writings on Politics, Gender and Hedonism*, 165–174. London: Verso.

Street Howe, Zoe. 2009. *Typical Girls? The Story of The Slits*. London: Omnibus.

Taylor, Neil. 2010. *Document and Eyewitness: An Intimate History of Rough Trade*. London: Orion.

Taylor-Gooby, Peter. 1985. *Public Opinion, Ideology and State Welfare*. London: Routledge.

Thompson, E.P. 1963. *The Making of the English Working Class*. London: Victor Gollancz.

Toynbee, Jason. 2000. *Making Popular Music: Musicians, Creativity and Institutions*. London: Arnold.

Toynbee, Jason. 2007. *Bob Marley: Herald of a Postcolonial World?* Cambridge: Polity.

Turner, Alwyn W. 2008. *Crisis? What Crisis? Britain in the 1970s*. London: Aurum.

Voller, Debbi. 1999. *Madonna: The Style Book*. London: Omnibus.

Voloshinov, V.N. 1973. *Marxism and the Philosophy of Language*. Napier: Seminar Press.

Walker, John, A. 2002. *Left Shift: Radical Art in 1970s Britain*. London: I.B. Tauris.

Whiteley, Sheila. 2000. *Women and Popular Music: Sexuality, Identity and Subjectivity*. London: Routledge.

Widgery, David. 1986. *Beating Time*. London: Chatto and Windus.

Williams, Raymond. 1965 [1961]. *The Long Revolution*. Harmondsworth: Penguin.

Williams, Raymond. 1977. *Marxism and Literature*. Oxford: OUP.

Williams, Raymond. 1981a. *Culture*. Glasgow: Fontana.

Williams, Raymond. 1981b. *Politics and Letters: Interviews with New Left Review*. London: Verso.

Williams, Raymond. 1983. *Towards 2000*. London: Chatto and Windus.

Williams, Raymond. 1989. *Resources of Hope: Culture, Democracy, Socialism*. Edited by Robin Gable. London: Verso.

Williams, Raymond. 2005. *Culture and Materialism*. London: Verso.

Willis, Paul. 1978. *Profane Culture*. London: Routledge.

Wilson, Colin. 1973. *The Occult*. St. Albans: Mayflower.

Wilson, Elizabeth, and Angela Weir. 1986. *Hidden Agendas: Theory, Politics and Experience in the Women's Movement*. London: Tavistock.

York, Peter. 1980. *Style Wars*. London: Sidgwick and Jackson.

Media Sources

"2001: An Ace Odyssey." *NME*, 6 January 2001, 13.

Adetunji, Jo. "Johnny Marr Tells David Cameron to Stop Saying He Likes the Smiths." 3 December 2010. Accessed 5 October 2015. http://www.theguardian.com/politics/2010/dec/03/johnny-marr-david-cameron-twitter

Anonymous. "PragVec and the Normal at the Factory." *City Fun*, Vol. 1, no. 3, 1978.

Anonymous. "Scam." *City Fun*, Vol. 1, no. 7, 1979.

Anonymous. "Shake Your Cosy Attitudes." *City Fun*, Vol. 2, no. 14, 1981.

Aronson, Ronald. "Marcuse Today." *Boston Review*, 17 November 2014. Accessed 25 June 2015. http://bostonreview.net/books-ideas/ronald-aronson-herbert-marcuse-one-dimensional-man-today

Aspinall, Vicki, interview in *The Angry Violist* zine no. 4, copies available online at http://angryviolist.wordpress.com/tag/vicki-aspinall/

Barber, Lynden. "The Sweetest Groove." *Melody Maker*, 29 May 1982.

Barry, Robert. "Who's Afraid of the Big Bad Music Industry? In Search of the Beast." *The Quietus*, 29 June 2011. Accessed 8 October 2015. http://thequietus.com/articles/06502-music-industry-beast

BBC. *Till Death Us Do Part* Series 7 Episode 4: "The Window," originally broadcast 26 November 1975. Accessed 29 April 2015. https://www.youtube.com/watch?v=gA0-fnOsZeo

BBC News. "On This Day 1950–2005—26 January 1982." Accessed 8 October 2015. http://news.bbc.co.uk/onthisday/hi/dates/stories/january/26/newsid_2506000/2506335.stm

Bell, Max. "Idealists in Distress." *NME*, 30 June 1979, 24–27.

"Beyond Punk!" special issue of *Mojo*, January 2004.

Birch, Ian. "Rough Trade Records: The Humane Sell." *Melody Maker*, 10 February 1979, 19.

Birch, Ian. "Scritti Politti." *Smash Hits*, 12 November 1981.

Blase, Cazz. "Women of the Punk Era—Part Three." *The F Word*, 24 April 2010. Accessed 8 October 2015. http://www.thefword.org.uk/features/2010/04/women_of_the_pu

Boyd, Lindsey. "Alternativevision." *Sounds*, 24 December 1977, 12.

Brass Lip fanzine issue 1 1979, interview with The Raincoats. Accessed 8 October 2015. http://www.tumblr.com/tagged/brass-lip

Brazier, Chris. "United They Fall." *Melody Maker*, 31 December 1977.

Brazier, Chris. "The Gang That Tries to Talk Straight." *Melody Maker*, 3 November 1979.

Burkham, Chris. "Cabaret Voltaire: Prepare to Meet Your Mecca." *Sounds*, 25 July 1981.

Bushell, Garry. "UK Subs." *Sounds*, 12 August 1978, 12–13.

Bushell, Garry. "Will Jim Take the Money?" *Sounds*, 5 August 1978, 19.

Bushell, Garry, review of Gang of Four, *Entertainment!*, *Sounds*, 6 October 1979, 43.

Bushell, Garry, live review of the Angelic Upstarts at the Rainbow, *Sounds*, 14 June 1980, 50.

Bushell, Garry, and Dave McCullough. "Cockney Rejects and the Rise of the New Punk." *Sounds*, 4 August 1979, 16–17.

Bushell, Gary. "The Gang's All Here." *Sounds*, 2 June 1979.

Butt, Ronald. "Mrs Thatcher: The First Two Years." *The Sunday Times*, 3 May 1981.

Campbell, Mike. "How Independent Artists and Labels Are Getting Squeezed Out by The Vinyl Revival." *Noisey*. Accessed 16 September 2015. http:// noisey.vice.com/blog/how-independent-artists-and-labels-are-getting-squeezed-out-by-the-vinyl-revival?utm_source=noiseyfbus

Cavanagh, David. "The Fall." Vol. 4, September 1992.

City Fun, Vol. 3, no. 6, 25 June 1983.

Cokyuce, Ozgur, interview with Ana Da Silva for *Punk Globe*. Accessed 8 October 2015. http://www.punkglobe.com/anadasilvainterview0710.html

Cook, Richard. "The Curse of The Fall." *NME*, 15 January 1983, 18–19.

Coon, Caroline. "Parade of the Punks." *Melody Maker*, 2 October 1976, 26–27.

Corbyn, Jeremy, interviewed on *The Andrew Marr Show*, BBC One, 26 July 2015. http://www.bbc.co.uk/programmes/p02y2ffn

Cotton, Max. "Where Did All the Comrades Go?" BBC Radio 4, 14 January 2013.

Cranna, Ian. "Product, Packaging and Rebel Music." *NME*, 13 January 1979, 22–24.

Dempster, Sarah. "Angst." *NME*, 6 September 2003.

Dewhurst, Tony. "The Fall's Mark E. Smith Talks Television, Politics and New Technology." *The Bolton News*, 7 October 2015. Accessed 8 October 2015. http://www.theboltonnews.co.uk/news/13809653.The_Fall_s_Mark_E_Smith_talks_television__politics_and_n/

Doran, John. "Interiority Complex: Exploring Manchester's Hinterlands with Lonelady." *Quietus*, 5 February 2015. Accessed 18 September 2015. http:// thequietus.com/articles/17173-lonelady-interview-hinterland

Drastic Measures—Rock Against Sexism fanzine issue 1, 1979.

Dwyer, Simon. "The Politics of Ecstacy." *Sounds*, 29 May 1982, 26, 29.

Express Staff Reporter. "Women's Lib Lost Me My Children." *Daily Express*, 6 December 1978, 4.

The Fall: The Wonderful and Frightening World of Mark E. Smith, BBC4, 2005.

Ferrier, Morwenna. "Jeremy Corbyn: From Home-Knitted Jumpers to Harrington Jackets, His Style Evolution." *The Guardian*, 19 August 2015. Accessed 22 September 2015. http://www.theguardian.com/fashion/2015/aug/19/jeremy-corbyn-style-jumper-newsnight

"From the Pressing Plants to the Concert Halls, We Want Some Control." *After Hours* fanzine, 1979.

Gardner, Noel, review of The Raincoats—*Odyshape* re-release, *Drowned in Sound*, September 2011. Accessed 8 October 2015. http://drownedinsound.com/releases/16469/reviews/4143468?relevant-artist

Gilbert, Jeremy. "What Hope for Labour and the Left? The Election, the 80s and 'Aspiration'" *OpenDemocracy*, 28 July 2015. Accessed 22 September 2015.

https://www.opendemocracy.net/ourkingdom/jeremy-gilbert/what-hope-for-labour-and-left-election-80s-and-'aspiration'

Goldman, Vivien. "New Musick: Dub." *Sounds*, 3 December 1977, 22, 24.

Goldman, Vivien. "Siouxsie and the Banshees." *Sounds*, 3 December 1977, 26–27.

Hann, Michael. "It's Bloody Great Being Alive." Interview with Wilko Johnson, *The Guardian*, 2 February 2013. Accessed 8 October 2015. http://www.guardian.co.uk/music/2013/feb/02/wilko-johnson-interview

Hann, Michael. "What to Say About The Real 80s Revival." *The Guardian*, 1 July 2003.

Hanna, Lynn. "Into the Valley of the Voodoo Doll." *NME*, 15 August 1981, 44.

Hanna, Lynn. "When Reality Rears Its Orchidacious Head." *NME*, 20 June 1981.

Harron, Mary. "Dialectics Meet Disco." *Melody Maker*, 26 May 1979.

Hasson, Thomas. "Like Choosing a Lover: Viv Albertine's Favourite Albums." *The Quietus*, 18 April 2013. Accessed 8 October 2015. http://thequietus.com/articles/12018-viv-albertine-the-slits-interview-favourite-albums

Herlihy, Jon. "Human Lib." *Flicks*, Vol. 1, January 1977.

Herrington, Tony. "Mancunian Candidate." *The Wire*, September 1996.

Hoskyns, Barney. "Hip Priest: The Mark E. Smith Interview." *NME*, 14 November 1981.

Hoskyns, Barney. "Where Radical Meets Chic." *NME*, 31 October 1981, 30–31.

Hussein, Meyrem. "Islington North MP Jeremy Corbyn is the Country's Lowest Expense Claimer." *Islington Gazette*, 8 December 2010. Accessed 8 October 2015. http://www.islingtongazette.co.uk/news/politics/islington_north_mp_jeremy_corbyn_is_the_country_s_lowest_expenses_claimer_1_748369

Irwin, Colin, review of The Fall—*Hex Enduction Hour*, *Melody Maker*, 6 March 1982.

"John McDonnell Talks to Jon Snow: In Full." *Channel 4 News*, 14 September 2015. Accessed 18 September 2015. https://www.youtube.com/watch?v=cGDla6aSwng

Jones, Owen. "Peter Hitchens Got Me Thinking: Do Lefties Always Have to Turn Right in Old Age?" *The Guardian*, 9 September 2015. Accessed 8 October 2015. http://www.theguardian.com/commentisfree/2015/sep/09/peter-hitchens-tory-trotskyite-left-right

Kay, George. "The Fall of Slick, Mark E. Smith's Hex Enduction Hour." *Rip It Up*, September 1982.

Keene, Leroy, interview with Scritti Politti, *Printed Noises* fanzine, 1979.

Kennedy, Joe. "Dance 'Til the Police Come: Post-Punk Politics in 2012'" *The Quietus*, 14 December 2012. Accessed 8 October 2015. http://thequietus.com/articles/10981-post-punk-politics-revival-now-not-shit-the-rakes

King, Jon, interviewed on the *Today* programme, BBC Radio 4, 14 January 2011.

Lake, Steve. "After The Fall." *Melody Maker*, 21 April 1984.

Leslie, Ann. "Femail—Another Middle Class Rebel Hits the Headlines—But How Much Is It a Case of Getting Back at Daddy?" *Daily Mail*, 7 September 1976, 10.

Letters. *Sounds*, 26 August 1978, 50–51.

Letters. *Sounds*, 24 February 1979, 59.

Letters. *Sounds*, 5 June 1982, 62–63.

Lock, Graham. "Big Macs Go for It!" *NME*, 4 February 1984.

Long, April, live review of The Rapture, *NME*, 11 May 2002.

Lowenstein, Oliver. *Dangerous Logic*, no. 1, 1978.

Lowenstein, Oliver. "A New Career in a New Town." *Melody Maker*, 18 January 1978.

Lowenstein, Oliver. "A Question of Identity." *Sounds*, 19 August 1978, 21.

Lowry, Ray, *City Fun*, Vol. 2, no. 14, 1981.

Lowry, Ray, *City Fun*, Vol. 2, no. 19, 1981.

Martin, Felix. "Love Them or Hate Them East London's Hipsters Have Fuelled a Vast Economy." *New Statesman*, 19 May 2015. Accessed 18 September 2015. http://www.newstatesman.com/politics/2015/05/love-or-hate-them-east-london-s-hipsters-have-fuelled-vast-economy

Martin, Gavin. "Revolting Soul." *NME*, 30 August 1986.

"Mary Whitehouse—Obituary." *The Telegraph*, 24 November 2001. Accessed 5 October 2015. http://www.telegraph.co.uk/news/obituaries/culture-obituaries/tv-radio-obituaries/6605110/Mary-Whitehouse.html

Mason, Rowena. "Tory Income Tax Lock a 'Gimmick', Says Ed Balls." *The Guardian*, 29 April 2015. http://www.theguardian.com/politics/2015/apr/29/tory-david-cameron-income-tax-lock-gimmick-ed-balls-general-election

Matlock, Glen, interviewed on the Shaun Keaveny breakfast show, *BBC 6Music*, 5 May 2011.

McCullough, Dave. "Shrieks from the Grove." *Sounds*, 8 December 1979.

McCullough, Dave. "The Nitty Gritty on Scritti Politti." *Sounds*, 13 January 1979, 11.

McCullough, Dave. "Turn of the Scrits." *Sounds*, 8 December 1979, 18.

McCullough, Dave. "Society's Scourge." *Sounds*, 17 May 1980.

McCullough, Dave. "Totale Turnaround." *Sounds*, 21 June 1980.

McCullough, Dave. "Flower Power Revisited." *Sounds*, 12 June 1982.

McTague, Tom. "Cameron Insists His Love for the Smiths 'Will Never Go Out' Despite the Band 'Banning' Him from Listening to Their Music." *Daily Mail*, 9 January 2015. Accessed 5 October 2015. http://www.dailymail.co.uk/news/article-2903557/Cameron-insists-love-Smiths-never-despite-band-banning-listening-music.html

"Mirror Comment—The Lunatic Fringes." *Daily Mirror*, 1 June 1976, 2.

"Mirror Woman Meets Germaine Greer." *Daily Mirror*, 27 May 1982, 9.

Morley, Paul. "They Mean It, Ma-a-a-nchester." *NME*, 30 July 1977.

Morley, Paul. "In Defence of Siouxsie and the Banshees." *NME*, 23 December 1978, 39.

Morley, Paul. "Pink Military: Post-Modernist Pop Music." *NME*, 12 January 1980, 6–7.

Morley, Paul, review of The Pop Group—*For How Much Longer Do We Tolerate Mass Murder?*, *NME*, 22 March 1980, 39.

Morley, Paul, review of Scars—*Author! Author!*, *NME*, 11 April 1981, 33.

Morley, Paul. "Singles." *NME*, 7 February 1981, 27.

Morley, Paul. "Dollar in Wonderland." *NME*, 2 January 1982, 17, 30.

Morley, Paul. "The Rolling Stones will Reign Supreme Until There is a New Counterculture." *The Observer*, 31 March 2013.

Morley, Paul, and Adrian Thrills. "Independent Discs." *NME*, 1 September 1979, 23.

Nesbitt, Huw. "The Author Speaks: Zoe Street Howe on Writing the Slits' Story." *The Quietus*, 1 July 2009. Accessed 8 October 2015. http://thequietus.com/articles/02022-the-author-speaks-zo-street-on-writing-the-slits-story

Ogg, Alex. "Beyond Rip It Up: Towards a New Definition of Post-Punk?" *The Quietus*, 1 October 2009. Accessed 5 October 2014. http://thequietus.com/articles/02854-looking-beyond-simon-reynolds-rip-it-up-towards-a-new-definition-of-post-punk

Panitch, Leo. "Can Jeremy Corbyn Redeem the Labour Party?" *Jacobin*, 11 September 2015. Accessed 18 September 2015. https://www.jacobinmag.com/2015/09/jeremy-corbyn-benn-miliband-leadership-election/

Paphides, Pete. "Kind of Green." *Mojo*, March 2011.

Parkes, Taylor. "The Fall and Mark E. Smith as a Narrative Lyric Writer." *The Quietus*, 19 March 2010. Accessed 8 October 2015. http://thequietus.com/articles/03925-the-fall-and-mark-e-smith-as-a-narrative-lyric-writer

Parkhouse, Will. "I Do Not Believe in Love: Viv Albertine on Life Post the Slits." *The Quietus*, 25 February 2010. Accessed 8 October 2015. http://thequietus.com/articles/03789-viv-albertine-of-the-slits-interview-on-new-ep-never-come

Parsons, Tony. "Go Johnny Go." *NME*, 3 October 1976, 29.

Pearson, Deanne. "Women in Rock." *NME*, 20 March 1980.

Penman, Ian. "Reflections on In(ter)dependence." *NME*, 25 November 1978, 29.

Penman, Ian. "Singles." *NME*, 18 November 1978, 31.

Penman, Ian. "The Fall." *NME*, 19 August 1978.

Penman, Ian. "All Fall Down." *NME*, 5 January 1980.

Penman, Ian, review of The Slits and The Pop Group split single "In the Beginning There Was Rhythm/Where There's A Will." *NME*, 15 March 1980, 21.

Penman, Ian. "Political Conscience Every Now and Then, Pub Every Night." *NME*, 27 June 1981, 21–22.

Penman, Ian. "Singles." *NME*, 17 January 1981, 19–20.

Penman, Ian. "Into Battle—Declaring War on the Pop State." *NME*, 8 September 1984, 30–31.

Perry, Mark. "Editorial." *Sniffin' Glue* 1, 1976, 2.

Petridis, Alexis, review of Franz Ferdinand—*Franz Ferdinand*, *The Guardian*, 30 January 2004.

Pidd, Helen. "Welcome to the Mass Movement of Giving a Toss About Stuff." *The Guardian*, 30 August 2015. Accessed 21 September 2015. http://www.the-guardian.com/uk-news/the-northerner/2015/aug/30/jeremy-corbyn-manchester-rally

Pouncey, Edwin. "Rough Justice." *Sounds*, 9 June 1984.

Power, Chris, review of *The Raincoats* re-release, *Drowned In Sound*, November 2009. Accessed 8 October 2015. http://drownedinsound.com/releases/14871/reviews/4138182

Prince, Rosa. "Jeremy Corbyn: Full Story of the Lefty Candidate the Tories Would Love to See Elected as Labour Leader." *The Daily Telegraph*, 22 July 2015. Accessed 8 October 2015. http://www.telegraph.co.uk/news/politics/labour/11710685/jeremy-corbyn-profile.html

Pye, Ian. "The Fall Go to The Wall." *Melody Maker*, 6 June 1981.

Pye, Ian. "An Old Raincoat...." *Melody Maker*, 21 August 1982.

Robertson, Sandy. "Hex Education." *Sounds*, 8 May 1982.

Robinson, Peter. "Indie Sexy Cool: The Coolest UK Clubs." *NME*, 12 April 2003, 26–29.

Rook, Jean. "Carvallo's Body Blow to Women's Lib." *Daily Express*, 1 July 1978.

Savage, Jon. "Cabaret Voltaire." *Sounds*, 15 April 1978, 16–17.

Savage, Jon, review of Gang of Four—*Entertainment!*, *NME*, 6 October 1979.

Savage, Jon, and Jane Suck. "New Musick." *Sounds*, 26 November 1977, 23.

Shaar Murray, Charles. "John, Paul, Steve and Sidney: The Social Rehabilitation of the Sex Pistols." *NME*, 6 August 1977, 23–26.

Shaar Murray, Charles. "In New York They're Tourists." *NME*, 21 June 1980.

Shaar Murray, Charles. "Ullo Alexei! Gotta New Audience?" *NME*, 6 March 1982, 14–15.

Sigerson, Davitt. "New Musick: Disco." *Sounds*, 3 December 1977, 28.

Smith, Mark E. on Dave Fanning's Radio Show, RTE (Ireland), Broadcast 18 October 1980.

Smith, Mark E. on KPFA Radio, San Francisco, Broadcast 10 July 1981.

Smith, Mark E. "Portrait of the Artist as a Consumer." *NME*, 15 August 1981.

Snow, Mat, review of Gang of Four—*Hard*, *NME*, 10 September 1983.

Snow, Mat. "Before and After The Fall." *NME*, 3 November 1984.

Stubbs, David. "Join the Chant? Pop's Endlessly Problematic Relationship with Politics." *The Quietus*, 21 April 2015. Accessed 29 April 2015. http://thequietus.com/articles/17715-politics-pop-music-general-election

Sutherland, Steve. "On the Sick List." *Melody Maker*, 27 November 1982.

Sutherland, Steve. "The Sane Old Blues." *Melody Maker*, 1 May 1982.

Sutherland, Steve, review of The Raincoats—*Moving*, *Melody Maker*, 28 January 1984.

Taylor, Steve. "The Popular Press or How to Roll Your Own Records." *Time Out*, 2 February 1979.

Temporary Hoarding, no. 10, December 1979.

Thatcher, Margaret. "It's Your Freedom They Hate." *Sunday Express*, 23 November 1975.

Thrills, Adrian. "Siouxsie in Wonderland." *NME*, 24 June 1978, 18–19.

Thrills, Adrian. "ABC." *NME*, 18 July 1981, 14–15.

Toop, David, interview with Green Gartside. *The Face*, June 1988.

Toothpaste, Lucy. *Jolt* 2, 1977.

Toothpaste, Lucy. "Women and Popular Music." *Spare Rib* 107, June 1981.

Ubaghs, Charles. "Post-Punk Distilled: The Raincoats' Debut Album 30 Years On." *The Quietus*, 26 October 2009. Accessed 8 October 2015. http://thequietus.com/articles/03050-post-punk-distilled-the-raincoats-debut-album-30-years-on-the-raincoats

Verrico, Lisa. "Are You Talking to Me?" *Dazed and Confused*, December 1998.

Wainwright, Hilary. "Political Organisation in Transition." *Red Pepper*, January 2013. Accessed 8 October 2015. http://www.redpepper.org.uk/essay-political-organisation-in-transition/

Wallace, Wyndham. "How the Music Industry is Killing Music and Blaming the Fans." *The Quietus*, 24 May 2011. Accessed 8 October 2015. http://thequietus.com/articles/06318-how-the-music-industry-is-killing-music-and-blaming-the-fans

Walsh, Steve. "Pop Group Mania." *NME*, 18 February 1978, 19.

Whitfield, Gregory Mario, interview with Tessa Pollitt. Accessed 26 August 2015. http://www.3ammagazine.com/musicarchives/2003/nov/interview_tessa_pollitt.html

Williams, Zoe. "Nine Lessons We Can Learn from Thatcher." *Compass*, 23 April 2013. Accessed 8 October 2015. http://compassonline.org.uk/news/item.asp?n=17179

Wood, Ian. "The Fall Stumble into the Void." *Sounds*, 8 April 1978, 26.

Zenfell, Martha. "'Love Sex, Hate Sexism?' Review of Rock Against Sexism Gig." *NME*, 7 April 1979.

JOURNAL ARTICLES

Alderson, David. "Back to the Future." *English Studies in Canada* 30, no. 4 (December 2004): 167–187.

Anonymous. "Definitions." In *Internationale Situationniste*, no. 1, June 1958. Translated by Ken Knabb. Available online at Situationist International Online. Accessed 16 June 2015. http://www.cddc.vt.edu/sionline///si/definitions.html

Campbell, Bea, interview with Edwina Currie *Marxism Today*, March 1987.

Cogan, Brian. "Typical Girls? Fuck Off, You Wanker! Re-Evaluating the Slits and Gender Relations in Early British Punk and Post-Punk." *Women's Studies: An Interdisciplinary Journal* 41, no. 2 (2012): 121–135.

Fryer, Paul. "Punk and the New Wave of British Rock: Working Class Heroes and Art School Attitudes." *Popular Music and Society* 10, no. 4 (1986): 1–15.

Golding, Peter, and Graham Murdock. "Privatising Pleasure." *Marxism Today*, October 1983.

Gosling, Ray. "Dream Boy." *New Left Review* 1, no. 3 (May–June 1960): 30–34.

Gracyk, Theodore. "Kids're Forming Bands: Making Meaning in Post-Punk." *Punk & Post-Punk* 1, no. 1 (September 2011): 73–85.

Hall, Stuart. "The Culture Gap." *Marxism Today*, January 1984.

Hall, Stuart. "Thatcher's Lessons." *Marxism Today*, March 1988.

Hesmondhalgh, David. "Post-Punk's Attempt to Democratise the Music Industry: The Success and Failure of Rough Trade." *Popular Music* 16, no. 3 (October 1997): 255–274.

Hobsbawm, Eric. "The Forward March of Labour Halted?" *Marxism Today*, September 1978.

Hoover, Michael, and Lisa Stokes. "Pop Music and the Limits of Cultural Critique: Gang of Four Shrinkwraps Entertainment." *Popular Music and Society* 22, no. 3 (1998): 21–38.

Johnson, Richard. "Edward Thompson, Eugene Genovese, and Socialist-Humanist History." *History Workshop Journal* 6 (Autumn 1978): 79–100.

Laclau, Ernesto, and Chantal Mouffe. "Socialist Strategy." *Marxism Today*, January 1981.

Littler, Jo. "Meritocracy as Plutocracy: The Marketising of Equality under Neoliberalism." *New Formations* 80–81, special double issue on 'Neoliberal Culture' (2013): 52–72.

Mort, Frank, and Nicholas Green. "You've Never Had It So Good—Again!" *Marxism Today*, May 1988.

O'Brien, Lucy. "Can I Have a Taste of Your Ice Cream?" *Punk and Post-Punk* 1, no. 1 (September 2011): 27–40.

O'Meara, Caroline. "The Raincoats: Breaking Down Punk Rock's Masculinities." *Popular Music* 22, no. 3 (2003): 299–313.

Sinfield, Alan. "Sexuality and Subcultures in the Wake of Welfare Capitalism." *Radical Philosophy* 66 (Spring 1994): 40–43.

Stahl, Matt, and Leslie Meier. "The Firm Foundation of Organisational Flexibility: The 360 Contract in the Digitalizing Music Industry." *Canadian Journal of Communication* 37, no. 3 (2012): 441–458.

Williams, Raymond. "On Reading Marcuse." *Cambridge Review*, 30 May 1969, 366–388.

Williams, Raymond. "The Writer: Alignment and Commitment." *Marxism Today*, June 1980.

Williamson, Judith. "Images of 'Woman'—Judith Williamson Introduces the Photography of Cindy Sherman." *Screen* 24, no. 6 (November/December 1983): 102–116.

Worley, Matthew. "One Nation under the Bomb: The Cold War and British Punk to 1984." *Journal for the Study of Radicalism* 5, no. 2 (2011): 65–83.

Worley, Matthew. "'Hey Little Rich Boy, Take a Good Look at Me': Punk, Class and British Oi!" *Punk &Post-Punk* 3, no. 1 (2014): 5–20.

Worley, Matthew. "Punk, Politics and British (fan)zines, 1976–84: 'While the World was Dying, Did You Wonder Why?'" *History Workshop Journal* 79 (2015): 76–106.

INTERNET SOURCES

Anonymous. "Louis Althusser." Accessed 8 October 2015. http://www.marxists. org/glossary/people/a/l.htm; Accessed 8 October 2015. http://www.brit-ishpoliticalspeech.org/speech-archive.htm?speech=131

Conservative Party Election Broadcast. "The International Prosperity Race." 19 April 1979. Accessed 5 October 2015. www.politicsresources.net/area/uk/ pebs/con79.htm

Faber website listing for *Totally Wired* by Simon Reynolds. Accessed 5 October 2015. http://www.faber.co.uk/catalog/totally-wired/9780571235490; Accessed 8 October 2015. https://twitter.com/corbynjokes

Jeremy Corbyn for Labour Leader. "Policy Documents." Accessed 21 September 2015. http://www.jeremyforlabour.com/policy

Momus. "Return to the Giant Slits." 29 September 2008. Accessed 8 October 2015. http://imomus.livejournal.com/403645.html

Neate, Wilson, interview with Simon Reynolds for Perfect Sound Forever February 2006. Accessed 8 October 2015. http://www.furious.com/perfect/simon-reynolds31.html

Nice, James. "The Blue Orchids Biography." Accessed 8 October 2015. http:// www.ltmrecordings.com/bobio.html

Official Charts. Accessed 27 May 2015. http://www.officialcharts.com/home/

Reynolds, Simon. "Melody Maker Review of the Blue Orchids compilation 'A View from the City'." http://ripitupfootnotes.blogspot.co.uk/2008/11/ footnotes-24-chapter-23-glory-boys.html

Reynolds, Simon. "Rip It Up—The Footnotes." Accessed 8 October 2015. http://ripitupfootnotes.blogspot.co.uk/2008/11/footnotes-24-chapter-23-glory-boys.html

Thatcher, Margaret. "Iain Macleod Lecture Entitled 'Dimensions of Conservatism.'" 4 July 1977. Accessed 5 October 2015. http://www.marga-retthatcher.org/document/103411

Unterberger, Richie, interview with Gina Birch. Accessed 8 October 2015. http://www.richieunterberger.com/birch.html

"Your Heart Out." Music Blog. Accessed 8 October 2015. http://yrheartout.blogspot.co.uk/2011/05/hiss-shake-leggs-eleven-pt-8.html

ORIGINAL INTERVIEWS

Author interview with Martin Bramah, 2011.
Author interview with Una Baines, 2012.

INDEX

A

ABC, 56, 99, 104
Adorno, Theodor, 17, 33
Albertine, Viv, 60, 156, 158–61, 170, 177
Alderson, David, 31, 32
Allen, Dave, 96–8
Althusser, Louis, 12, 13, 31, 85
Anderson, Jon, 158
Anderson, Perry, 85, 93
'Animal Rhapsody', 175–177
anti-culturalism, 13, 19–20, 47, 48, 159, 160, 177
anti-fascism, 118
anti-psychiatry, 118
Ari Up (Ariane Forster), 17, 155, 158, 161, 162, 166, 169, 170, 172, 177, 178, 182
'Armalite Rifle', 88
Art and Language, 77–9, 81–2, 83, 104, 160, 168
Aspinall, Vicki, 160, 163, 164, 168, 174, 180, 181
Atkinson, Terry, 78, 79

autodidacticism, 7, 53, 116–7, 121, 129, 130, 141, 142, 169

B

'Baby Song', 164–5, 167
'Bad Education', 140, 142, 143
Baines, Jess, 46
Baines, Una, x, 7, 61, 117, 118, 120, 125, 132–4, 136, 138–45, 148, 173
Bakhtin, Mikhael, 26, 27
Barber, Lynden, 99, 104
Barthes, Roland, 106
Bayton, Mavis, 59, 160
Birch, Gina, 99, 158, 160, 163, 166, 168, 173–5, 178, 179–81
Birch, Ian, 90
Blake, William, 136, 175
Blanco y Negro, 67
Blue Orchids, x, 2, 3, 7, 16, 22, 28, 47, 55, 58, 61, 88, 115–18, 120, 121, 131, 132, 134, 136–45, 147, 148, 159, 169, 177, 179, 180, 189, 196

© The Editor(s) (if applicable) and The Author(s) 2016   221
D. Wilkinson, *Post-Punk, Politics and Pleasure in Britain*,
DOI 10.1057/978-1-137-49780-2

Bob Last, 54, 64, 66, 80, 103, 106
Bourdieu, Pierre, vii, 14, 28, 29
Bovell, Dennis, 51
Bramah, Martin, 7, 22, 58, 116–18,
    120, 121, 132–43, 145, 148
Branson, Richard, 63, 64
Brass Lip, 163
Burnham, Hugo, 82, 97, 98, 104
Bushell, Garry, 52, 54, 55, 86, 88,
    103, 129

C
Cabaret Voltaire, 31, 49, 50, 54
Callaghan, Jim, 38
'Call Me Up', 90
Cameron, David, 4
Campbell, Bea, 113
Captain Beefheart, 159
Carroll, Cath, 60
Carroll, Kay, 123
Cash, Johnny, 125
City Fun, 1, 2, 49, 60, 131
Clarke, John, 55
Clarke, John Cooper, 117
Clark, T.J., 79
Clash, The, 15, 48, 80, 85, 103, 118,
    158, 173, 178
'The Classical', 128
class, vii, 5–7, 21, 26, 28–9, 30, 37, 39,
    43, 51, 52–5, 58, 61, 66, 78, 83–5,
    93, 97, 107, 115–131, 136–7,
    141–2, 146, 147, 158–9, 192
Cohen, Leonard, 3
Communist Party of Great Britain, 42,
    47, 62, 63, 78, 81, 83–4, 91,
    100–1, 105, 165
Conservative Party, 9, 37, 40, 44, 49,
    68, 69, 85, 199
'Contract', 15, 63, 65, 95, 177
Coon, Caroline, 60, 61, 164
Copeland, Miles, 127

Copeland, Stewart, 127
Corbyn, Jeremy, 147, 198–200
counterculture, vi, 5, 7, 8, 12, 14, 16,
    20, 22, 25, 26, 29, 30, 31, 38,
    42, 44–9, 51, 56–65, 70, 79–84,
    87, 105, 107, 115–21, 125, 128,
    133, 138, 147–8, 157–60, 176,
    177, 189, 190, 196, 199
Cowling, Maurice, 44
Crass, 56, 163
culturalism, 13, 15–18, 21–4, 30, 46,
    47, 64, 66, 79, 81–3, 121, 127,
    144, 159, 161, 168, 169, 171,
    175, 177, 179
cultural materialism, vii, 5, 8, 11–14,
    23, 26, 28, 29, 67, 157, 195
Currie, Edwina, 101
Curtis, Adam, 83
Curtis, Ian, 117, 146

D
Dada, 47, 79, 159
da Silva, Ana, 155, 160, 166, 168,
    173, 174, 178, 180
'Damaged Goods', 80, 90, 97
dancehall, 182
Davies, Ray, 119
Davis, Angela, 23
de Beauvoir, Simone, 183
'Deer Park', 128
Deleuze, Gilles, 86
Dempster, Sarah, 191
demystification, 20, 51, 82, 87, 160,
    169, 173, 175
Derrida, Jacques, 86, 94
de Sade, Marquis, 125
Desperate Bicycles, 105
Devoto, Howard, 51, 117
Doors, The, 125, 136
Dorothy, 180, 181
Dostoyevsky, Fyodor, 125

'Doubt Beat', 92, 93
Dr Feelgood, 89
'Dumb Magician', 134–6
Duran Duran, 104, 179
Dworkin, Dennis, 42

E
Eagleton, Terry, 141
'Earthbeat', 171, 172
education, vii, 5, 7, 15, 16, 21, 28, 30,
    42, 52–3, 78, 83–5, 97–8, 104,
    107, 115–21, 126, 128, 130–31,
    136, 141, 144, 159, 190, 192
EMI, 1, 64, 103, 104
'The Eternal', 146
'Ether', 97

F
Factory Records, 2, 49, 54, 64–5, 192
Factory Star, 143
Falklands war, 104, 119
The Fall, 7, 16, 19, 22, 28, 47, 53–5,
    61, 115–23, 125–33, 137, 140,
    146, 147, 159, 180
Fast Product, 54, 57, 64, 80, 103.
    See also Bob Last
fatalism, 37, 38, 133, 134, 142, 148
Faust, 128
feminism, 7, 18, 20, 42, 59–61, 94,
    95, 116, 118, 120, 136–40,
    155–7, 160, 161, 163–5, 172–7,
    181, 200
'Fiery Jack', 117, 125, 126, 151
Fisher, Mark, 122
'Fit And Working Again', 116, 151
'5.45', 97
Ford, Simon, 123
formations, 20–1, 41, 48–56, 77, 121,
    129, 144, 147, 155, 157, 170,
    177, 189, 195

Forster, Nora, 158
Foucault, Michel, 13, 86
4AD, 64
Franz Ferdinand, 191
freedom vi, 3, 5, 14, 15, 17, 19, 21–5,
    29, 38–41, 44–7, 50, 56–62, 66,
    77–82, 86–8, 90, 93-100, 104-7,
    117-9, 125–7, 135–8, 141, 143,
    144, 147, 156, 157, 161–4, 173,
    175, 176, 182–3, 189, 194,
    196, 197
Frith, Simon, 17, 20

G
Gang of Four, 2, 3, 6, 7, 17, 20,
    28, 29, 48, 51, 53, 54, 58, 60,
    61, 64, 77–88, 90–2, 94–6,
    98, 99, 103, 104, 107, 108,
    120, 130, 160, 163, 166, 174,
    189–91
Gartside, Green, 28, 54, 56, 77–85,
    90–4, 98–101, 103, 105, 106,
    108, 178–80
gay liberation, 39, 43, 45
Gilbert, Jeremy, 190
Gildart, Keith, 116, 119
Gill, Andy, 20, 78, 80, 81, 83,
    85, 88, 89, 94–9, 103, 104,
    107, 130
Gitlin, Todd, 27
Gogan, Sue, 99
Goldman, Vivien, 51, 54
Gorz, André, 41, 46
Gosling, Ray, 18, 22
Gracyk, Theodore, 47
Gramsci, Antonio, 11
Graves, Robert, 121, 137
Greengrass, Paul, 83
Greer, Germaine, 61
Guattari, Felix, 86
Gurdjieff, G.I., 117, 121, 141, 142

H

habitus, 14, 28, 58, 80, 90, 99, 117, 155, 158
Hall, Stuart, 101, 102
'Hanging Man', 133, 134
Hanna, Lynn, 120
Happy Mondays, 147
Harron, Mary, 82, 86
Heath, Edward, 25, 38
Hebdige, Dick, 5
'Hegemony', 101–3
hegemony, 11–12, 23, 28, 98, 102
Hendrix, Jimi, 158
Henry Cow, 91, 118
Hesmondhalgh, David, 3, 4, 63, 66, 144, 194, 195
Hesmondhalgh, Julie, 199
Hewitt, Paolo, 145
Hobsbawm, Eric, 52, 97
Hoover, Michael and Stokes, Lisa, 79, 87, 103
Horne, Howard, 17, 20
Hoskyns, Barney, 90, 122
humanism, 14, 23, 42, 43, 101, 159, 164, 167
Human League, 104

I

'I Found That Essence Rare', 90
'I Love A Man in Uniform', 95, 104
'Independence', 90
independent labels, 1, 7, 15, 47, 51–2, 55, 63–7, 103–7, 127–31, 177–82, 190, 194
indie, 128, 172, 183, 189, 196
institutional autonomy, 15, 19, 21, 22, 58, 144, 194
institutions, 6, 14–20, 25, 42, 43, 45, 47, 50, 51, 64, 65, 142, 147, 172, 189, 190, 195, 197

'In The Beginning There Was Rhythm', 73, 171, 186
Irwin, Colin, 122–3
Island Records, 183

J

Jackson, Ben, 38
'Jacques Derrida', 93–4
James, M.R., 122
Jam Today, 56, 160
Jarman, Derek, 49
Jinks, Nial, 81, 83
Johnson, Wilko, 89
Jones, Owen, 112
Jones, Paul, 34
jouissance, 57, 106
Joy Division, 49, 54, 146

K

Kamera, 128
Kennedy, Joe, 191, 192
King, Jon, 78, 83, 87, 130
Kinks, The, 119
Kleenex, 65

L

Labour Party, 7, 13, 37–9, 40–2, 65, 85, 101, 115, 147, 190, 191, 197–200
Lacan, Jacques, 106
Laclau, Ernesto and Mouffe, Chantal, 101
Laing, Dave, 29, 61
Last, Bob, 54, 64, 66, 80, 103, 106
Lauper, Cyndi, 3
Lawrence, Jon and Sutcliffe-Braithwaite, Fiona, 149
Leavis, F.R., 24, 66
Lee, Sara, 96, 97

left culturism, 16, 130
Lester, Paul, 97
libertarian left, 6, 8, 13, 14, 22–3, 25,
	37–67
'Life On The Line', 174
'Lions After Slumber', 99, 100
Littler, Jo, 85
Livingstone, Ken, 43, 65
Locke, John, 79
Lock, Graham, 180
Loewenstein, Oliver, 49
Lonelady, 193
'The Long Night Out', 145, 146
Lovecraft, H.P., 117
'Love und Romance', 169
'Loving Feeling', 181
'Low Profile', 142
Lowry, Ray, 53, 106
Lydon, John, 48, 49

M

Machen, Arthur, 122
Madonna, 181
Magazine, 51
Mailer, Norman, 128, 129
Manchester Musicians Collective,
	28, 118
Marcuse, Herbert, 14, 23–5, 42, 43, 78,
	87, 88, 95, 123, 131–3, 172, 176
Marcus, Greil, 87
Marley, Bob, 163
Marxism, 11, 13, 20, 23–4, 26, 28,
	39, 40, 45, 77, 79, 83–5, 91–3,
	97–9, 100–1, 104, 106, 116,
	131, 167, 190
Marxism Today, 100, 101, 190
Marx, Karl, 42, 65, 87, 89, 111
McCullough, Dave, 53, 80, 90, 91,
	127, 136, 146, 167, 168
McGuigan, Jim, 22, 46
McLaren, Malcolm, 48

McRobbie, Angela, 155–6
Medhurst, John, 68
Mekons, The, 64, 146
Merleau-Ponty, Maurice, 183
Middles, Mick, 115
Middleton, Richard, 34
Milner, Andrew, 29, 102
mobile privatisation, 40, 41
modernism, 16, 19, 47
Mo-Dettes, 65, 66
Moi, Toril, 183
Momus, 172, 178
Morley, Paul, 2, 51, 55, 106, 118,
	144, 196
Morley, Tom, 78, 99
Mort, Frank and Green, Nicholas, 101
'Mr Pharmacist', 119
Mulhern, Francis, 16
Murray, Charles Shaar, 48
mutual improvement, 141–2
mysticism, 7, 61, 132, 134, 135,
	140–2, 148, 160, 169, 170

N

'Natural's Not In It', 88, 90
nature imagery, 131, 143
Naylor, Liz, 49, 60, 61, 65
Negus, Keith, 4
neoliberalism, 5, 7, 8, 12, 23, 37, 44,
	107, 126, 134, 147, 155, 160,
	182, 189, 193, 195, 197, 198
Neu!, 128
Neville, Richard, 45
New Left, 6, 14, 16, 17, 22–5, 41–5,
	118, 198
New Order, 99
new pop, 2, 6, 19, 54–7, 64, 66, 67,
	77, 78, 99, 100, 103, 104, 106,
	119, 129–31, 135, 136, 144,
	145, 148, 171, 172, 177–80,
	190, 196

New Right, 12, 38, 44, 53, 56, 60, 78, 85, 93, 94, 107, 119, 157, 196
new sensibilities, 56–8, 82, 162, 173, 174, 193
Nice, James, 65
Nicholson, Viv, 165
Nico, 145
The Normal, 2
'Not Great Men', 96
Nu-metal, 191
Nuttall, Jeff, 45, 83

O

objectification, 8, 95, 168, 174, 176, 182, 183
O'Brien, Lucy, 88, 156
O'Dell, Dick, 178
'Odyshape', 164, 166–8, 180
'Off Duty Trip', 173–5
Ogg, Alex, 63
Oi!, 6, 52, 54, 55, 60, 129
'Ooh Ooh La La', 175
Orton, Fred, 79
Ouspensky, P.D., 121, 132

P

Palmolive (Paloma Romero), 159
'P.A.s', 91
The Passions, 163
Peake, Mervyn, 117
Pearson, Deanne, 170
Peel, John, 82
Penman, Ian, 1, 2, 56, 57, 106, 116, 117, 171
Perry, Mark, 62, 127
personal politics, 42, 44, 57–8, 78, 81, 96, 105, 121, 135, 140–3, 157
Pimlott, Herbert, 25
pleasure, vi, 3, 5, 14, 17, 21–5, 29, 39, 40–1, 43, 44, 47, 50, 56, 57, 59,

60, 62, 66, 78, 81, 82, 87–5, 98, 99, 101, 102, 105–7, 115, 117, 121–3, 125–6, 131–6, 138–41, 143–5, 148, 155–8, 165, 168, 173–7, 180–3, 189, 196, 200
Poison Girls, 163
Police, The, 127
political correctness, 147
Pollitt, Tessa, 159, 182
Pollock, Griselda, 79, 95
Pop Art, 19, 20, 48
the Pop Group, 49, 55, 62, 98, 165, 170
populism, 13, 18–19, 44, 54, 66, 77, 118, 119, 130, 131, 145, 179, 180, 189
postmodernism, 6, 8, 56, 64, 101, 181, 190, 192
post-punk, 1–8, 11–31, 37–67, 78, 81, 82, 87, 90, 92, 99, 103, 105, 115–48, 155–61, 163, 164, 172, 178, 183, 189–200
post-structuralism, 2, 13, 28, 31, 77, 79, 83, 85–6, 91–4, 99–103, 106, 116, 117, 171, 180, 183, 190
PragVEC, 2, 99
Presley, Elvis, 120
Press, Joy, 125, 173
primitivism, 57, 172
'Psykick Dance Hall', 123, 124
Public Image Limited, 49, 192
punk, 1, 46, 48–50, 52, 59, 61, 62, 80, 88, 92, 105, 120, 122, 138, 158–60, 170, 173, 177
Pye, Ian, 179

R

The Raincoats, 7, 28, 47, 48, 57, 60, 61, 88, 99, 116, 146, 155–8, 160, 163, 164, 166–8, 173–5, 178–81, 183, 189, 190, 196

Rastafarianism, 163, 169
The Red Crayola, 178
Reddington, Helen, 59
'Return the Gift', 90
Reynolds, Simon, 4, 30, 31, 46, 47,
    50, 52, 53, 57, 62, 64, 81, 86,
    87, 89, 91, 94, 96, 98, 100, 103,
    115, 124, 125, 134, 143, 145,
    147, 148, 166, 169–71, 173,
    175, 176, 178, 180, 182, 183,
    189, 190, 195, 196
Rhodes, Bernie, 48
riot grrrl, 183
Robertson, Sandy, 121
Robinson, Tom, 118, 163
rockabilly, 125, 126
'Rock-A-Boy Blue', 106
Rock Against Racism, 18, 62, 99, 107,
    118, 163
Rock Against Sexism, 163, 173
romanticism, 16, 17, 79, 82, 175
Roman Totale XVII, 117
Rose, Jonathan, 121, 130, 141
Rough Trade, 3, 8, 15, 24, 54, 57,
    63–7, 98, 103, 104, 106, 108,
    126–30, 143, 144, 147, 166, 172,
    177–80, 189, 193–6, 197, 199
Rowbotham, Sheila, 42, 43, 58, 59, 157

S
Samuel, Raphael, 44
Sandbrook, Dominic, 37, 38
Saunders, Robert, 68, 69
Savage, Jon, 22, 48, 50, 54, 57, 59, 86
'Scritlock's Door', 105, 106
Scritti Politti, 2, 3, 6, 7, 28, 29, 47–8,
    50, 51, 53, 54, 57, 62, 64, 77,
    78, 80–5, 90, 91, 93, 98–101,
    104, 106, 107, 116, 120, 126,
    129, 135, 167, 171, 178, 179,
    189–91

'Scritto's Republic', 92, 93
Segal, Lynne, 43, 45, 59, 155, 157
Selfish Cunt, 191
sensuous reason, 56, 78, 87–90, 92,
    94, 95, 174, 176, 200
Sex Pistols, 1, 15, 48, 54, 88, 158
Shelley, Percy Bysshe, 100
Sinfield, Alan, 5, 9, 12, 14, 16, 22, 29,
    46, 83, 116, 130–1
Siouxsie and the Banshees, 51, 54, 59
Situationist International, 50, 64,
    79, 108
skiffle, 126
The Slits, 7, 17, 28, 47, 54, 56, 60,
    61, 151, 155–8, 160, 161,
    163–5, 167, 169–72, 174, 177,
    178, 182, 183, 189, 190
Smith, Mark E., 7, 19, 28, 53, 54,
    115–31, 135, 140, 142, 143,
    145–7, 179, 189
Smiths, 4, 67, 129
Snow, Mat, 104
Socialist Workers Party, 62
Soper, Kate, 170
'Spend, Spend, Spend', 165–6
Step Forward, 59, 127
Stone, Sly, 180
Street-Howe, Zoe, 156, 160–2,
    165, 177
structuralism, 101, 190
structure of feeling, v, vii, 14, 21, 26,
    28, 41, 42, 45, 48, 82, 85, 88,
    93, 99, 101, 117, 131, 146, 156,
    157, 171, 172, 178, 181, 192,
    198, 200
Strummer, Joe, 198
Stubbs, David, 46
subcultures, 5, 10, 13–15, 17, 20, 44,
    48, 53
'Sun Connection', 132–5
surrealism, 51, 91, 159
Sutherland, Steve, 145, 179

T

Taylor, Neil, 65
Temporary Hoarding, 62, 99
Thatcherism, 3, 7, 13, 37–67, 77, 85,
    93, 101, 115, 119, 121–3, 125,
    128, 132, 134, 135, 141, 200
Thatcher, Margaret, 1, 25, 37, 40, 44,
    145, 157, 166, 177, 200
This Heat, 49, 50, 163
Thompson, E.P., 97, 136
Thompson, Mayo, 66
Thornton, Sarah, 192
'To Hell With Poverty', 90
Toynbee, Jason, 15, 18, 26, 28, 58
Travis, Geoff, 15, 54, 65–7, 106, 108,
    178, 180, 193
T Rex, 159
Turner, Alwyn W., 38
'Typical Girls', 161, 162, 164–6, 169

U

utopianism, vi, 8, 14, 22–4, 42,
    49–51, 55, 82, 88, 117, 182,
    190, 193, 195–7, 199

V

Velvet Underground, 48, 80, 117,
    145, 174
Vicious, Sid, 125
Virgin Records, 63, 106
Voloshinov, Valentin, 27

W

Wah! Heat, 127
Wainwright, Hilary, 42, 43, 197

'Walkabout', 171
Walker, John A., 79
weird fiction, 117, 122
welfare-capitalism, 3, 5, 9, 21, 37–44,
    49, 85, 199
Westwood, Vivienne, 48
Whitehouse, Mary, 44, 60
Whiteley, Sheila, 59
Whitman, Lucy (Lucy Toothpaste),
    60, 156, 158, 174
Wilde, Oscar, 144
Williamson, Judith, 180, 181
Williams, Raymond, v, vii, 5, 11–13,
    16, 21, 23–6, 28, 38, 40–3,
    49–50, 52, 66, 85, 101–2, 104,
    105, 194, 196, 200
Williams, Zoe, 156
Willis, Paul, 17, 46, 59, 133
Wilson, Elizabeth, 45
Wilson, Harold, 38, 46
Wilson, Tony, 2, 64, 192
Wise, Alan, 115
Wishart, Trevor, 118
Witts, Dick, 115, 118
'Woman Town', 95
Woodcraft Folk, 159
Wood, Ian, 54, 130
work, 87, 89, 123, 128, 131–3
Workers Educational Association, 117
Worley, Matthew, 49
Wyatt, Robert, 63

Y

Yes, 158
yippies, 82, 159
York, Peter, 30, 45, 55
The Young Ones, 39

Coleg Gŵyr Abertawe
Llyfrgell
Gower College Swansea
Library

Lightning Source UK Ltd.
Milton Keynes UK
UKHW020712120220
358602UK00010B/509